The Gift of Knowledge /

Ttnúwit Átawish Nch'inch'imamí

The Gift of Knowledge / Ttnúwit Átawish Nch'inch'imamí

Reflections on Sahaptin Ways

VIRGINIA R. BEAVERT
Edited by Janne L. Underriner

University of Washington Press
Seattle and London

The Gift of Knowledge / Ttnúwit Átawish Nch'inch'imamí was published with the assistance of a grant from the Naomi B. Pascal Editor's Endowment, supported through the generosity of Nancy Alvord, Dorothy and David Anthony, Janet and John Creighton, Patti Knowles, Katherine and Douglass Raff, Mary McLellan Williams, and other donors.

TULALIP TRIBES

www.tulalipcares.org

This book was also supported by a generous grant from the Tulalip Tribes Charitable Fund, which provides the opportunity for a sustainable and healthy community for all.

Printed and bound in the United States of America
Design by Katrina Noble
Map by Robert Elliott
Composed in Minion Pro, typeface designed by Robert Slimbach
21 20 19 18 17 5 4 3 2 1

Cover photograph: *Wáwtuktpa* (At Camp), ca. 1922 (the author is the child and her mother is seated). Courtesy of Yakama Nation Museum
Frontispiece: The author with her mother, Ellen Saluskin (Hoptonix Sawyalilx̱), and stepfather, Alex Saluskin, ca. 1941. Courtesy of Virginia Beavert Family Photo Collection.

University of Washington Press
www.washington.edu/uwpress

Library of Congress Cataloging-in-Publication Data on file

The paper used in this publication is acid-free and meets the minimum requirements of American National Standard for Information Sciences—Permanence of Paper for Printed Library Materials, ANSI Z39.48–1984. ∞

To Ronald, Julie, and Brian Saluskin, and all of their children, grandchildren, and great-grandchildren, to Rudolph Saluskin II (deceased), and all of his children and grandchildren, and to Steven Saluskin.

Contents

List of Illustrations *ix*
Map of Hunting, Fishing, and Food-Gathering Sites *x*
Preface *xi*
Acknowledgments *xv*

1. The Culture That Made Me Who I Am Now / Inmí Tiinwít Wapíitat 3

2. My Story / Inmí Ttáwax̱t 15

3. Life Circles / Wyá'uyt Wak̲'íshwit 31

4. Experiences and Reflections / Pina'ititámat Wak̲'íshwit 103

Conclusion / Wának̲'it *159*
Appendix: Guidance for Academic Researchers *163*
Ichishkíin–English Glossary *171*
References *175*
Index *177*

Illustrations

2.1 Ellen W. Saluskin (Hoptonix Sawyalilx̱) and daughter Virginia 16
2.2 The roaring waters of Celilo 25
2.3 Ready to Dig Camas 28
3.1 Ruth Coyote with a traditional cradleboard 35
3.2 Anna Hoffer with a modern cradleboard 35
3.3 A *pátł'umx̱sh* (wedding veil) 52
3.4 Male dowry items 53
3.5 *Wápshat ámtanatnan* (braiding of the bride's hair) 54
3.6 A bridal shower enactment 55
3.7 Wedding feast 56
3.8 *Pamalíit* (modern wedding) 56
3.9 *Ashxyatúu* 57
4.1 *Mimanú Wáashat* (Owl Dance) 106
4.2 Owl Dance at the Celilo Falls Salmon Feast 106
4.3 Bone game being played at Moxee Hop Ranch 110
4.4 *Palyúut* (bones used to play bone game) 112
4.5a *Tł'ut pachúpa* (guessing both white bones are to the center) 114
4.5b *Tł'ut pachúpa* (guessing both white bones are to the center) 114
4.6a *Papúchan* (guessing both white bones are to the outside) 115
4.6b *Papúchan* (guessing both white bones are to the outside) 115
4.7a *Tł'ut nax̱sh wíkayklanan* (guessing a single bone holder) 116
4.7b White bone to the outside 116
4.8a *Tł'ut Nax̱sh Wíkayklanan* (guessing a single bone holder) 117
4.8b White bone to the inside 117
4.9 Drying lamprey eels at the camp of Billy Barnhart 141
4.10 Watch these women ride 148
4.11 *Yikít k'úsima* (Yakama wild horses) 153
4.12 *Yikít k'úsi* (a wild horse) 154
4.13 *Shapáashaptpama k'úsi* (a pack horse) 154
A.1 Samish Canoe Races at Tulalip, with Kit Kendall 167

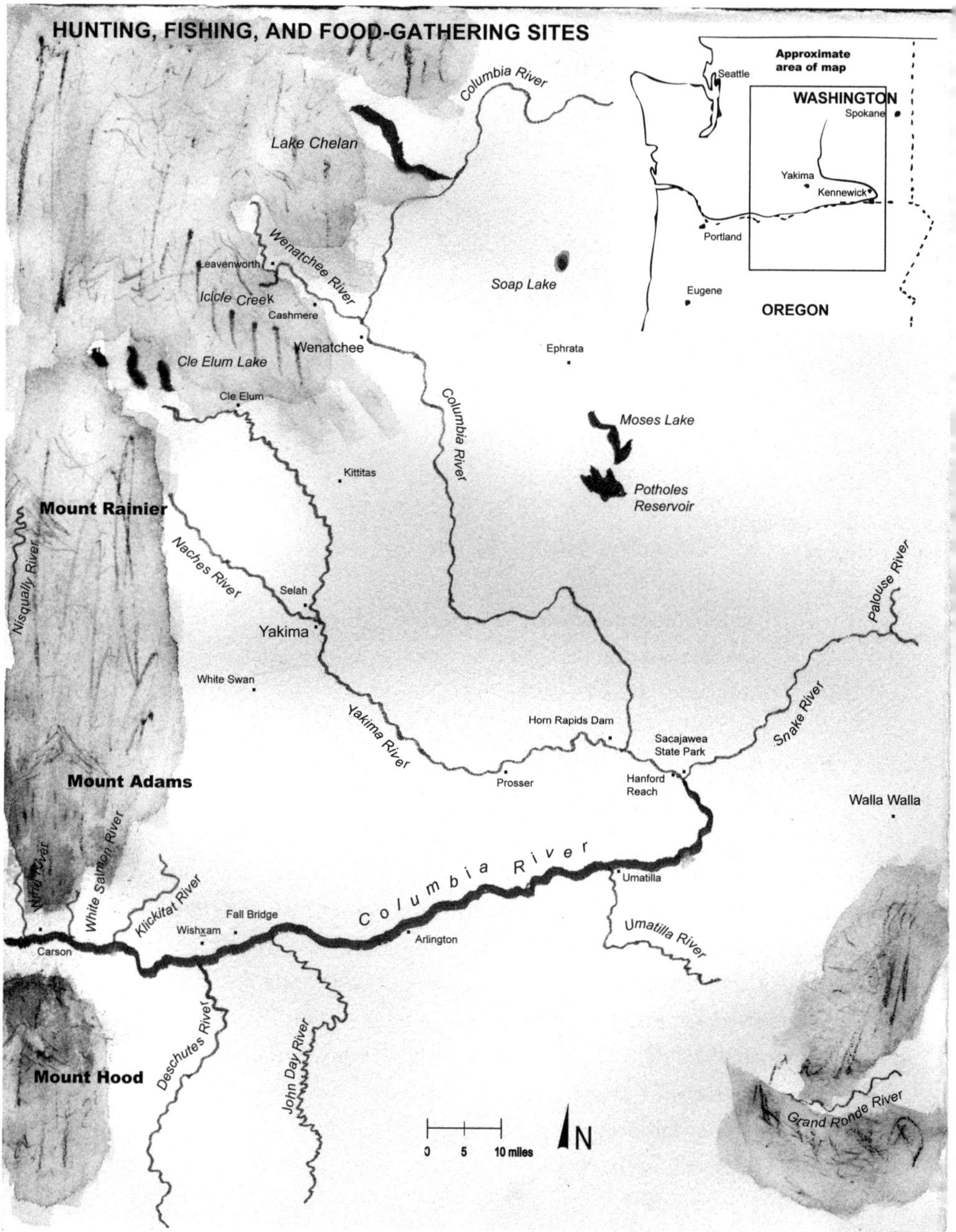
HUNTING, FISHING, AND FOOD-GATHERING SITES
Approximate area of map
Seattle
WASHINGTON
Spokane
Yakima
Kennewick
Portland
Eugene
OREGON
Columbia River
Lake Chelan
Wenatchee River
Leavenworth
Icicle Creek
Cashmere
Wenatchee
Soap Lake
Ephrata
Cle Elum Lake
Cle Elum
Columbia River
Moses Lake
Kittitas
Potholes Reservoir
Mount Rainier
Nisqually River
Naches River
Selah
Yakima
White Swan
Palouse River
Yakima River
Horn Rapids Dam
Sacajawea State Park
Snake River
Prosser
Hanford Reach
Walla Walla
Mount Adams
White Salmon River
Wind River
Klickitat River
Columbia River
Umatilla
Fall Bridge
Wishxam
Arlington
Carson
Umatilla River
Deschutes River
John Day River
Mount Hood
0 5 10 miles
N
Grand Ronde River

Preface

This is the story of my life and the traditions of my family. From birth I was immersed in the Ichishkíin language, culture, traditions, history, and modern life of the Sahaptin People, who reside in the Pacific Northwest of the United States of America. All of these elements are related to the importance of maintaining and preserving the foundation of Indian life. One wise man said, "Without language there is no culture, without culture there is no language."

This is also my way of answering questions asked of me over the years by people in my community, linguists, and others. Writing has enabled me to gather in one place language that I feel is slipping away from my people. Young people are the future caretakers of this country. It is essential that they obtain an education in science and linguistics to keep pace with the modern world, to protect their natural environment and preserve their identity. Soon, the Sahaptin Elders will be gone and no longer available to consult about language and culture. This is my contribution to the younger and future generations. It is for their benefit that I write this.

I begin by addressing the history of academic research on my language from the perspective of a Native person who has been involved in this work as an assistant to non-Native researchers and now as a linguist myself. I talk about my language and how it works from the perspective of a Yakama person who has spoken and used the language her whole life, and about my path to becoming a linguist and educator.

Subsequent chapters are about my early life and the traditions in which I was raised. I first reflect on growing up through stories of my family, my early traditional and public schooling, and descriptions of traditions and the areas where I was raised. I then detail some of the most basic ways of our ancient culture and lifeways through description of the circle of life, from conception to death. Finally, I discuss other parts of traditional life: sweathouse, bone game, horses, and foods. In an appendix, I offer suggestions to scholars and academic researchers, Native and non-Native, working in the field of Native language documentation, preservation, and revitalization. An Ichishkíin–

English glossary lists terms used in the text for learners and teachers. It is my hope that they will be used in the classroom and at home.

I write this for the Ichishkíin-speaking communities in hope that this documentation of our lost traditions will provide a resource from which to learn our ancestors' ways and language. Detailing the traditional practices offers a much needed historical and social accounting of each. And explaining the words we use to talk about our traditions and how these words explain the deeper meaning of what we do gives our communities the vocabulary they need to practice our traditions. Included are various dialects and ways shared by other Ichishkíin-speaking communities, as well as texts and descriptions of dances, songs, and practices in Ichishkíin.

This work contributes to the fields of sociolinguistics and theoretical linguistics, as well as historical and cultural anthropology. Despite the best efforts of some anthropologists and linguists, all earlier academic work done on Yakima Ichishkíin was conducted by researchers from outside the community and is inevitably seen and presented through the lens of the English language, Euro-American culture, and the Western tradition of "objective" scholarship. I am in a unique position to present the research on my language as a contribution to academic scholarship but from a very different perspective: that of a Native speaker and scholar. Implicit in my view of scholarship is the way researchers should work with Native people; therefore, I address how linguists can better work with community members, as well as the protocols and etiquette expected by Native people in working with non-Natives.

In cowriting *Ichishkíin Sínwit: Yakama/Yakima Sahaptin Dictionary* with Sharon Hargus (Beavert and Hargus 2009) and working together with Joana Jansen to create "A Grammar of Yakima Ichishkíin/Sahaptin" (Jansen 2010), it became clear to me that I wanted to document the Yakama traditions I was raised in. In doing so here, I have included dialects and practices shared by other Ichishkíin-speaking communities to preserve their language so these communities will benefit from this work. Practices distinct to each Ichishkíin-speaking community are becoming diluted, and this is causing confusion among younger generations.

It is my hope that this book will better inform Ichishkíin communities about language and traditional protocols. For example, our Elders tell us that our Ichishkíin language is needed to enable us to obtain the natural medicines we need to heal our bodies and to gather our roots and prepare our foods. We must speak our language to the plants when we gather. Ceremonies must be conducted in Ichishkíin. These things people do not understand anymore. So I include the language necessary to carry out traditions as our ancestors did, as well as descriptions of changes and variations in practices and of female and male language when practice is affected by gender.

Some of the texts are provided in English only, and some are written in Yakima Ichishkíin accompanied by an English translation. The English is equivalent in meaning but is not a literal word-for-word translation. In some places, there is additional information in English in brackets that is not in the corresponding Ichishkíin passage.

The reader may also find some places where the spelling of words does not exactly match the spelling in the *Ichishkíin Sɨ́nwit* dictionary. This could be a difference of dialects, as I sometimes use my father's Umatilla words, or could be related to formality of speech. Our writing system is comparatively young, and spelling conventions are still being established.

I include my own Native language to let the readers know how the language is actually used. In the *Ichishkíin Sɨ́nwit* dictionary we describe the meanings of words, using English. In our curriculum materials and grammar we present language and structures for teachers and learners (Jansen and Beavert 2010, Jansen 2010). It is important to also record how our words and phrases are used when we talk about traditional and modern life. This work presents the language in this way.

Acknowledgments

I stay in Oregon now to continue working on my language. I have found support here and am grateful to the University of Oregon for helping Native tribes to preserve and revitalize their culture and Native languages. I thank my colleagues here for understanding my commitment to help keep my language and culture alive, in particular, Scott DeLancey for encouraging me to pursue my graduate and research work; Janne Underriner, for providing further support for my work; Scott Pratt, whose vision brought Yakama Ichishkíin to the University of Oregon; and to the Office of Research and Innovation and the College of Arts and Sciences for supporting its being taught.

I am grateful to Jeff Magoto and the World Language Academy for their commitment to helping my students by including our language in their establishment. I was astounded to find myself sitting at the table with teachers of languages from around the world. I said to myself, "It has finally happened. My Native language is finally recognized as a human language."

Thank you to Lorri Hagman and her colleagues at the University of Washington Press for publishing this story about my growing up in an Ichishkíin-speaking environment and witnessing deep culture that no one in modern life has been able to comprehend. The University of Washington Press's publication of *Ichishkíin Sínwit: Yakama / Yakima Sahaptin Dictionary* helped me keep the spelling of Ichishkíin words correct throughout this book.

Thank you to those who contributed something of themselves to this book: illustrators Judith Fernandez and Jaeci Hall; my niece Julie Ann (Julie) Saluskin, and my nephew Brian Saluskin, for their support and their contribution of Beavert family photos; Charlene and Javin Dimmick for providing their wedding photos; and Brittany Parham, Robert Elliott, Joana Jansen, and Jeff Magoto, who have chronicled Ichishkíin activities through photos over the years, some of which made their way into these pages. The Yakama Nation Wildlife, Range and Vegetation Resources Management Program and the Yakama Nation Museum and Cultural Center provided photos of wildlife on my reservation and of me and my mother (one of the very few photos of us existing today). Photos also came from the Yakima Valley and Ellensburg

Public Libraries, the Special Collections Library at the University of Oregon, and the Confederated Tribes of the Umatilla Indian Reservation. Thank you.

I cannot thank you enough, Northwest Indian Language Institute staff, for your assistance with material preparation and editing of my story: Janne Underriner, for keeping me on track and editing and organizing this book; Joana Jansen, for editing translations for English and Ichishkíin; and Regan Anderson, along with Brittany Parham, for checking Ichishkíin spellings and for typing and keeping things organized. Thank you, Sharon Hargus at the University of Washington, for your hours spent reading and editing Ichishkíin.

Thank you to the University of Oregon students who participated in the modern version of traditional marriage and diapering, and for the baby board: Anna Hoffer, Abel Cerros, Joliene Adams, April Anson, Brittany Parham, Bruno Seraphin, Keith Walker, and Jaeci Hall.

Páyu kw'ałanúusha Robert Elliott for developing the wonderful map depicting the Yakama migration trails and gathering sites.

Thank you to John Curtis for duplicating the traditional set of "bones" for our illustrations demonstrating how bones are held in the hand to outwit the opposing team in the bone game played by Sahaptin Natives.

Many thanks to the Yakama Veterans Organization and to Heritage University for supporting me during my hard time at the beginning of my journey to higher education at the University of Arizona, and to the professors there who mentored me: Terri McCarty, who encouraged me to apply for my master's degree; Akira Yamamoto, who made me realize how important the Yakama language, culture, and people are to me; Mary Willy, for explaining suffixes and prefixes in Navajo language, which helps me teach Ichishkíin; and Ofelia Zepeda and Philip CashCash for your support and encouragement.

I extend my gratitude to Kathleen Ross (my sister) at Heritage University, and all of the nuns who pray for me and my family. Thank you, Mary James and your *átway-am*, Ed James, for all of our happy times putting together teaching materials for Ichishkíin language and for encouraging students to never give up their education and their studying and learning to speak, read, and write Ichishkíin.

Without the support from the following elected officials I would not be writing this thank you today: Yakima Tribal Council members no longer with us, Hazel Umtuch Olney, Clifford Moses, and Wilfred Yallup; past General Council elected chairs, Phillip (Bing) Olney and Joanne Menineck, and current General Council chair, Yalawísh; and current Tribal Council Education Committee chair, Delano Saluskin. Thank you, Yakama Indian Education Center director, Shx̱maaya Arlen Washines, and his staff for their foresight in supporting Indian education and the academic world by expediting financial support and assistance to Native students.

Thank you, Bruce Rigsby for writing our first Ichishkíin alphabet with my stepfather Alexander Saluskin, which enabled us to teach reading and writing in the Native language for the first time. And thank you to all Ichishkíin students who have and do utilize this tool and go farther in the language because of it.

I would like to express my appreciation to my colleague and friend, Deward Walker, Jr., for the work we did together on the legend book and projects afterward.

In conclusion, what would my life be without my elders? One-hundred-twenty-year-old X̱axísh Sawyalix, who loved and cared for me from early childhood to the age of puberty. She sent me to school every day (although sometimes I became distracted en route by watching a bluebird hatch her eggs). Thank you Mom, Hoptonix Sawyalilx̱ Wanto Saluskin, for teaching me the culture, traditions, and languages (Nez Perce and Ichishkíin). I want to thank Hawáaya Alexander Saluskin for adopting me as his daughter, and for encouraging me to obtain a degree in anthropology in order to study how Native languages work and how to pass this on to the younger generation through educating them.

Thank you Dad, Harris (Henry) Wataslayma Beavert, for loving me although we were living far apart, and for the entertaining history and legends you shared when we camped out in the mountains with all those single women huckleberry pickers.

Thank you Wantux̱ Oscar Beavert, my dear brother, for your love and support during my childhood and puberty, when no one told me about things girls needed to know.

Kw'ałanúushamash Elder Annie Jim. When my brother Oscar died, I was devastated with grief. She told me to go to Mother Earth for healing.

How do you thank all the people who supported you to accomplish your contribution to help others? There are many kind people who helped me along during my lifetime. I have acknowledged some here by name, yet there are others I could not fit into this space. I am grateful to you all for your contributions to my life and this book.

The Gift of Knowledge / Ttnúwit Átawish

Nch'inch'imamí

CHAPTER 1
The Culture That Made Me Who I Am Now

Inmí Tiinwít Wapíitat

Łt’úkna wa tamánwit niimípa tiináwitpa, ku ttuush íchi íkuuk ikks ttáwax̱t kúsh pa’atł’yáwisha, “Atḵ’ix̱sháx̱itash awkú namách’a íchi shúkwat mish iwachá míimi tx̱ánat íchi tiináwit, átḵ’ix̱shatash shúkwat áwnatash ku chaw shínɨm isápsikw’ata.” Ku cháwnash awkú pa’ɨ́nx̱a mish awkú pamíta kwɨnkínk, ashkú aw nch’íwisha inmí ttáwax̱t, kush íkushx̱i ink wachá, cháwnash mun px̱wípx̱wishana túkin íkw’ak tiináwitki ashkú shapáttawax̱ni tx̱ánana miimawítki.

The laws are strict in our Indian way of life, and now some of the younger generation are requesting of me, “We too want to know our old ways, to learn how things were long ago, we want to know, because nobody taught us.” But they do not tell me what they are going to do with that knowledge, and now that I am growing older I see that I used to be like that; I never worried about our way of life, because I was raised with that knowledge, in the old way.

Iksíksknik nash ttáwax̱tknik sɨ́nwix̱a Íchishkiin kush áḵ’inunx̱ana íkush pakúsha tíinma, kush chaw wa tł’aax̱w túpan wapsúx̱, chaw, awkłáwnash aw áshukwaasha kw’ɨnk ash kw’ɨnk wachá sápsikw’ani. Íkw’aksimmash awkú tíix̱wata íchna tímashpa.

I spoke Ichishkíin all the time and I witnessed what the people were doing, but I am not knowledgeable about everything, I only know what I was taught. That is what I have included in this writing.

I have been asked over the years, especially when I first began documenting Ichishkíin and again now that I am older in my career, "What does your language mean to you, in terms of cultural heritage and identity?"

My language means that I, my relatives, and tribal members are human. We speak, process, and comprehend the Ichishkíin language in the same way other humans process their languages. The traditions and cultural heritage passed down by the Sahaptin people through generations identify our country and our inherent right to occupy our geographical place. It supports that we, the Native/Ichishkíin people of this land did not migrate to the United States of America from any other country. We are its original inhabitants.

I have been asked how tribal communities can maintain, preserve, and revitalize a language. I was exposed to my Native language before I could talk. The laughing and talking and singing of my immediate family members were probably the first sounds I heard. There was the comfort of love surrounding me. The most important thing is speaking and singing a lullaby to children when they are young. In this way the language never leaves the child.

Knowing my traditions, wanting to better understand them and share them, documenting them so our future children will know them, all of this has led me to become a linguist; has led me to the work I do now. I walk hand in hand with knowing the ways of my family and writing them down for those to come. This is why I became an Ichishkíin language teacher and linguist.

I want to talk about the language and the people who speak Ichishkíin, about the land that has known this language since time immemorial, about those who have documented it, and how I found my way to being a part of documenting and revitalizing it. I am able to tell the history of academic research on my language from the perspective of a Native person who has been involved in this work as a "helper" or "assistant" many times. The academic research that has been done on Yakima Ichishkíin presents a picture of Ichishkíin to the outside world, and some of it is useful to my community also. But I think that it is time to write about some of these questions and ideas from the other side, as a Yakama person and a Yakama scholar.

LANGUAGE BACKGROUND / SHÚKWAAT ICHISHKÍIN SÍNWIT

The Sahaptin tribes living on Indian reservations in Oregon, Idaho, and Washington once roamed freely where there were no dividing lines to separate or impede people from traveling in order to socialize with each other. According to archaeological evidence, Native Americans have lived here on the Columbia Plateau for eight thousand years or more (Hunn 1990). Early culture depended entirely on hunting, fishing, and gathering wild plants for food.

The Sahaptin tribes extend over a large territory in western Idaho, northern Oregon, and southern Washington; migration northward and westward in recent centuries caused a wide scattering of bands. Sahaptin is a language of great dialectal diversity. Anthropologist Bruce Rigsby (1965) describes three main language groups: Northeast, Columbia River, and Northwest, which is spoken in the Yakima River drainage and includes the Yakima dialect. Ichishkíin and Nez Perce languages make up the Sahaptian family. It is in the Plateau branch of Penutian, as are Klamath and Molalla (DeLancey and Golla 1997).

North-central Oregon bands include the Warm Springs, Tayx, Tenino, John Day, Wayam, and others. Eastern-central Oregon tribes and bands include the Walla Walla (Walula) and Umatilla in Pendleton, Oregon, and the Palus of southeastern Washington, following the Snake River to where it connects with the Columbia. The Wawyuuk bands roamed the territory north of the Columbia, and had a permanent village across from Hanford (which in 1943 became Hanford Nuclear Reservation).

Northwest Sahaptin proper includes most of those who now reside on the Yakama Reservation: a small Sk'in Tribe (Fall Bridge and Pine Creek people); the large Yakama and Pshwánapam bands (Kittitas-Ellensburg); and east and west of the Cascade Mountains, the X̱wáɫx̱waypam (Klikatat) bands of the Lewis, White Salmon, and Klikatat Rivers. The mid-Columbia River bands of Priest Rapids and Saddle Mountain, who occupied areas clear up to Soap Lake, are Sahaptin speakers and practice similar traditions.

The Taytnapam and Upper Cowlitz River bands, a large group of Sahaptin speakers, resided on the west side of the Cascade Mountains (from the city of Packwood to Randle, Washington), and a smaller group, the Mɨshiil (Mishal, west of Mount Rainier National Park), called the Upper Nisqually River bands, spoke the Sahaptin language. Some were enrolled on the Yakama Reservation; others were enrolled with the Nisqually Tribe under a different treaty.

When the Elders talk about these people, they tell their children to be careful whom they marry because some of us are blood relations. However, they encourage marriage between Sahaptin bands who retain their family values, including language and culture.

The country of the Sahaptin People ranges along the western border of the Columbia Plateau in the base of the Cascade Range; eastward, it extends from the slopes of the Cascades summit to an elevation of only 650 feet along the Middle Yakima River Valley. The Yakama Indian people lived in the watershed of the Yakima River, their primary stream, which begins in the Cascade Mountains and is joined by other streams such as the Tieton,

Cowiche, Toppenish, and Satus as it flows southeast to join the Columbia River near Richland, Washington. The Yakama people spoke different dialects of the Sahaptin language. They lived in small villages close to the waterways to feed their stock and for other domestic uses of water. Water has always been an important part of the religion Sahaptin people practice.

John R. Swanton (1952) reported that in 1780, the population of people in this area was three thousand or more and they were called Yakitma (Runaway). According to Ruby, ethnologist Frederick Webb Hodge , stated "that the native name of the Yakamas was Waptailmin or Pakiutlema, which means 'people of the gap.' Union Gap, south of present-day Yakima, Washington, was the site of their main village" (1986:272). L.V. McWhorter (1952) indicated that the Spokane and Nespelem people gave the name Yah-ah-kima to those who lived in the Upper Yakima area, and K'tittáas (Rock People) to those who lived around Ellensberg, Washington. He reports other meanings for Yakima/ Yakama: "growing family," "black bear," "big belly," or "pregnant ones."

The country is broken by the Yakima Folds, volcanic faults. Long narrow ridges extend eastward from the Cascades to sagebrush land. On the north side is the Wenatchee Range, and farther south along the Goldendale Ridge are the Horse Heaven Hills. Prehistoric habitation sites are found in caves and rock shelters throughout the Yakima River drainage, and small seasonally occupied campsites are scattered throughout the backcountry. Large permanent village sites appear along the major watercourses from early prehistoric time and exist today as Toppenish, Zillah, and Yakama, for example. There are also numerous prehistoric villages along the Yakima River. These include Awátam, the area that includes Sunnyside Dam, located at Union Gap; Wenas village in the Selah district; Medicine Valley at White Swan; and Siɬá, a village across the Yakima River from Zillah. Ancient campsites or villages appear today as clusters of *wɨlchí*, saucer-shaped circular depressions, about three feet deep and from twenty-five feet to forty in diameter, that are the remnants of earth lodges. Later there was a shift to rectangular-shaped lodges, sometimes with rounded ends, a prototype of the present *káatnam* (longhouse). The most recent discoveries describe shallow, circular depressions outlined by ridges of stone that mark summer lodge sites, similar to the teepee rings found throughout the plains country.

At the time of this writing, according to the Yakama Nation's 2014 census data, the current Yakama Nation enrollment is eleven thousand members; according to the Yakama Nation Ichishkíin Sinwit Program's 2012 language survey, thirty-eight Elders from the ceded areas and reservation are fluent first speakers of any of the fourteen identified dialects of the Sahaptin language group. Exposure to the language occurs most often in the *káatnam*—for example, at the *ká'uyt* (First Foods ceremony)—and in some Shaker churches' traditional activities. (The Shaker Church is a Christian-based religion that originated with a man from the Washington coast. When dying he saw a vision that returned him to the living. Shaker parishioners sing and ring bells and they heal through their sight and hands. Their hands tremble when they are healing. They are illuminated by candles.)

Ichishkíin language is taught in high school classes and middle and elementary schools on the reservation. Additionally, first- and second-year classes of Yakima Ichishkíin are taught at the University of Oregon at Eugene and at Heritage University in Toppenish, Washington.

MY BACKGROUND AND WORK IN LINGUISTICS / INMÍKI TIINWÍTKI WAPÍITAT WAWSHUSHYAŁAMAMÍYAW

I have worked with almost every linguist who has studied the Ichishkíin language, at first in the role of language expert or consultant, later as a fellow linguist. In addition, both my mother, Ellen Saluskin (Hoptonix Sawyalilx̱), and stepfather, Alex Saluskin, were instrumental in documenting Yakima Ichishkíin as language consultants to Bruce Rigsby and helped to develop the Ichishkíin practical alphabet.

Initially I worked with linguists as a resource person and contributed my cultural knowledge. The household I grew up in was Indian-speaking only, and traditional. *Nakáłas* (my grandmother, mother's mother), Timinsh, was a shaman, as were *natútas* (my father) and *na'íłas* (my mother); my great-grandmother (mother's grandmother), X̱ax̱ísh, was an herbalist doctor and midwife. During my childhood, I was surrounded by people who spoke our tribal dialects and languages—Nez Perce, Umatilla, Klikatat, and Yakima Ichishkíin—so all I knew were the languages and traditions of my family and environment. Until I was eight years old, my life was focused solely on learning about food gathering, medicinal plants, and wildlife. From that point my traditional education became coupled with my formal Western education, alternating years between the two until I entered tenth grade. It was during that time I began working with linguists.

WHEN I BEGAN TO WRITE OUR INDIAN LANGUAGE / ASHKÚ WIYÁ'UYNA TÍMAT ICHISHKÍIN SÍNWIT

The first written work on our language was done by Father Charles Marie Pandosy (1862), and was a sketch of the language of Pshwánapam bands living along the Yakima River at Kittitas Valley. This was before my time. My work on the language began at age twelve, in 1934. I met linguist Melville Jacobs while I was working with his student, anthropologist Margaret Kendall. I was the liaison, interpreter, and contact person for her because I spoke many of the dialects of the people she interviewed. Dr. Jacobs was impressed when he discovered I was a fluent speaker of the Klikatat language, and he began teaching me to read and write the orthography he had developed for the Klikatat language when he was collecting Klikatat myths (Jacobs 1929, 1934, 1937). He had also developed a sketch of Klikatat grammar (Jacobs 1931). Being able to read stories he had recorded allowed me to facilitate the work. Little did I know this was the beginning of my linguistics career!

After my early schooling, however, I stepped away from linguistic work for a time. During World War II, I joined the Women's Auxiliary Corps. When the Auxiliary Corps became part of the regular Army, I joined the U.S. Air Force, and became a wireless radio operator at the B-29 bomber base at Clovis, New Mexico. During that time I nearly forgot my Native language. One day I was on my way home on furlough and I was caught in a Greyhound bus strike. I had to call home for somebody to rescue me. My mother answered the telephone and she became excited and began talking Sahaptin, but I could not understand her, and I kept asking her "What, what?" She finally lost her patience and yelled at me in Ichishkíin, "*Míshnamat tx̱ánasha?*" (What is the matter with you?). Something popped in my head, and I understood her. I had nearly lost my Native language because I was not using it.

I was honorably discharged from the Air Force on November 28, 1945. I immediately enrolled in school to become a medical secretary. After that, I thought that I was done with formal education. During that time, my stepfather, Alexander (Alex) Saluskin, had retired from the tribal council and was working as an archivist at Fort Simcoe, an old Army Fort converted into a museum. Alex was half Yakama and half Salish, and was a multilingual speaker of numerous Sahaptin and southern Salish dialects. He had held positions of responsibility within the tribe, and was a respected and knowledgeable man. He met Bruce Rigsby, a linguist and anthropologist from the University of Oregon, at Fort Simcoe. They decided to collect stories in the Yakima language, and Dr. Rigsby developed a phonetic practical writing script, the Practical Yakima Alphabet, for the language. Alex worked for four years with Dr. Rigsby recording Elders' words and legends on the Indian reservation, sometimes on tape but often just writing down what they heard. Dr. Rigsby helped me to develop a plan to teach reading and writing of the Yakima alphabet, my main interest in language preservation.

Alex and I worked from Bruce Rigsby's notebooks (Rigsby 1964–71) and the stories that Alex and Rigsby had collected to create word lists. This eventually became the first dictionary of my language (Beavert and Rigsby 1975). Rigsby also collaborated with linguist Noel Rude on a grammatical sketch of the Ichishkíin language (Rigsby and Rude 1996). My mother, Ellen Saluskin, and I worked with Noel Rude as consultants. I translated her words to English and worked with Rude in investigating specific grammatical constructions.

Also during the 1970s, I was hired by Deward Walker, Jr. of the University of Colorado to collect and translate several Ichishkíin dialects for a legend book project. I interviewed Elders from across the reservation and recorded the legends they knew on cassette tapes—recordings that later disappeared and were never found. I translated their legends into English for the book *The Way It Was: Anakú Iwachá: Yakima Legends* (Beavert and Walker 1974).

Working with anthropologists over the years—Margaret Kendall, Helen Schuster, Deward Walker, and Linda Klug—allowed me to connect to and work with numerous people on the reservation. As the years progressed, Elders passed, and I began to notice that the younger generation (including myself at the time) was more involved in modern Anglo life, which impacted the language as it was spoken in fewer and fewer contexts.

CENTRAL WASHINGTON UNIVERSITY / PSHWÁNAPAM

Alex felt his health was worsening, and he worried about the future of our language. He asked me to return to school and major in anthropology. He thought this would give credibility to the Sahaptin language. He asked me to carry on the project that he and Dr. Rigsby had started. I was reluctant to give up my current occupation, but finally relented.

I enrolled at Central Washington University and although it took a number of years, I received a bachelor's degree in anthropology in 1986. My incentive was to help my people do something about our Native language.

Going back to school at middle age was awkward. If not for the support and encouragement from my professors and others at Central Washington University, I would have given up. I took my first linguistics class, phonetics, from Dr. Linda Klug. She introduced me to how sounds were used in my language. As a speaker, I had never thought about where the sounds were produced in my mouth.

Larry Porter, a young American Indian professor in the department of education and his wife, a Yakama tribal member, supported my work on the legend book project. Larry Porter and James Brooks, president of Central

Washington University, both helped me. They made sure I was provided with good housing, and they helped me find a teaching position in ethnic studies to pay for my tuition.

While I was at Central Washington University, we spearheaded funding for the first edition of the *Yakima Language Practical Dictionary* (Beavert and Rigsby 1975) and *The Way It Was: Anakú Iwachá: Yakima Legends* (Beavert and Walker 1974). The funding came from the U.S. Bureau of Indian Affairs in Washington, D.C., implemented by a concerted effort made by Dave Warren of the Pima Tribe.

During this time, Dr. Warren received a grant from the Bureau of Indian Affairs to select five Native American Indians from across the United States to spend the summer of 1974 at the University of Mexico, where he had received his doctorate. We participated as members of a panel group. Each day we met for half a day discussing cultural information with the University of Mexico anthropology and cultural studies faculty. It was there I learned and came to understand many things about the Mexican people and their culture in Middle America. I had the opportunity to talk with many indigenous people, to hear from them about their religion, culture, and politics.

Also in 1974, I obtained a small grant at Central Washington University to study linguistics at Dartmouth for a summer. There a group of Indian students adopted me as their grandmother! Three things happened that summer that influenced my life. My linguistics instructor, who was also a French teacher, taught me linguistic terms for body movements (while dodging things he threw at us). He also taught me to teach language with unusual, entertaining visuals. Outside of my studies, students were organizing to march on Washington, D.C., and the Indian students wanted me to participate with them in the rally. I decided to stay put that day and not join them, as I was at Dartmouth for a different reason. The third and truly serendipitous event that occurred was that I found linguistic materials by Melville Jacobs gathering dust in the basement of the Dartmouth library. When I returned to Central Washington University, we notified the Jacobs Foundation, which retrieved the materials.

Dr. Warren also funded my history and language research project for two summers, 1977 and 1978, at the Smithsonian in Washington, D.C., and for two summers, 1977 and 1979, at the Newberry Library in Chicago. I was fortunate to find unidentified artifacts at the Smithsonian. As no one knew where they were from, I was charged with the task of identifying the objects. I relied on phone interviews with Elders, especially my mother, to help me identify and catalog the artifacts. They were mainly domestic and recreation instruments used a long time ago. I donated my research material to the Yakama Tribe. At the Newberry Library, I concentrated on language and history. I found maps drawn by early explorers and interesting Yakama-related artifacts. I catalogued those identified by Elders and again donated my research material to the Yakama Tribe. Today they are housed at the tribe's museum.

RETURNING TO THE RESERVATION / TÚX̱NIŁMT INMÍYAW TIMÁNI TIICHÁMYAW

I moved back to the Yakama Indian Reservation in 1981 from nearby Ellensberg, seeking employment and a place to live. The Yakama Nation Indian Advisory Board recommended me to teach a class at Wapato High School to students who were failing English and could not graduate. The curriculum, for teaching the Yakima Ichishkíin language as well as English for comparison, was already developed. They just needed a teacher. But I was also completing my studies at Central Washington University in anthropology and was teaching Native American culture in an evening class at Eisenhower High School in the city of Yakima. When I completed my studies, I took the job in Wapato.

During this time my mother became a widow and moved in with me, in my small apartment. Soon after, we moved into a house at a place called Wanity Park, housing for tribal members. As there was no one to care for my mother in her own home, she became totally dependent upon me. We were together until she died when she was 103 years old. She was my mentor and historical informant. She also restored my direction toward my native knowledge, culture, and language.

UNIVERSITY OF WASHINGTON / SIYÁTŁPAM

I became interested in learning more about the linguistic structure of my language after working with Sharon Hargus of the University of Washington and Akira Yamomoto of the University of Kansas in the 1980s and 1990s. Since that time, Dr. Hargus and I have collaborated on numerous papers (Hargus 2001; Hargus and Beavert 2001, 2002a, 2002b, 2005, 2006a, 2006b, 2012, 2014) and on the *Ichishkíin Sɨ́nwit: Yakama/Yakima Sahaptin Dictionary* (Beavert and Hargus 2009).

I first met Sharon Hargus in the early 1980s, when I visited the linguistics department at the University of Washington. We discussed my interest and developed a plan that allowed me to work on Ichishkíin there, complete with an office across the hall from hers. We began documenting verbs on a manual typewriter because I did not know how to use the computer. This was the beginning of the second edition of the *Yakima Language Practical Dictionary*, expanding it beyond the nouns, names of wildlife, plants, and personal nouns included in the first edition. We wanted to develop a document adequate for use in the classroom.

During that time, the University of Washington hosted a gathering of Washington State tribes to discuss their recommendations about academic education for American Indian students. Sharon provided me with room and board so that I could attend the conference. I listened to the Elders and learned a lot about their concerns regarding the problems facing the youth on Indian reservation lands, including the loss of their Native languages. There I met my lifelong friend Vi Hilbert. She was working with linguist Thomas Hess to document her language. At that time Vi was the director of the Lushootseed Language Program and was working on the first dictionary of Lushootseed, a Coast Salish language.

HERITAGE UNIVERSITY / NCH'I SAPSIKW'ATPAMÁ

Heritage College, formally Fort Wright College and since 2004, Heritage University, was originally a Catholic school centrally located in Spokane. When the nuns moved their school and established it on the Yakama Indian Reservation in 1982, they were assisted by two Yakama Indian women, Martha Yallup and Violet Rau, who were graduates of Fort Wright College. They moved the school into an old abandoned school building located on West Fort Road, in Toppenish.

Soon after their relocation to the Yakama reservation, Heritage College was advertising for an instructor. I applied and was hired as an adjunct professor to teach American Indian culture and history. It was ideal, only three miles from my home. My classroom was in Grange Hall, across the road from the school. On an impulse, I walked in, uninvited, to a college staff meeting and recommended that the institution teach the local Native language to Indian students, since the college was located on the Yakama Indian Reservation.

The president of Heritage College, M. Espirita Dempsey, saw the need for Ichishkíin language instruction on the reservation. We needed funding so she applied to the Mellon Foundation, with the support of Tribal Council Chairman Wilfred Yallup. This was a strong statement considering that only two members of the Yakama Tribal Culture Committee, Hazel Umtuch Olney and Clifford Moses, showed support for the project. At that time, teaching Yakima Ichishkíin outside the family was not favored by the tribe.

The following year our teaching efforts were supported through the funding Dr. Dempsey successfully secured from the Mellon Foundation, which has provided additional support for the development of our dictionary and for the Ichishkíin language fellowship at Heritage University.

STUDYING AT THE UNIVERSITY OF ARIZONA / SKÚULIT LÁX̱UYX̱TPA TIICHÁMPA

While I was teaching the alphabet at Heritage I realized that students needed more than rote learning. Although I am a fluent speaker of the Yakima language, and I had learned to read and write using the practical writing system, I lacked the academic training for teaching language. I soon realized that I needed to return to school to become a better instructor of Ichishkíin. The financial assistance of Heritage College and my connection with the local Indian veterans organization supported my graduate education at the University of Arizona so that I could become a professor of Ichishkíin.

The first year I attended the American Indian Language Development Institute (AILDI), I took Dr. Akira Yamamoto's introduction to linguistics course. Also attending were Sahaptin speakers and learners from Warm Springs, Oregon. We were Ichishkíin teachers interested in curriculum development for teaching the language. Dr. Yamamoto's class complemented curriculum classes taught by Drs. Mary Willie and Ofelia Zepeda, native speakers and teachers of their languages. Together they clarified how their languages worked. This helped me to look at my own and identify how it was structured. Dr. Yamamoto was working with Yavapai speakers then, which gave him a better understanding of how Native culture and language work together. His famous saying, "When there is no language, there is no culture, and when there is no culture, there is no language," has stayed with me to this day.

The AILDI language program help lay the foundation of my teaching work at Heritage University. I graduated from the University of Arizona in 2000 with a masters of education in bilingual/bicultural education. In 2006 I returned to AILDI as a National Science Foundation fellow together with my student, Roger Jacob. We studied language documentation and grant writing together.

THE NORTHWEST INDIAN LANGUAGE INSTITUTE / KÚTKUTT ICHISHKÍIN SAPSIKW'ATPAMÁPA

In 1997, Dr. Janne Underriner invited me to help the Northwest Indian Language Institute (NILI), newly created at the University of Oregon. I worked with tribal people there to develop a summer program to teach language and culture to Native teachers. Through NILI, I also met Joana Jansen, and I have worked with her on linguistic articles on morphology, a grammar of my language, and various teaching and curriculum projects (Jansen and Beavert 2010; Beavert and Jansen 2011, 2013; Jansen 2010).

My involvement with NILI was helpful in identifying cultural knowledge of the Columbia River, Nespelem, Warm Springs, and Umatilla tribal members, and made apparent how much of our traditional culture was becoming lost. This realization prompted my decision to pursue my doctorate in linguistics at the University of Oregon. While there I achieved what are perhaps my most important accomplishments. One is teaching Yakima Ichishkíin to students whom I hope will go back to the reservation and teach.

Roger Jacob and Greg Sutterlict, two of my apprentices, have attended the University of Oregon to do just this. We developed and taught a Yakima Ichishkíin class through the Yamada Language Center's world languages department. Together we designed a three-way teaching model that included developing teachers (language apprentices), a linguist, and an Elder first speaker. Roger Jacob and Greg Sutterlict were the classroom language teachers who focused on developing learners' oral skills; Dr. Joana Jansen gave weekly lectures on Ichishkíin linguistics with activities and helped develop curriculum and assessments; and I taught culture, listening, reading, and writing skills utilizing the practical writing script developed by Dr. Bruce Rigsby. This model has morphed into what now is the Ichishkíin language course within the department of linguistics, where materials continue to be developed and made accessible to Yakama community members.

Perhaps the most important work to come out of my time at the University of Oregon was the evolution of this book. Here I could record for future generations the lifeways that I had learned from my family. I devote the remainder of this book to doing that.

CHAPTER 2
My Story

Inmí Ttáwax̱t

I was born in a bear cave in the Blue Mountains in Oregon. I did not have a name yet when they brought me home. My brother Oscar was studying geography in school. He was studying about the state of Virginia. When they asked him to name his sister, he called me Virginia. The best friend of my aunt Mussie, who was attending a Catholic School in Tulalip, near Everett, Washington, was named Roslyn, and that became my middle name. Aunt Mussie also had the honor of piercing my ears. I am Virginia Roslyn Beavert.

I was a newborn when the Indian government nurse checked me over at the Umatilla Indian Agency at Pendleton, Oregon. She added "Baby Beavert, daughter of Mr. and Mrs. Harris Beavert" to the Umatilla enrollment list (as a Umatilla Indian) without the knowledge of my parents. When I discovered this later, I took my name off.

When I was not yet two years old, I got lost in Gifford Pinchot National Forest. My uncle and father were hunting deer at Psawaswáakuɬ (Twin Buttes) and my mother and her aunts and older sister were picking huckleberries there, too. There was another family camping there who had a young girl they called Maggie. We later came to learn that she knew the edible berries and plants in the forest. She and I were playing together, and all of a sudden we disappeared. Our families could not find us. The ranger enlisted outside help to form a search party. After some time my father was convinced that we were dead, to which my mother said, "Don't cry. She's not dead yet." They found us after two weeks. We were happy and healthy. We were safe because Maggie had found her power and it protected us.

I did not know this story growing up. I found out about it at a winter dance. A woman was called out to the floor. This was Maggie Jim. She was celebrating her power at the dance. (She had just saved her husband and

FIGURE 2.1. The lost child returns: Ellen W. Saluskin (Hoptonix Sawyalilx̱) and daughter Virginia, ca. 1922. Courtesy of Yakama Nation Museum.

herself from drowning in the Columbia River. Her husband could not swim, and she pulled him and herself across to safety.) When she realized I was in attendance, she told our story. This is how I learned about having been lost. I talked to my mother about the story and she told me it was true. She said my moccasins were practically worn out and I had berry juice all over my face and dress, which was well worn too. She said we survived. This picture shows my mother and me after I was found.

My great-grandmother raised me and my *yáya* (older brother) Oscar when my mother divorced my father. Oscar was named after my mother's father, Oscar Wantux (Wanto became the common spelling of the name). My brother was the first-born child, born just before the allotments distribution ended. The General Allotment Act (the Dawes Act of 1887) divided reservation land into parcels of land per person or per family. Parceling land into allotments allowed non-Indian people to purchase reservation land. Oscar, born in 1914, was seven years older than I. We were full brother and sister. When grandmother went to town for groceries, *yáyanimnash inakwúukshax̱ana* (*yáya* looked after me) while she was gone.

Grandmother would entertain my brother and me with Coyote stories.

She took me with her to gather our food in the mountains and told me about how these plants were like human beings. They had life, and they felt pain the same as people.

My mother divorced my father because he became an alcoholic when his employer, a white farmer, taught him how to make whiskey. He started sampling it and he could not stop. When he began to sell their hard-earned material things to support his habit, my mother was forced to divorce him. For me, this was *anut'átwit* (becoming an orphan), a tragedy no child should ever experience. I remember clinging to my father's leg and begging to go with him: "*Táta chaw wyáalakwɨm. Táta, nánam*" (Daddy, do not leave me—take me with you). He answered me in his gentle voice, "*Chaw, tx̱ának iłamípa*" (No, you must stay with Mom). He detached my fingers, one by one, from his pants, and walked away. My mother was yelling at him, "*Ku cháwnam mun ánach'ax̱i túx̱nɨmta íchɨn*" (Do not ever come back here again). That is all I remember. Everything was blank after that until I woke up one morning lying on a bed on the floor. Sitting by me, weaving a root digging bag, was my *nakáłas* (mother's mother), X̱ax̱ísh. She was my great-grandmother, who became my companion until she died in 1929 when she was 120 years old. It was in preparing her gravestone at the Indian Agency that I learned her age.

My mother told me that I loved my father very much. *Lalíwanaash natuta-asmíki maysx̱máysx̱* (I missed my father every day). My grandmother knew this and she let me know she loved me in every way. She would stroke my hair and say, "*Chux, chux, káła*" (I love you, my grandchild). I do not remember how old I was before I finally forgot the longing for my father.

My father became a *shíikash* (Shaker) soon after he and my mother divorced. He was among the last people to preach and sing the Shaker songs in Sahaptin. He quit drinking liquor, which was the reason he had *iwatátwya* (strayed from his marriage vows). My mother told me he had been a good husband and provider until *ipaláyna* (he drank liquor). He never abused her, and he was a kind person. He was respected by many people during his lifetime. Young people asked him for private counseling and he became a mentor for many young men and for girls. He could tell many legends and historical stories.

I spent most of my time as a child in Sih' (Sandy Place), located close to the Yakima River, across from the city of Zillah. A person who belongs to Sih' is called Siłá. When someone asked you "*Mɨ́nik nam wa?*" (Where do you come from?) you would reply, "*Wash nash Siłá*" (I am a person from Sih'). That is where I grew up living with my great-grandmother, X̱ax̱ísh. This is where my great-grandparents, Sawyalilx̱ and X̱ax̱ísh, lived.

Sawyalilx̱ was a Medicine Man, a great healer of ailments. He once healed a native African immigrant Elder who lived in Toppenish. The man's family paid my great-grandmother a boar and a sow for healing him. There were only a few families who were of African American descent living in Toppenish at that time. X̱ax̱ísh was a fluent speaker of Chinook Jargon, a local trade language. She raised pigs to trade with the settlers who lived in Zillah and around Toppenish. The Indians did not eat pork because it was taboo, unclean food. Later, during summer Bible school at the mission, I learned that other people in faraway countries also did not eat pork.

The family raised many horses that had been received as payment for my grandfather's healing work. Many swift racehorses were bred from those given to Sawyalilx̱ as payment. My uncles, aunts, my mother, and grandmother also owned many *k'úsima* (horses). When I was about six years old, my uncle Johnny George decided it was time for me to learn to ride a horse. He threw me on a fat grey horse and slapped it on the rump and the horse took off with me screaming on his bare back, desperately hanging onto his long mane. Uncle Johnny whistled and the horse stopped and returned to the barn. I did not fall off. After that, he taught me to mount a horse by stepping on the hock, grabbing a handful of mane, and lifting myself on. Uncle taught me this for protection in case I was accidentally caught far away from home or camp on foot. In those days, horses were always wandering around loose. I could catch one, ride home, and later return the horse to where I had found it. Most of the children were taught safety precautions of this type.

All of the children were instructed in how to take care of horses on hunting or food gathering trips with their relatives. This training saved many people. It was the grown child who looked after the horses; feeding and watering and taking them to the meadow to graze. Trips to the meadow could take longer than anticipated; you could become disoriented by a storm or by the evening becoming night too soon. Children were horse watchers in the mountains. When I went along with the women on root-digging and berry-picking trips, my responsibility was to water, feed, and tether the horses. The boys did the same during hunting and fishing season. This was our responsibility until we became old enough to participate as grownups.

My mother had an experience when she was young where horses saved her life in the mountains. She was taking care of them during a berry picking trip to the Trout Lake area. An Elder told her to take the horses to a certain meadow to graze. She was to leave them and walk back to camp. It was already past noontime and she did not question the request. She rode her own horse bareback, and towed the horses together with a rope halter, the head of one horse to the tail of the one in front, and navigated them in that way.

It was getting dark when she reached her destination. She hurried back toward camp but it became so dark she could not see the trail and was forced to get down on her hands and knees and feel her way. Soon she heard the timber wolves at a distance; they came nearer and nearer. She said she began to feel sorry for herself and was thinking that her relatives did not love her; that they wanted her to die. As she was feeling her way along the trail she felt something warm and soft. It was the nostril of her horse, Tak̲awaakúɬ, who had come back to rescue her. She took hold of his tail and he led her back to the meadow. The wolves were following them all the way.

In the meadow all the horses gathered around her. Her horse lay down, and she slept on his belly to keep warm until morning. The wolves were not able to reach her because the horses surrounded and protected her. In the morning she went back to camp and no one mentioned anything. No one apologized to her or wanted to know how she had made out. She explained that that was the cultural way. They wanted her to find a spiritual power from the mountains. While she was asleep she acquired that power. She was a healer for women.

I mentioned above that I was raised in Sih'. Sih' was a paradise for me! This village was a haven for many people. The vegetation is mostly cottonwood, willow, chokecherry, currant, rosebush, alder, and serviceberry (Juneberry). An artesian spring that formed a lake emptied into the Yakima River. There was much wildlife activity because Sih' was a breeding place for the *x̱átx̱at* (wild duck), *ákak* (goose), *áy'ay* (magpie), *tyiittyíit* (swallow), *lumt kákya* (bluebird), *x̱mɨmsá* (hummingbird), and many other birds. There was plenty of food for all of them. The speckled and rainbow trout spawned in the creek that emptied from the lake. Eels spawned in the small stream that flowed between the river and Sih' village. In the dense shrubbery at night, in the open lush grass around the lake, whitetail deer came to eat grass and to drink water. This is where a Yakama Native died and rose again and became a Prophet for the Longhouse religion for the Indian people residing along Taptíil, the Yakima River.

I explored every trail and riverbed. I knew where the birds nested, and where the fish spawned. I was especially interested in the eels. I scooped them up from the sand by handfuls, and examined the tiny baby eels that looked like earthworms, only they were darker. Then I would carefully put them back and cover them up, because I remembered how delicious dried, pounded eels tasted for lunch during huckleberry-picking time. There were all kinds of beautiful flowers blooming in different seasons: *lúmtli* (blue iris), *x̱áɬya* (yellow sunflower), blue chicory, yellow bird's-foot, *pukp'úk* (dandelion), *achaashpamá* (primrose), *isikw'ałá* (violet), *tamsháashu* (wild rose), and *tamalú* (peppermint). There were also several *apɨlsáas* (wild apple trees) and *pluumsáas* (prune trees) that bloomed and produced small *tmáanit* (fruit).

My great-grandmother never let food go to waste. She utilized all kinds of fruits—from wild fruit trees and other plants—by drying it. I enjoyed helping her pick the wild fruit because we rode around on horseback and picked them. The dried *tmɨsh* (chokecherries) were pounded together with pulverized dried *yáamash* (deer) meat into *tútni* (pemmican).

She made *ch'lay*, a pulverized dry *tkwínat* (Chinook salmon) seasoned in *shúshaynsh* (steelhead) fish oil. *Ch'lay* is an important part of our diet. Steelhead oil is the only oil that should be used to preserve *ch'lay*. The younger generation is using vegetable oils and the *ch'lay* turns rancid.

Yesterday I drove past Táptat (Prosser) on my way to K̲mɨł (Richland), and I thought about my great-grandmother. She had a large dry-shack near the dam on the edge of the Yakima River where she butchered and dried salmon. There were only Indian homes there at that time. In the summer, we lived in a small Army tent near the dam, where I ran and played joyfully up and down the edge of Yakima River. Because I was a curious child, I watched the fishermen spearing fish in the rapids. I can still remember how the fishermen looked, undressed down to their breechcloths, spearing the fish that swam up the Yakima River. When someone caught a salmon there was a loud whoop and holler from the other fishermen. There was a lot of laughter and teasing when the fish was large and the fisherman had difficulty landing it. Later, it was declared illegal to spear the salmon, and Indian fishermen fished off the platform using hoop nets.

Further down the river is a place called Wanawísh (Horn Dam), where the Yakima River flows into the Columbia. My grandmother used to dry salmon there too. It is the traditional fishing site for the Wawyúuk Sahaptin tribe and their relatives, called Plash K̲'mɨł (White Bluffs) people. I do not remember my childhood activities there, but I am related to many people from Wawyúuk.

White Bluffs on the Columbia River at Hanford Reach in Richland, Washington is the major spawning grounds for the Chinook salmon. Hundreds of Sahaptin people gathered there during spawning season to hook the salmon after they completed breeding. I translated a recording of my mother, Hoptonix Sawyalilx̱ (Ellen Saluskin), for an anthropologist who was documenting tribal activities at Hanford Reach. Legislation was introduced in the 1970s to trench the beach in order to widen the river so that materials could be shipped upriver on the Columbia. My mother provided testimony about the cultural importance of this area. She recalled that, when she was a girl camped at Hanford Reach with her family, she saw many tribes gathered to preserve *mit'ula* (dog salmon), the last food source of the season, before they returned to their homes. They waited until the female laid her eggs and the male fertilized them with sperm before the fisherman speared the salmon, to insure the sustainability of the species. Hanford Reach is the most important spawning place for the Columbia River salmon. When the Hanford Reach spawning ground is destroyed, a great number of Chinook salmon will disappear. Today, tourism is a threat to Hanford Reach, as it destroys sacred plants and medicines in areas where spiritual rituals are held. (Copies of my mother's tapes and information about the health hazards caused by contaminants of nuclear waste can be found at the Hanford Reach Museum Archives at Kennewick, Washington.)

Every year, after food harvest time, the Sahaptin people conducted a special ceremony at Alderdale, in Washington, which was a conveniently located place for the tribes to congregate. They set up a *káatnam* (longhouse) by the Columbia River because this was a convenient place to gather and invited the tribes to bring the young men and women who were eligible for marriage.

The longhouse was built to accommodate many people. Wagonloads of people moved in and established campsites. There was a lot of excitement in the air. The singers were practicing the songs. The leader instructed the new singers to make sure they sang the proper songs. The *walptáykt* (social songs) for this ceremony are similar to the longhouse songs.

To prepare the dance floor within the longhouse for dancing, they carried dirt inside and put several layers on the floor, and stomped on it until was firmly packed down. The men and women who were involved in conducting this ceremony were knowledgeable in the culture, and they knew which were the proper songs for the drummers to sing. The gathering was called Pápawawshtaymat (Engagement Dance); other tribes call it Pátkwaychashat. The meaning for this ceremony is important. Pápawaawshtaymat was a public display of selecting a mate for the young man in the family. It was a way to unite Indian heritage and culture, to maintain territorial food-gathering, hunting, and fishing places.

My parents were married in this traditional way. Traditional marriages, also known as Indian trade marriages or arranged marriages, were recognized as legal marriages not only by our families and communities but also by the government. They were legally binding in the eyes of the court. This was so on the Yakama Indian reservation until 1950. Traditional Yakama marriages required mutual agreement between both sides of each family. Approval was generally followed by an Indian trade between the immediate family members of the bride and groom.

Arranged marriage and the Engagement Dance ceremony were two of three practices recognized in traditional Yakama marriages. The third practice, *klíwawyat* (the serenade), occurs when a marriage partner seeks another because the present partner is barren. The original spouse has the choice to remain or leave. Both sides of the family participated in each of these traditions. The wedding trade was fundamental to arranged marriages. The trade secured the inheritance of future children. It was through these traditions that the Sahaptin tribes secured their land base.[1]

Many changes have impacted land ownership in the transition from traditional to modern time. Now the federal government is withdrawing its responsibility to protect Indian trust lands for treaty signing tribes. I am concerned as I observe our trust lands gradually being depleted, as "outsiders" whose ancestors are not Yakama are allowed to inherit land. Where will the Yakama people go when the land is all gone?

My parents' marriage was legalized by a *pápshx̱wiit* (Indian trade) between my father's Umatilla family and my mother's Yakama relatives. My father, Henry (Wataslayma) Beavert, was half Umatilla and half Columbia River-Yakama from Táp'ashnak̲'it (Bickleton, Washington), a little town at Horse Heaven Hills. His grandfather, Shɨ́shaash (Porcupine), came from a village on the north side of the Columbia River, across from the present city of Umatilla, Oregon.

Shɨ́shaash came to the Yakima Valley to ask for my mother to be the bride for his grandson. The Umatilla family did not send their children to school, and they followed the traditional ways strictly. My father did not go to school. He was raised in a slightly different culture, and he spoke a different dialect and no English. My mother, Hoptonix Sawyalilx̱ Wanto, was born and raised in the Indian village, Sih', on Taptíil, the Yakima River. My mother spoke Yakima-Klikatat and my father spoke Umatilla-WallaWalla, the dialect spoken by the Plateau people in Oregon. This environment in which Indian people did not speak one word of English at home caused all of us who lived in our village to learn each dialect and language. I am glad I learned to speak and understand the different dialects from the Columbia River.

My mother's grandfather, Sawyalilx̱, objected to Shɨ́shaash's request because he did not believe Hoptonix was old enough for marriage, since she had just turned twelve years old and had not had her First Menses initiation ceremony. The other Elders in her family argued that they were bound by the traditions of the Yakama people. In the end, they agreed to the marriage because despite the mixed views of the Elders in her family, my mother had participated in the Marriage ceremony, Pápawawshtaymat. So they traded my mother's *tmayíksh* (female dowry) for my father's *inawawíksh* (male dowry). Those were the days when Sahaptin, Nez Perce, Umatilla-Cayuse, and Columbia River tribes and bands—which include Umatilla and Warm Springs in Oregon and the Yakama in Washington—practiced arranged marriage rituals to establish broader political, social, and kinship relationships.

For my parents, being married in this traditional way did not mean the marriage lasted forever. My mother left our home soon after she *ichákwiłka malíish* (got her divorce). She went to Nez Perce country in Idaho, to stay with her *káatsa* (paternal relatives) and later married an educated man named Alexander Saluskin. He was Salish on his maternal side. His mother was Chashtkw'l, Louise Timentwa. His father was George Saluskin, a Yakama Indian. Alexander was raised by his Salish grandmother at Icicle River above Cashmere, Washington, near the city of Leavenworth, in the Cascade Mountains. His father and mother were married in a small Catholic chapel at Cashmere, where a park and museum now exhibit the chapel and small one-room school. Those buildings were relocated from Icicle Creek where a Catholic priest established his church to teach the Indian people. Alex used to take all of us there to show us where he had gone to school. He would show us the seat he had sat in doing his schoolwork. There is an old Indian cemetery located on the north hillside at Cashmere where his mother's ancestors are buried. Alex's mother spoke the Salish Winátchi language and she learned the Yakima dialect from her husband.

George and Louise were forced from their home. They moved to Awátam (Parker, Washington) at Pax̱útakyuut, where they took allotments and settled down. There were two sons that I knew about, Alexander and David Saluskin. I was a teenager when I met David. He was a federal government policeman on the Yakama Reservation. Sometimes my friends and I would linger on our way home after a movie. We all lived in the city limits and went to the movies together. My parents would not let me go alone. When David was on duty, he would send my schoolmates home then drive me home in his fancy police car.

Nakáłas (my mother's mother) Timinsh, Emma Sawyalilx̱, was the daughter of Sawyalilx̱ and X̱ax̱ísh. She was married to Oscar Wantux (Wanto), *napúsas* (my mother's father). He was the son of Old Wantux and Tux̱amshish. Wantux spoke Yakima-Klikatat and his wife spoke Lower Snake River Palouse-Nez Perce. He taught me how to speak Nez Perce. Soon, my grandfather's two brothers, and his nephew came to stay with us. They were fluent speakers of Nez Perce. Our village became lively again. My adopted uncles were farming the land my father used to plow and plant with grain. The horses were being tamed and were ridden again.

My Aunt Mussie, who had been away at boarding school, had returned home, and took over the cooking and housekeeping of our household. She had learned domestic science in a Catholic school at Tulalip, on the coast. My Aunt Mussie was the one to explain how things worked in the outside world. She explained that life would be different when *nakáłas* (my mother's mother) was no longer there for me, which I didn't understand because I thought grandmother was going to be with me forever.

Wúukshanaash (I stayed home) during my childhood, except when Grandmother X̱ax̱ísh took me with her to the Columbia River or to the mountains to pick berries or to visit my *tax̱nútwayma* (first cousins) when we were finally old enough. We all were born a few years apart, and we could not visit other homes until we were old enough and *tmáakni* (well behaved).

MY EDUCATION: PUBLIC SCHOOL AND TRADITIONAL AND LONGHOUSE WAYS

When I was old enough, truant officers threatened to take me away to government school so my stepfather enrolled me at Lincoln Public School in Toppenish, Washington. (Later, after grandmother died, my family put me in a First Christian Mission boarding residence and from there I attended White Swan Public School until tenth grade.) I walked from grandmother's house to school every day. There was no bus service during that time. In the wintertime I went by horseback, and tied my horse outside the school grounds where they had a small barn. *Nakáłas* X̱ax̱ísh wrapped my legs in burlap sacking to keep my legs warm, because she could not afford galoshes (that is what we called snow boots). She accepted donations from people in town, and sometimes I wore clothes way too large for me. People might think we were pitiful; but I did not care what I wore, as long as it kept me warm and I was with my *káła*.

My first year in school would seem comical to some people; I could not speak or understand English. If it were not for a very patient and kind teacher, I probably would have given up and gone home forever.

I had four friends in grade school. We were outcasts, because we were the ethnic minorities: Nisei Japanese, Black/African American, Spanish, German-Dutch, and Indian. I was the first fullblood Indian student to enroll in Lincoln Public School. We were drawn to each other because the white students would not play with us. The Japanese and Dutch girls became my best friends mainly because we walked home together. Sometimes the Dutch girl asked me to go home with her. Her mother would serve us whipped cream sweetened with sugar on fresh baked bread. They lived in a tiny white house with two bedrooms. Her mother kept the floor white by scrubbing it with lye. We had to

FIGURE 2.2. The roaring waters of Celilo, ca. 1948. Courtesy of Virginia Beavert family photo collection.

remove our shoes when we went inside. Her parents did not speak English. I do not remember what her father did for a living. The area where they lived was populated by Germans; it was called German Town.

My Japanese friend lived close to my house, only three miles away. Her father and mother raised vegetables. She had two brothers in high school, and they spoke English quite fluently. My Japanese friend's name was Tomiei (Tomi-yay).

Most of my *tax̱nútwayma* (cousins) were boys. I had one particular female cousin who was a *nax̱tiłá* (cry-baby); her name was Walulmay, Eileen George (Redhorn). When we became adults, we became best friends. She was a fluent Ichishkíin speaker, and she also spoke the Blackfeet language. She fell in love with a young traveling preacher from Blackfeet, Montana, Jesse Redhorn. Her father, Tsasat, was my uncle Jesse George. She had four brothers—Johnson, Andy, Thomas, and William—and one half brother, Ned. This was the immediate family of Yakama George Sawyalilx̱ and X̱ax̱ísh's son, X̱ayawat, Johnny George. My grandmother X̱ax̱ísh's sister, Tkwasayat, had a son, Johnny McCoy, who had two daughters; they were half Wíshx̱am and half Yakama and they lived at a village across from The Dalles, Oregon. Because my uncle Johnny was a *cháynach* (newly-married man) married to a Wíshx̱am woman, his inlaws were allowed the privilege to fish at the Wɨ́shx̱am fishing site. My stepfather, Alex Saluskin, took the family there to fish during spring fishing season. My cousins Esther and Margaret McCoy spoke both Yakima and Kiksht, and we were able to converse with each other in Ichishkíin because I did not understand Kiksht. Margaret spent most of her time at the First Christian Mission located on the Yakama reservation near White Swan. Esther and I were born on the same day, and when we were too young for school, we played all day along the beach at Wɨ́shx̱am on the Columbia River.

NP'ÍWIT NCH'IWÁNAPA

CELILO STORY

Wúux̱miki ashkú wɨshúwanx̱ana skúulitat kush áḵ'inunx̱ana Na'íłas aw ishapáts'ɨmksh shuwatpamá x̱apiłmí ku ínpimx̱ itámaatsha niimí wíx̱wɨlx̱wɨl wax̱wnayki, kush áshukwaana tsa'atsímkaash panátta skúulitknik.

In the springtime when I was getting ready to go to school, I saw my mother sharpening her butchering knives and I saw my stepfather taking our canvas army tent out of storage. I knew that soon they would take me out of school.

Ínpats Rudy, iwachá íx̱wi iksíks kush ánatkwaninx̱ana, íkwaknash wachá inmí kútkut. Na'íłas iḵḵanáywix̱ana apísh aníx̱ana. Ílax̱yawix̱ana tkwínat ku aníx̱ana ch'láy.

My younger brother Rudy was a little child and it was my job to look after him. Mother was busy taking care of our [winter food source] cache. She dried the salmon, and she made *ch'lay,* pulverized salmon rendered in steelhead oil.

Ínpimx̱ inp'íwix̱ana ɨmaawípa waníki Sk'in, ankwnák kaasmí wáx̱wayki iwayáwayksha Nch'i Wánapa.

My stepfather fished on the island called Baby Board, where the railroad bridge extends across the Columbia River.

Míshx̱it tíin myánashma papx̱winúux̱ana Nch'i Wánapa Siláylunan. Inmíyaw, X̱ápaawish Siláylupa iwachá anakúsh tun wáḵ'ish tíin.

I wonder what the [other] Indian children's thoughts were about the Columbia River fisheries called Siláylu [Celilo Falls]. To me, the falls at Celilo was like a live human being.

Atashkú wisháchikx̱ayka Wánayaw, kúuknam áyktax̱nay x̱ápaawishnan.

When we used to arrive at the Columbia River you could hear the sound of the waterfalls.

T'áalknam ix̱átamatł'umx̱tax̱nay ínɨmtnɨm x̱apaawishmínɨm.

The sound of the falls would envelop you and you would become deaf.

Anakúshnam ɨmítyaw i'áshanita wáwnakwshash ínɨmtnam.

It's like the sound permeates your entire body.

Úytnam, nax̱sh łkw'í ku sts'át chaw pnúta, ku níiptipa łkw'ípa cháwk'a áykta.

At first, the first day and night you won't be able to sleep, and the second day you will no longer pay attention to the sound.

Íkush iwachá Siláylu, anakwnák tíinma panp'íwix̱ana, pa'aníx̱ana tkwátat anwíktay.

That's how it used to be at Celilo Falls where the Indians fished for salmon to put away for winter survival.

Ambrose Whitefootmí, ku niimí, íkw'aknash ikwɨ́ áp'ɨx̱sha.

At the railroad bridge there were three dry shacks: the Selam's, Ambrose Whitefoot's, and ours, that I remember.[2]

Tł'áax̱wma panisháatuna miimawít. Walím ílkwshki pakúukix̱ana áyatma. Pnúnx̱anaatash tiichámpa, kuutash winaníix̱ana wanapamá chíishki. Awkłáw Na'íłas aníx̱ana saplɨ́l pax̱aapí tawtawliinmípa pax̱aapáwaaspa. K̠'ínupa anakush-páynk páshtɨnma paníchx̱ana saplɨ́l.

We all lived the old way. The women cooked on an open fire; we slept on the ground, and bathed in river water. Except my mother baked biscuits in a tin-can oven [a mod-ernized method] that resembled the kind the white women stored their bread in.

Páyshx̱it Nakáłasin mɨnán pá'ɨyax̱anya uu paysh pɨstɨx̱łáyin pá'anyanya.

My grandmother probably found it somewhere, or the blacksmith made it.

FIGURE 2.3. Ready to dig camas: Ellen Saluskin, first left, with Mary John, Isabel Menineck, and Ellen's son Rudy, taking part in a root festival prior to digging bitterroots for the Toppenish Longhouse, ca. 1949. Courtesy of the Ellensburg Public Library, INA-048.[3]

Íkushnank x̱átash myánashma ax̱aashnúux̱ana, wínat Siláylukan wúux̱miki.

That was what the children anxiously looked forward to, a trip to Celilo in the springtime.

Úytnam wiyánawiikta kúnam áykta íkwɨlkin ínɨmsha wána. Chawtúyay tuun yíktay, t'aalk. Chiish ix̱ápaawi pshwápshwapa ku iwíit'iishksha.

When you arrive, you hear the river roaring. The sound is deafening as several separate waterways have water plunging over giant rocks and splashing down below.

Children were *sápsikw'ani* (taught) the traditional culture of Sahaptin at home. Until around 1975, small children were not allowed at important ceremonials. That included the First Foods communion ceremony, called Ká'uyt (root feast). My cousin, Shuyawt, Louie Sweowat, and I were instructed by my *káła*, X̱ax̱ísh, and Louie's great-grandmother, Lix̱ups, who were full sisters. They *walptáyka* (sang) the food songs together and we would *wáasha* (dance). They taught us how to properly *asht káatynamyaw* (enter the longhouse), *ku mɨnán awínshma ku áyatma* (and where the men and women) were to sit. The grandmothers sang the prophet songs and recited the teachings of the holy man. They told us to learn the songs and carry on the ways and the teaching.

Sometimes I became so confused when listening to the instructions about the longhouse! The words were so strange and came so fast that when we were told to rest, both Louie and I took the chance to ask questions. They passed around snacks of dried fish fillet, dried fruits, and nuts. Then they began to *ititatámasha* (chant the parables) from the teachings of the local holy *shapátux̱ni tiin* (prophet). We listened. Listening is an important part of the training. They told us to listen with our heart. It took a while to understand what that meant. Perhaps I still do not understand a lot of the meaning in those chants. I was advised not to analyze those words. The Elders say, "When you hear it long enough and listen with your heart, it will gradually become part of your life." I often wondered why Louie and I were selected for this training.

My mother introduced me to food gathering when I became sixteen years old. My mother was a leader of women food gatherers. Figure 2.3 shows her (first left) with Mary John and Isabel Menineck and my younger brother, Rudolph Saluskin, on a digging trip for *pyax̱í (Lewisia rediviva)* and *sikáwya* (*Lomatium* sp.). (Note that the caption reads "Ready to dig camas" even though the roots being dug are *pyax̱í* and *sikáwya. Camas* was a generic term used for all roots.)

I learned a few songs that we sang at our own longhouse during that time, and I learned three death songs and two spiritual chants that my people believe are sacred and should not be shared with outsiders. My longhouse participation has been limited to my family members' funerals, giveaways, memorials, and other celebrations, and during food ceremonials and other social community activities. Sensitive traditional knowledge is often misunderstood and therefore I include only general references here.

I grew up listening to the tutelage of the Elders at Sih' village and am grateful for this knowledge about how important the Native ways are to our people. I am also grateful to have learned the different dialects spoken during these sessions. It has impacted my life profoundly.

NOTES

1 In March 1963, Congress passed Federal Public Law 280, allowing Washington State to take jurisdiction over the Yakama Tribe's trust land and certain domestic affairs. Until 1963, the inheritance procedure was controled by the federal government. A federal judge held hearings to determine inheritance by recognizing Indian trade marriage. The requirement that the heir be descended from an original landowner was strictly enforced. This law protected the land from infringement by outsiders.

2 The term *tyáwtash* (dry shack) includes the enclosed sleeping quarters and cooking space.

3 Figure 2.3 shows Ellen Saluskin teaching prayer song to Mary John and Isabel Menineck, who were apprentices. Mary John became leader of women root diggers at White Swan Longhouse located at White Swan, Washington.

CHAPTER 3
Life Circles

Wyá'uyt Waḵ'íshwit

When I asked the Elders for their wise instruction, this is what one Elder said:

"Anakú Tamanwiɫá itmíyuna íchɨnki tiichámki ku itamánwya tíinan ku tɬ'aax̱w tuun kákyanan, ku páshapatkw'anatya paníipt, ɨwínsh ku áyat; aytúks ku taláyi. Kúshx̱i pátamanwya pɨ́t'x̱anuknan kwnak pánicha tɬ'áax̱wnan tuun ku pánya wáḵ'ishwit kúshx̱i páshapattawax̱na panápu. Ánach'ax̱i pá'anya hawláak wayinwayinɫámaman, ku tiichampamánan wáḵ'ishwit. Chiishpamánan páshapawinama wanapáynk atáchiishknik íkwɨn ishíchyaw. Piimách'ax̱i pawá panápu. Íkushat áwa pɨnmínk náwtmiyush kwɨnkínk tɬ'aax̱w tun watwáa piná'ishax̱ta tmíinwa."

"When the Creator made plans for this world, he created all the people and creatures, and he made them walk together —man and woman, female and male animal. And He created the mountains where he placed all different kinds of beings and he gave them life, and he made them walk together. Then he made the winged ones and the ground people and gave them life. He made the water people and placed them in the water, from the ocean to the nest. They, too, are paired—male and female. That is how he planned it; that is how life is to continue to replenish itself."

Ának íkwɨn íshax̱a sɨ́nwit: "Páyshnayat chaw kúunak tamánwitnan átmaakta kuna íx̱wi wáta shapáshuyni."

After she said that, she added, "When we do not follow and do not respect his law, then we will suffer."

FAMILY PLANNING AND PREGNANCY / TMÍYUT TTAWÁX̠TWIT KU IYÁKWIT

Children were spaced every five years. Because food was scarce at times, which meant a shortage of roots and berries, salmon, and deer and buffalo meat, families had fewer children than now. Birth control was practiced—by both the man and the woman—in order to avoid hardships raising children. Taboos were practiced for many stages of married life—during conception, after childbirth, and during child-raising. Today, people believe life of this kind is too strict. But it was our way of life before the change came to the Indian people. This made people strong, and they were able to survive many hardships up to the present, and still hold onto what they have left.

There were many prohibitions a new mother and father needed to observe from pregnancy to the birth, especially with their first baby. During the time his wife was pregnant, the father-to-be was banned from killing anything. He could not hunt or fish. We are told that when an animal is dying it goes into several phases of contortions; it rolls its eyes around and crosses its eyes and it goes into convulsions. They say this will reflect on the newborn, as it might be born cross-eyed, epileptic, or inherit other inflictions experienced by the dying animal.

When parents observed the teachings, there were very few babies born with crossed eyes, with cleft mouths, or with epilepsy. Historically, this cannot be proven, but now more babies are born with afflictions that were rare a hundred years ago.

Parents abstained from having sex until after the baby was weaned. As mentioned above, it was not wise to have too many children because of the dangers of drought and starvation. Following the ancient ways, parents spaced their children five years apart. Some women I interviewed told me that when a baby was conceived too soon after a woman had given birth, it usually died. Orphaned babies were given to a prominent family to rear, often to a leader who was a good provider for all of the people.

New parents observed the ways of each side of their family. When parents were away on food-gathering expeditions, children (toddlers and older) stayed with grandparents. In this way children learned the Old Ways from their grandparents in lessons their clan or tribe observed.

CHILDBIRTH / X̠IIT

At the end of a woman's pregnancy she was isolated in a Birth Hut which was conical in shape and similar to the present sweathouse, and located some distance from the main village. She lived in the birth hut for five days, during the birth and then after the child was born. It was a private affair. A midwife attended the birth and an Elder stayed with her to teach her proper infant care. One or two experienced women assisted with difficult childbirths or performed other important chores. The chores involved heating flat stones to warm the patient's abdomen, carrying water, bathing the newborn, and performing the umbilical cord surgery as well as the ear piercing when the baby was a girl.

When the baby was a girl the maternal grandmother gathered soft milkweed puffs for diapers and for the mother's napkins; when the baby was a boy the paternal grandmother did these things. The paternal grandmother wove a cattail cradleboard for the baby's first cradleboard. For a boy, the board was designed with a male motif; a girl's board was designed with female colors, beadwork, et cetera. The cradleboard was designed to fit the baby's body so that the body would grow straight. Yakama people did not practice circumcision. During this time the mother was tutored by the Wise Ones about the responsibilities of motherhood and the proper care of the child.

The baby's *ishísh* (umbilical cord) was preserved for the child. The mother covered it with soft buckskin made into a tiny pouch, beaded with a special design, then hung on the baby's first cradleboard hoop. When older, a male child would wear it on a cord around his neck for the rest of his life; girls would store it in a keepsake box. The Old People told us: "It [the cord] is the connection to the mother and Mother Earth; for as long as you keep your umbilical cord necklace with you, you are aware of your identity and your relationship to God and to Creation."

NEWBORN / MYÁLAS

An infant is born without culture. The newborn experiences the essence of culture instantly. Newborns experience the feel of temperature—cool water over the body. They become hungry, and experience the need to cuddle against a familiar, loving body. The newborn is handled and washed as part of the transition from the womb to the beginning of a new culture. The grandmother takes the Indian baby to the spring and dunks him or her in the cold water to teach that life on Earth will not be easy. Some Elders say that this ritual awakens latent cells in the child's body which makes the infant healthy and strong. Even this first familiar exposure has an effect upon the newborn's development as he or she experiences life outside of the womb. We learn culture throughout our entire lifetime until the last breath is taken by the body. Parents are also the teachers of culture, and the process of change will influence the lives of many people who are part of a child's life. We learn culture in many ways.

Parents and family are a child's first experience with cultural teaching. Often a male or female infant's first word is *aḵúu* (daddy). As young individuals progress through life, they learn from other experiences with peers, playmates, friends, and even their enemies, how to cope with their environment and how to protect themselves and those who depend on them. In modern life today, this involves school, books, television, movies, each impacting the child's life.

Life does not begin during birth for an Indian child. According to the Elders, life begins before conception. The infant's future is planned way before his mother and father are brought together in marriage. A dowry is started by the mother, aunts, and grandmother. The collection is added to each year. By the time the child is old enough to marry, his or her dowry consists of many things.

CRADLEBOARD / SK'IN

The baby's first *sk'in* (cradleboard) was made of *chch'iw* (cattail) gathered by the grandmother. The newborn's father made the backing for the first cradleboard from a cottonwood section that he planed into a thin board wide enough to accommodate a growing baby. He bored holes around the edge of it for lacing, designing it according to his family's tradition. Then he would select a branch for the cradleboard hoop from a willow or hardwood tree. This was the father's responsibility; he could not have anyone do this for him. When finished with these tasks, he gave the base of the cradleboard to the maternal grandmother if the baby was a girl, or to the paternal grandmother if it was a boy. The grandmother put the finishing touches on the board by putting on the cover, the hood, and mattress. The head must have a round doughnut-shaped pillow to shape the head properly, and a small raised padding under the knee so that the baby will grow nice long, straight legs. The bottom of the covering is lapped over and laced with enough material to accommodate the growth of the baby. The children covet their baby boards.

The grandmother wrapped the infant for the first visit with the relatives. By that time, the mother was capable of carrying on her usual activities in the home. The Elders say, "The cradleboard is the baby's home until he begins walking." Sometimes a child will sleep in the cradleboard until it is two or three years of age. A new cradleboard is made for each child. It is not proper to put a baby into a used one.

FIGURE 3.1. Ruth Coyote (Cayuse Tribe) with a traditional cradleboard of the kind made for baby boys. Typically boys' boards were made by the father's mother. Photo by Lee Moorhouse. Special Collections and University Archives, University of Oregon Libraries, Eugene, PH36, photo ID# 4392; and the Confederated Tribes of the Umatilla Indian Reservation.

FIGURE 3.2. This modern cradleboard was made in a traditional style by Anna Hoffer, left. It is a girl's cradleboard. Students are from the author's Ichishkíin language class at the University of Oregon, 2016. Courtesy of Joana Jansen.

DIAPERING / X̱TÍNIT

When a Native child grows up in a traditional environment, his or her parents' marriage is sanctioned in and by a Wedding Trade. Children from traditional marriages are highly regarded. Shortly after a child is born from such a marriage, he or she is acknowledged at a Páx̱tinit (Diapering ceremony). Relatives from both sides of the extended family, maternal and paternal, participate in and attend these ceremonies. When the child is a boy, the paternal family initiates this trade and the maternal side initiates it when the child is a girl. Gifts are exchanged between both maternal and paternal relatives, and gifts are brought for the child. This practice honors the heritage on both sides of the family. The philosophy in this activity is to unite the families and tribal territory; and to preserve the values of culture, language, and religion.

NAMING / WANÍKT

X̱ax̱ishmí Tɨmnanáx̱t
Tx̱ánat iwá lahaháamyaw ititámani
pakwɨ́ɫksim tɫ'áax̱w tuumíyaw
anakw'ɨ́nk iwá wak̲'íshwityii.
Nch'iinmí tamanwitmí naknúyii
alitlak̲'itmíknik tɫ'yawitnmíyaw.

Quoting Yakama Prophet as told by X̱ax̱ísh
Existence is the eternal form of life
counted far back since immemorial.
It is equal to all living things with
spirit. The invisible power looks
after all from the determined time of
birth to the time of death.

The second ceremony during childhood is the Naming ceremony. When the child or teenager is old enough to understand, the family selects an ancestral name that fits the personality of the child who is to receive the name. In the case of a girl, she might develop habits reminding the family Elders of a passed-away family member. It is common for a girl to acquire a name from her mother's family. If a boy child likes to hunt or fish, or has a talent for taming wild horses, then he would acquire the name of a passed-away man with similar talents on his father's side of the family.

Traditionally, the Naming ceremony was performed at a memorial service for the passed-away person, although names could be given at other occasions too. When an individual is old enough to understand the importance of their name and are able to remember it, they are given a name. This can occur after puberty and into adulthood. During the year before the ceremony, the family sets aside things to give as gifts at the memorial to relatives of the person who has passed away. The ceremony includes a giveaway, dinner, and then the naming; the dinner and giveaway are provided for by both families of the passed-away one.

After dinner the person who will be named is dressed and brought out for the occasion. An Elder "crier" or announcer, a person who holds special knowledge about this ceremony, then cites the heritage of the name being given to the person and calls forth the gift recipients. The person receiving the gift gives a short description of the personality of the passed-away person whose name is given and his or her relationship to that name.

In modern settings when ancestral names are lacking, a name is taken from nature, for example the name of a bird, flower, or animal. Sometimes an Elder will loan his or her name to a youngster, and when the Elder dies, the loan name becomes legal at the memorial of the Elder.

My mother acquired her name during the Winter Dance. Her grandfather was a medicine man and he gave her a spiritual name. She became his assistant when he performed the Healing ceremony. A spiritual name is known only by the Shaman. She was also provided with an everyday name, X̱apt'íniks. I was named by a shaman in a Winter Dance also. This was during the time when the Christian church was trying to ban shamanism. Most of the Elders in my family were shamans, except my great-grandmother X̱ax̱ísh. A medicine man named Timothy George gave me a spiritual name. Later my mother named me after her paternal grandmother, Tux̱ámshish.

EARLY CHILDHOOD TRAINING / SÁPSIKW'AT

The Old People were teachers of strict lessons, and they told the child about the Whipman, who was the enforcer of broken rules. The Whipman earned his food with his craft, teaching children proper behavior. The Whipman was not a common individual in the community. He was selected for his knowledge and experience in dealing with child psychology and enforcement. While he inflicted punishment, he evaluated the situation and expressed his reasons for the punishment.

The Whipman traveled on horseback to visit each village to check on the children. When a child in one village was naughty, he was summoned. He began the whipping ritual with the child who had misbehaved first, using a special whip of ten long willow branches tied together with twine. The children who were with that child when he or she misbehaved were also whipped but with a smaller bundle of willows to remind them that they should have cautioned the offender. The Elders told me that this was to help the children to be aware among themselves that they should keep others from committing mischief. When a child was about to break a rule, the other children would tell him or her to quit, because they did not want to sit before the Whipman. The one who misbehaved had to bite the whip, and dance up and down while the Whipman sang the song about bad behavior. Afterward, the child had to declare he or she would never do it again, and then kneeled before the man and received the lashes the Whipman wielded on his or her bare back. The rest of the children would then line up to kneel before the Whipman and receive one or two light strikes. The children were under the customary rule of the Whipman until they were declared old enough to begin learning about maturing into adulthood, around the age of fifteen or sixteen.

The Storyteller also played a role in training children in our ways. She went from house to house, like the Whipman, to earn her food. The Storyteller was knowledgeable in child psychology and she was capable of pointing out the dangers of life using a story. At the end of each story there is always a lesson and behaviors a child must remember to avoid. She was like a professor, teaching important lessons, while the Whipman was like a policeman. They were paid by the families they visited with special food set aside in a cache gathered especially for them.

The Storyteller came to tell legends in the wintertime; before she began her duty, the family set a tule mat table for her and put down an assortment of dried salmon, deer meat, nuts, and dried fruits. Then she would eat and tell ancient legends handed down for generations about when animals and things could act and talk like people do today. The legends were about proper behavior. For example, one told how Mɨsɨ́s (Chipmunk) did not listen to Káła (maternal grandmother) when she told him not to wander too far away from home. When he disobeyed, T'aataɫíya (Witch Woman) grabbed him and almost ate him. But Mɨsɨ́s jerked away from her and ran home. Her claws left those scratch marks on his back.

The Coyote, in legends, is portrayed as the creator of certain things, but God is the Creator of "all things." When legends talk about history and life before the physical evolution of human beings, and the consequences of certain actions, the Watiɫá (Storyteller) says: "This is going to happen to anyone who breaks the rule of customary conduct." The decision then becomes the responsibility of the individual about his or her future and how he or she is going to live it.

CHILDHOOD CULTURAL INSTRUCTION AND PUBERTY / TNUNAḴ'ITPAMÁ SÁPSIKW'AT

An Elder is an important part of a child's entire life as they are the transmitters of cultural knowledge. Training is begun at an early age when the Storyteller recites the ancient legends while pointing out lessons about what is right or wrong. The details in the stories illustrate the punishment bestowed upon the animal creature for misbehavior. Stories answer questions like, "How did Raccoon acquire those stripes on his tail? And why was Beacon Rock, who used to be a handsome young man, turned into a useless mountain?" (Beavert and Walker 1974). Tales with lessons warned children about the dangers of life, like "the wicked Witch" who will "catch you and throw you into her basket. She will take you home and eat you. She gathers naughty children who do not mind and get into trouble."

In the past, during the onset of puberty, children were extensively instructed by people who were knowledgeable in the traditions and culture of the tribe. It was a critical period of life for the adolescent. Both boys and girls were taught about responsibilities that would affect their entire future.

Boys of this age were taught to respect girls. They were told about growing up, and about the changes they would experience in their bodies during puberty. There were special ways to behave around girls, especially their relatives. They were raised to respect all girls and women. The boys I knew during my childhood and teen years were always respectful to me. I grew up with all boy cousins. My teenage boy friends (not boyfriends) from the Nez Perce tribe treated me like a little sister. The one whom everyone believed was my special boy friend treated me differently than the boys treat their girlfriends today. There was no touching, no kissing, no sexual behavior. And I expected that kind of treatment, so I trusted all of the boys during my growing-up days. It was different from today, when children learn about sex early from the media or their peers. They believe it is natural, and when the urge is there, they do it, like the animals. I have observed some girls riding around on boys' backs, their legs wrapped around the boys' bodies, or taking other positions that seem natural to them and give suggestive sexual signals. Today sex is practiced by children still in puberty. Society is out of control, and that is the reason we have so much dysfunction and disease.

Boys were instructed by their uncles. They were made aware of men's responsibility as providers for the family and for those who cannot provide for themselves. Orphans, the disabled, and the aged were the responsibility of the men, who were the providers. Indian leaders in earlier times appointed men and women as food gatherers; the men were selected in accord with their skills as providers, or as warriors who could protect the people.

The boy was also tutored in geography so he could locate where the best hunting and fishing areas were found. He learned the customs regarding food acquisition, and the taboos that affect spiritual and physical family life. A young man was taught to respect his manhood by keeping the body and spirit clean. Learning the language of the sweat lodge, the songs and prayers about growing up and becoming a good hunter, fisherman, or a warrior became his goal.

The Holy Man, who instructs in the sweat lodge, emphasized the importance of respect for all things created by God. "The Earth takes care of all living things. The Earth is our Mother and she represents womanhood, and therefore we must respect all women." Spoken in Native words, the concept is pure poetry.

SHÍX̱WIT SÁPSIKW'AT	TEACHING VALUES
Tiin ttáwax̱t iwachá átaw anakú íkushkink watwáa panaknúwya tanamútɨm ku maykwáanik pápats'aka piimínk pimáshukt mɨ́ts'ay. Anakw'ɨnk íkuuk shuyaputɨ́mptki áwanikx̱a "heritage."	Indian heritage was prized when it kept the culture and religion intact and held the family structure together. This is what white people call heritage.
Íkw'ak kushkínk nch'ínch'ima myánashnan pasápḵitwanx̱a pashapáttawax̱ɨnx̱a pináshuki.	That was the reason the Elders were teaching the youth—nurturing them gradually to acknowledge their identity.
Iksíks áswan iwachá sápsikw'ani tun áwata pɨnmínk kútkut íchna tiichámpa. Míshkin kw'ɨnk ináktkwaninta, nisháykt, áyat ku pɨnmínk myánashma. Kúshx̱i pt'íniks iwachá sápsikw'ani. Anakú itx̱ánata áyat, mish pɨnk pinánaktkwaninta, ku kúshx̱i pɨnmínk nisháykt, ɨwínsh, myánash.	A young man was taught what his responsibilities were when he became an adult—how to care for his home, wife, and children. The girl was taught her responsibilities as an adult—to care for her home, husband, and children.

Anakú patax̱núnaḵ'ita, kuuk átx̱anax̱a tiináwit tamánwit twánat. Chaw piimínk tmyútay, awkłáw nch'inch'imamí míshkin kw'ɨnk iwáta náktwanini.

When young people become adults they must follow the spiritual teachings. Not their own, only what the Elders or spiritual people passed on to them.

From the day an Indian child was born, before the new laws came into existence, he or she was groomed for family life. A boy was taught all of the skills required to support not only his immediate family; he learned to provide for those who are living in poverty and need someone to depend upon for their everyday needs. For example, a good provider was expected to share his food with the old people, disabled ones, and orphaned children. Consequently, during his childhood he was taught all of the skills required for a good provider. Not every male child could be a Leader, however.

Each person had a role in the community. Each individual child was selected for his or her early potential skills and was taught to develop those skills as he or she progressed into adulthood, both to contribute to humanity and to prepare for the afterlife. Children were taught from the beginning that the life he or she carried was not his or her own. It is a gift from the Creator. The child is taught to take care of life, to respect it, and to respect everything on this earth that has life because all things are like brothers and sisters. When a man killed an animal for food, he thanked that animal for its life so that his own life might continue to exist. It is believed that everything humans consume was planned that way. The hunter thanked the Creator for the food and the animal for his life. The fisherman spoke to the salmon as it quivered under the club, thanking him for his life and thanking the Creator.

TMÁYWIT TILÍWALIT

Míimi, anakú uyt myánash pt'íniks itax̱núnaḵ'ix̱ana, ánichx̱anapat wíyat nisháyktknik tamátł'umx̱i ɨlíitɨliitpa. Kwnak nax̱sh áyatin pánaktwaninx̱ana. Anakú itilíwalix̱ana uyt, cháwakut pináwapashata pɨnmipáynk wáwnakwshashpa.

THE COMING-OUT CEREMONY

A long time ago, when a girl had her first menses, they put her far away from other people in a little hut. There was a woman there to take care of her. When her blood flowed, she was not allowed to touch herself on any part of her body.

Chaw pinátwanpta u piná'ayata. Kushnáyk'ay áyatin pánaktkwaninx̱a pt'íniksnan, "Áwnam tx̱ána áyat. Cháwk'anam wa myánash. Cháwk'anam łḵ'íwitsimita, áwnam pinásapsikw'ata náktkwanint nisháykt." Awkú áyatin pánix̱a sɨ́nwit anakú itx̱ánata ɨwínshyi, mish áwata tx̱ánat, kúshx̱i myánash anít, ku náktkwnint tsɨ́mti myálashnan.

She was not to comb her hair or scratch herself. That was why the woman helper was there—to counsel the girl: "You are now a woman. You are no longer a child. You will not just play, now you are going to learn how to take care of a home." The woman would advise her about married life, sex, pregnancy, and how to care for an infant.

Anakú i'átɨmta kwnink ɨlíitɨliitknik laak iwáta shukwínsh tł'aax̱w íkw'ak wapsúx̱wit tax̱nunaḵ'itpamá. Kuuk áwku iwá ts'aa ámanitay.

When she comes out of that hut, she will have all that knowledge. That is when she is responsible enough for married life.

Íkush íkw'ak áwacha miimá sápsikw'at tiinmamí.

That is how the old ways of the People were passed on.

The maternal family had a meeting after the *tmay* (unmarried girl) had her first menses and was adequately trained for married life. When the girl left the Menses Hut, she was informed about married life and family responsibilities. Word was sent out that she was eligible for marriage. She was prepared for the Engagement Dance, a "coming out" ceremony.

The family during the girl's confinement prepared for the Engagement Dance, which would include a giveaway. The girl was eligible for marriage now. She was wise in her future role as a wife and mother. She had been thoroughly counseled about the taboos before and during pregnancy. She would have no difficulty raising her child, or with her responsibilities toward her husband.

When a boy's family asks for a wife for him, the boy's parents have no voice in the matter. It is the same for the girl's parents, providing the union is acceptable to the girl's family. Instead, the decision is made by the Elders in each family. Both families must be equal in status, and both children must be from tribes that practice the same culture and have the same values. A special child was watched by other families during his or her adolescence for assurance of a good match when the proper time came. Most arranged marriages lasted a lifetime. Separation and divorce were very rare.

Today, young people select their own spouses without considering traditions practiced by the Sahaptin people. The result changes the tribal structure of family, inheritance, culture, and membership. This is another interesting subject. Some tribes follow strict laws regarding tribal membership and inheritance to protect their tribal land base. When tribal officials do not implement the policy by making exceptions caused by personal motives, then the law is violated. The man or woman who marries outside of the Sahaptin culture may not suffer, but these marriages impact the blood quantum for enrollment, inheritance, and the future of the children.

ARRANGED MARRIAGE / PÁPAWAWSHTAYMAT

PÁPAWAWSHTAYMAT

Chaw shin ishúkwaasha mun iwiyá'uyna pápawawshtaymat, awkɬáw Ititámat Naknuwiɬáma, anakwmák tɬ'aax̱w pa'íkwstɨmix̱ana átaw tx̱ánat.

Átway Miimamamí ititámat áwacha lch'íi, anakwíɬ wá niimí ɬamtíx̱. Pawíshtka átaw ɬkw'i, tx̱ánat, tɬ'yáwit, myálas anít, píitɬ'yawit, páwanikt, pápatkw'akyut, anatún átaw tx̱ánat piimyúk tiináwityaw.

Cháwnam páysh áwyax̱tax̱nay mɨnán ikushnanák túpan Museumpa, awkɬáw tun iksíks anakw'ɨnk kpaylimá tiin aníya.

COMING TOGETHER

No one knows when the Coming Together ceremony originated, except for the Time Ball Keepers, who recorded important happenings.

The now-deceased ancestors' Time Balls were as large as human heads. They recorded the special daily events, deaths, births, wars, name-givings—any important happenings for the Time Ball Keeper's people of traditional values.

You probably won't find those kinds of Time Balls in a museum, except for modern versions that people attempted to start.

Kwnamánk miimá tɨmnanáx̱tknik tiin ishúkwaana mɨnán áwacha ɨshchɨ́t wiyánintpama. Lahaháam winaatshapamamíknik áx̱miknik, wíihaykt wanapáynk, ku úyknik ɨshchɨ́t íkuuk akwíitamsh kpaylíma íchɨn támiwnat xwałx̱waypammamiyaw tiichámyaw.

From these ancient recordings on the hemp ball called "the count," the people knew which paths were for traveling where. They traveled from far distances to important gatherings. From up the Columbia River far away from as Wenatchee country they came down the Columbia and over the mountain into Klikatat country. [Where there is now a modern highway was once one of the old Indian trails.]

Kpáylk ashkú áwishapnix̱ana Nch'ínch'imaman kush ttúshma pa'ɨ́nx̱ana, "Cháwnash ínch'a áshukwaasha, ashkú wíyat panánana tímani tiichámknik kush chaw shínɨm tamuna íkw'ak."

Recently [in the 1970s], I asked Elders about these stories and they told me, "I don't know about those things because they took me away from the reservation and nobody told me those stories."

Ku ḵáaw, nch'ínch'i chaw itḵ'íx̱na átaw tiináwit isíkw'at. Kútya ttúush patɨmnáx̱na anakú pawachá iksíks ttáwax̱t, piimanách'apat wiyánch'ima kwnáx̱i ánanana anakú piimínk pyap uu pat ánaniinya pápawawshtamatkan.

And separately, Elders did not want to reveal important traditions. However, a few shared that when they were still children, their parents took them along when they took an older sister or brother to the Páwshtaymat.

Until the twentieth century, the young man and woman were taught about the responsibility of family, marriage, and child-raising. They knew from the very beginning what their life destiny contained. When the family decided to select a spouse for a child, they were careful about which family they wanted to connect their family unit to. A marriage was arranged and announced, and a date was set for the formal Indian trade.

In the arranged marriage the paternal family groomed their son or grandson from childhood to puberty in the responsibilities of family life. He learned appropriate skills to fulfill his destiny in his future life. The paternal family observed how families trained their young women, and the paternal family began to make a selection. It was important for families to form unions that were beneficial for survival in terms of territory and hierarchy. After the paternal family made their selection, the oldest male family member went to meet with the girl's family to discuss marriage. He would cite his family heritage, language, and culture. When the maternal Elder and his family approved of his proposal, they prepared for the marriage ceremony.

PÁPASHIX̱ANIT MYÁNASH

Anakúx̱it mun anwíktpa, paysh tyamíḵ'itnaḵ'itpa, anakú tiin iwshtúx̱ɨnx̱an anamɨník pawɨsháchikx̱ana tkwátat waḵ'ítanat, kuuk pa'aníx̱ana páwyaḵ'ukt ɨ́matalampa. Nch'i káatnam pápatukɨnx̱ana pápawawshtaymatay. Íkw'ak iwaníksha íkush anakú panákpnita tmay, ku ináawin páwyawshtayma ku paysh chaw pápawaynatata íkw'ak awkú patx̱ánata pawaláḵ'iki. Mayk íx̱wi kwnínk awkú kuuk átx̱anata nɨmnawíit pápɨshx̱wiit, anakú papúuchnik ɨwínshknik ku áyatknik pápawyakyuta pápatx̱taymata inawawíksh tmayíkshyaw.

ENGAGEMENT AND MARRIAGE

At a certain time of the year, probably springtime, the people gathered together, bringing food, and they built a large longhouse at Umatilla for the Meeting of Two People dance ceremony. It is called that because when the girl is brought out, the boy goes out to meet her, and if he is approved she lets him stay but if she turns away, he has to find someone else. After the engagement, the family has the Indian Wedding Trade. Man and woman sides trade with each other; male dowry is traded for female dowry.

ENGAGEMENT DANCE: A COLUMBIA RIVER VERSION AND A MODERN CEREMONY NARRATION

PÁPAWAWSHTAYMAT

Náx̱shk'a awachá tx̱ánat anakú myánash atax̱núnaḵ'ix̱ana myálasknik myánashyaw kuuk tíinma pa'aníx̱ana ayáyat wanapáynk. Papátukx̱ana nch'ii káatnam ku pawɨsháchikx̱ana ts'áax̱wknik mɨ́nik íkwɨn. Panáchikx̱a myánashma.

ENGAGEMENT DANCE

There was another ceremony when the first child came of age, and the Sahaptin People held this ceremony along the Columbia River territory. They set up a large longhouse, they camped there. They brought their oldest child.

Áwacha kwtɨnpamánksim walptáykt, chawíyat anakúshx̱i waashatpamá, awkłáw kuts'k mayktúnx̱. Íkuuk kwtɨnpamánk pa'itwásha waashatpamáyaw.

The songs were special for this ceremony, they resembled the longhouse songs, but slightly different. Nowadays the songs are mixed together.

Awkú papátukx̱ana káatnam íkwna wanapáynk anakwnák iksíks tawn iwá iwaníksha Arlington. Paysh áwa tiin waníkt kush chaw áshukwaanisha.

They would set up the longhouse there along the Columbia River where there is a small town called Arlington. It has an Indian name I cannot remember.

Aw tł'áax̱wkan miin pawánpix̱ana tíinmaman anakuumínk áwa kúshx̱i tiináwit. Ku pawɨsháchikx̱ana ku yakút ɨníit pawiptúkx̱ana kwnak.

They notified all tribes who practice the same tradition. They came and set up their camp there.

Anakú pawíi'uynx̱ana walptaykłáma pawát'ax̱ana kiwkíwlaas, kuuk panáshx̱ana myánash.

When they started the activity, the drummers would signal with the drum, and people brought their child.

Tináynaktknik walptaykłáma pimá'ikwstɨmix̱ana, pa'áwx̱anaykx̱ana kiwkíwlaas píkshani, ku wát'uychnik túskaas ttmayíma waayk wáashpa pa'áwx̱aynakx̱ana.

The singers positioned themselves in the west side, they stood in a straight line, side by side, holding their round drum and, the maidens stood in front, across the floor, in a straight line, side by side.

Anáshtiknik wapáwni amíishma patútix̱ana its'wáyki anakúshx̱i ttmayíma, waayk wáashpa. Anakú tiin wáashat iwíi'uynx̱ana, tł'áax̱wx̱i shin iwáashax̱ana. Ku mun chatikłá iwáwiinax̱ana kw'alálkw'alalki, kuuk panákpnix̱ana myánash ku panákslikx̱ana wáashpa.

On the east, the boys stood dressed in a straight line just like the girls, across the longhouse floor. When the dance started—first started—everyone danced. When the Bell Ringer gave the signal that was when the Elder brought her child out and danced across the floor.

Ttmayíma pawá ayáyat wapáwani tunx̱túnx̱ kálu tł'píipyi ku k'pɨ́tmi ɨwáywyi, wímshyakshi, ku luts'aanmí, ɨstíyaasi luxlúx taalaanmí, kkáatnam wápshaash áwa wáw'umki nuksháyki.

The maidens wore different-colored bright clothes decorated with beads, earrings of shell, gold and shimmering silver bracelets, long braids wrapped in otter skins.

Kúshx̱i waayk wáashpa pawá ináwawma, wilyakíyi, tunx̱túnx̱ lalupaanmí táatpas ku pipshmí ɨwáywishyi. K'pɨtmí shapáwaltawish tútanikpa papúuchnik tpɨ́shpa. Íkush awkú pimáwapaawax̱ana patkwaycháshatpa.

The boys were the same way, dressed in colorful chaps, wearing different-colored ribbon shirts, bone breast plates, beaded decorations in the hair hanging down on each side of the face. This is how they dressed at the Engagement Dance.

Íkush áwa tx̱ánat wanałamamí, anakwmák panisháykshana wánapaynk.

This was how the ceremony was performed by the people of the Columbia River, who lived along the river.

Átaw iwá chiish tiinmamíyaw. Tł'áax̱wnan tuun inaknúwisha. I'íyatł'pix̱a tamaníkshnan anakw'ɨ́nk wa niimí x̱nit, ku úyknik inísha waḵ'íshwit. Kwɨnkínk kw'ɨnk awkú piná'iwya'ishax̱sha.

Water is a vital part of Indian life. It takes care of everything. It waters the garden where all the foods exist, and it gives them life. That was how they were able to replenish themselves.

Tł'aax̱w tun iwá pɨ́ts'aki. Anakúsh íchi íkuuk átk'isha tímani sɨ́nwitnan: "Sɨ́nwi-t-nan," "á-tk'i-sha."

Everything is connected, like we see in the written word: "*Sínwi-t-nan,*" "*á-tk'i-sha.*" [Each of these connected pieces carries meaning.]

Kúshx̱i tiinmamí myánash kw'ɨ́łx̱i áwa páshwini. Pmách'ax̱i wat'úychan sápḵitwani pimá'ishax̱asha. Kwɨnkínk pawachá sáp'awyi shapátkw'alshtx̱i. Cháwtya shix̱ ḵ'ínupa, awkłáw mish myánash iwachá sápsikw'ani, ku mish kw'ɨnk myánash pinátmaaksha ku itmáaksha sápsikw'atnan ku pɨnmínk nch'ínch'ima. Íkush pawachá wáachyi ikks ttáwax̱tma, kúshx̱i piimínk wyánch'ima náx̱shpa nisháyaaspa.

The parents put equal value on children. They are preserved to benefit the future. This is the reason this Engagement ceremony is important. They are not judged for beauty; it depends on *how* they are raised, and it depends upon whether the child respects himself, the ceremony, and his family. They were closely observed, even when they stayed with the grandparents in their home.

Cháwpam px̱wíta tł'aax̱w tiin itwánashana. Ttuush tiin ihananúynx̱ana tiináwit twánat ku pináwɨnkpx̱ana túnx̱yaw tx̱ánatyaw.

Do not get the idea that all people followed this tradition. Some Indian people thought it was too much trouble, and they preferred to adopt different cultures.

Kushkínk áwacha nax̱sh sɨ́nwit pá'anix̱watpa twakwstɨ́myi, "Anakú inmí áyat myánash i'ámanita kwimyúuk anakw'ɨnmínk áwa tunx̱ ttáwax̱t. Cháwk'a awkú iwáta inmí myánash. Itwánata awkú kuunák ɨwínshnan."

It was for that reason, the Sahaptin people declared this, in the treaty, "When my daughter marries someone who is of different race, she is no longer my child. She must go with the man."

This annual celebration dance, called Páwawshtaymat or Pápawawshtaymat (Coming Together), was an older means of marriage selection. There was no special place where it occurred; it was announced to all the tribes and they came together, bringing children who were of eligible age and properly trained. They built a longhouse to accommodate everybody, and the singers came. The singers were like the religious drummers, but the songs were called social songs although they may sound similar to the religious longhouse songs.[1]

Anticipation was rampant. The finest regalia were brought out. The relatives observed other families, and how those children behaved. Children were treasured.

On the west side of the longhouse floor, seven teenage girls line up a few steps in front of the drummers. They are dressed in their finest bright-colored wing dresses, with shiny shell earrings, necklaces made of bone, and beaded moccasins. On the east side seven boys dance facing the girls, wearing beaded *sapák'ɨlks* (breechcloths), *wilyakí* (chaps), and *ɬk̲'am* (moccasins). Their long braids are decorated around the face with tiny braids intermixed with shiny beads and a white fluffy eagle feather tied at the tip. These boys and girls are already committed. There are several female couples dancing on the south side in the longhouse, and the men on the north side of the longhouse in pairs with the young men. The aunts and uncles usually escort the initiates. There are seven drummers, similar to the religious services in the longhouse.

The bell ringer makes a lot of noise with his bell and the drummers raise their drums in the air and sing loudly when a couple is approved by the *twáti* (leader and judge) when he lays the staff over the boy's hand, which is placed on the girl's right shoulder.

The *twáti* stands to the right of the singers. He is dressed like a medicine man, and he carries a long *twat'ikáwaas* (staff) wrapped in furs with an eagle feather tied to the tip of the staff.

The aunt will take the girl's *wákatsal* (left) arm with her right, and dance with her out on the floor. The uncle or grandfather will link his *nɨwít* (right) arm with the boy and dance out on the dance floor. They will wait; the uncle will pick out the girl, and he will lead his nephew to meet the female couple. The boy will extend his left hand on the girl's shoulder; the bell ringer signals by ringing his bell loudly, raising it in the air and the drummers raise their voice and raise the seven drums into the air. Everyone cheers loudly. If the girl's escort approves of the boy, she will remain dancing in place, but if she does not approve, she will whirl the girl away from the male couple and dance away with the girl. This might happen if the family had made their selection in advance, and they were waiting for the right one. But if she approves, they remain dancing until the *twáti* with the long staff covered with fur and an eagle feather at the tip walks out on the floor and lays the staff over the boy's hand, and everybody cheers again. The drums stop, and the woman's side will bring out a robe and cover the couple and they walk off together to the man's family. This activity continues for several days and nights until all or most of the boys and girls are paired off. This traditional ceremony is similar to the public announcement of an engagement by a couple in modern times.

SÁP'AWIT

Áwacha niipt tamánwit ikksmíyaw. Anakú patx̱ánax̱a ts'aa px̱winútpa tax̱núnaḵ'yi ku ts'aa sápsikw'ani, kuuk nch'ínch'ima pawaḵítɨnx̱ana mámknik nisháyaasknik áwa myánash ts'aa shapákyuut piimyúuk ttáwax̱tyaw kw'ɨnkínk úyknik myánashma áwata shúkii anakúsh náx̱shk'a mɨ́ts'ay. Kuuk ɨwínshknik iwínanux̱ana tmay myánashyaw. Páyshpat "ii" ákux̱ana, ku awkú piimínk tiin patíix̱wax̱ana, "Awna wɨshúwata átaw ḵḵanáywitki."

Chɨmyanashyíima awkú panákwɨshuwanx̱ana aswanmí inawawíksh.

Kúshx̱i pt'iniksmí wyánanch'ima ánakwɨshuwanx̱ana pɨnmínk tmayíksh. Papúuchnik ɨwínshknik ku áyatknik pápawyakyuuta pápatx̱taymata inawawíksh tmayíkshyaw.

Íkush awkú iwachá míimi. Íkushkink ḵ'tɨt áwacha tiin ttáwax̱t, anamáal íkush sáp'awyi panaknúwya piimínk mɨ́ts'ay anakuumínk áwacha kkúshsim tiináwit.

Ának awkú pápatx̱taymax̱ana chɨmmyanashyíima. Íx̱wimash isíkw'ata.

SELECTING

There were two laws for the young people. When young people are close to maturity and ready for teaching, the Elders searched for families they wanted to attach to and extend their heritage—extend further with children. The bride went to live with the groom's family. When they were approved, then the relatives announced to everyone, "Now we must get ready for the big event that follows [the Wedding Trade]."

The parents, then, would get the male dowry ready to trade.

At the same time, the girl's Elders were getting the female dowry ready. The man and woman sides trade with each other; male dowry is traded for female dowry.

That is the way it was long ago. That was how the Indian heritage remained strong, as long as they were meticulous and managed to keep their roots within the same culture.

Afterward, the parents exchanged gifts.
[Dowry items, listed in Ichishkíin and English, are included in the glossary.]

A few weeks later, the families completed the ceremony with the traditional Indian trade, when the boy's *inawawíksh* (male dowry) was exchanged for the girl's *tmayíksh* (female dowry). The marriage ceremony was an exchange of valuable artifacts and goods of equal value. After the ceremony, the girl went with the boy's family to familiarize herself with their culture. If the girl was too young, she lived with an aunt. Later, the couple was moved to the girl's family's home, where he would learn their ways.

It should be noted that this ceremony is no longer practiced. The people who knew the songs are gone. The young drummers are mixing these social songs with the longhouse religious songs, and nobody knows the difference anymore. The material contained in the boy's and girl's dowries have become too expensive. Collectors of artifacts have put too high a monetary value on these items. The traders who operate secondhand stores, and lending shops exploit the Indians by offering to buy these items for only a few dollars, and then turn around and sell them for triple the price to collectors.

As mentioned earlier, *tmayíksh,* the female dowry, included dresses made of buckskin or cloth decorated with shells or beads, dried roots and berries packed inside a five-gallon *pshatatpamá* (cornhusk bag) that is very valuable today, beaded and woven handbags, cedar baskets, and woven hemp containers. Later, shawls, broadcloth clothing, and combs were included. *Pátł'umx̱sh* (the bridal veil) was made of dentalium shells woven into a cap with a long trail down the back. In front there was a fringe made of colorful beads and old brass coins hanging down to cover the eyes.

Figure 3.3 shows the wedding veil worn by one of my language students at her wedding.

The *inawawíksh* (male dowry) included things that represent the male contribution to family life. The young man's training for manhood included fishing and hunting with his uncle. He was instructed how to recycle the raw materials from this into useful things such as rawhide parfleche, the Indian suitcase called *shá́ptakay*, and buckskin robes made of animal skins. Bones from deer and fish were made into eating utensils. Dyed porcupine quills were used to decorate costumes. The *twinúushush* (feather headdress) was made from eagle feathers and the war dance *wapalikáatsat* (roach headdress) from the hair of the porcupine. A young man hunted and provided dried meat and fish to fill the *shá́ptakay*. His family, for their contribution to his wedding day, acquired herds of *k'úsima* (horses) and *músmustsin* (cattle) for his dowry, to represent material things. These were traded with the immediate family of the bride for her female dowry.

FIGURE 3.3. A *pátł'umx̱sh*, the traditional wedding veil that was part of a girl's dowry. Courtesy of Charlene and Javin Dimmick.

INDIAN WEDDING TRADE / PÁPSHX̱WIIT

During the late nineteenth century and into the early twentieth century, only the immediate family members participated in the Wedding Trade. The dowry that was put away was valued for the amount of work that went into producing it: the tanning of hides, cedar basketry and cornhusk weaving, beadwork or jewelry production. Assembling a dowry also included the gathering and processing of food and ensuring its freshness (some breadroots get wormy after a while).

Now, in the early twenty-first century, Indians must go before a minister of a church and obtain a state license to be considered married. Being legally married allows for a spouse to inherit the estate when a husband or wife dies. Children can also inherit. Indian Wedding Trade marriages were recognized by the government until 1957, after that these Indian or "blanket" marriages were not considered legal. The legality of marriage became central to inheritance. So when the government realized that many tribes were issuing individual real estate tracts to their members, blanket marriages became problematic because they offered no legal proof of marriage.

The shift from Indian trade marriages to legal marriages has changed the ways that modern generations value Indian goods. The market has placed a

FIGURE 3.4. Male dowry items, 2016. Courtesy of Roger Jacob.

value on traditional (dowry) items that is so high, only collectors can afford to own them. At auction, cedar baskets can run up to many thousands of dollars. Other artifacts are priced based on the value of their authenticity and tribal origin.

For modern weddings, male dowry items are put into a typical trunk or suitcase rather than an expensive and out-of-reach *sháptakay*. The female goods are typically made of modern materials, like baskets woven from raffia instead of bark.

Today there are still many traditional beadworkers but beads are of lower quality, many of them plastic and glass. Root bags are woven with yarn or string instead of *taxús* (Indian hemp).

Commercial dealers know about Indian burials and trades, so they escalate the prices of needed blankets and shawls to sell to the Indians. Once I purchased a string of (what the salesman claimed were) real beads for fifteen hundred dollars! I treasure it, even if it may not be the real McCoy. The same

FIGURE 3.5. *Wápshat ámtanatnan* (the braiding of the bride's hair), 2010. Courtesy of Joana Jansen.

salesman did not know the value of real Canadian blankets and I purchased one for twenty dollars—a collector would have known the value to be five or six thousand dollars!

This greed and devaluing of traditional lifeways must be among the changes and grief the Prophet spoke about. We have separated the Elders from the family. Some parents abandon their children to orphanages where they are raised by people of different races and they learn different ways and languages. Despite this, men still hunt and fish and sell their game, and women sell roots and berries to earn enough money to pay their bills. We will survive. Our women are strong, the men will become responsible, and children will return home.

MARRIAGE CEREMONY / PÁPSHX̱WIIT

The bride's relatives spread many articles of value for her to sit on; her hair was braided, smeared with bear grease, to make it shiny or easy to comb. Wooden combs were put in her hair, and she was showered with small beads, coins, and jewelry to represent *apín* (head lice).

Afterwards, these items were taken by the guests who came to witness the event. Figures 3.5 and 3.6 show the bride being prepared in this way.

A big feast was given by the bride's family where the bride and groom were honored. Her family provided seats made of blankets and beaded bags, and guests were served on the very best dishes and silverware. Each participant

FIGURE 3.6. A bride is showered with small beads, coins and jewelry to represent *apín* (bugs), in an enactment by students from Virginia Beavert's Ichishkíin language class at the University of Oregon, 2016. Courtesy of Robert Elliott.

dressed in their best outer clothes, which were given to the hostess, and in return, they were provided with female goods, like sets of dishes and dried roots and berries to take home. After the food was served, the containers were taken home by the groom's people. Figure 3.7 is a drawing of this ceremony.

These traditional practices are incorporated into many weddings these days as well. Figure 3.8 shows the wedding party of one of my students. This ceremony was more modern but incorporated traditional practices. A minister performed the ceremony. Traditionally a medicine man would have officiated and seven Native drummers and a bell ringer would have been seated behind the wedding group.

Traditionally, after the ceremony, the bride was taken to her new husband's village, where she was tutored in their language and culture. If they were still too young to live as man and wife, they were given proper instruction. When the bride became familiar with the traditions and language of the groom, his family invited the bride's relatives to come to their village. They welcomed the bride's family the same way that they had been served. They prepared a big feast. The visitors stopped about one hundred yards from the home and organized the goods they had brought to trade with the man's side. These were trinkets representing the bridal shower, called *ashxyatúu*. The families brought camping utensils, knives, spoons and forks, small aluminum vessels,

FIGURE 3.7. The wedding feast, where the bride and groom were honored. The families sat on seats of blankets on tule mats. Courtesy of Judith Fernandes.

FIGURE 3.8. *Pamalíit* (modern wedding), 2010. Courtesy of Charlene and Javin Dimmick.

FIGURE 3.9. *Ashxyatúu:* women join together, holding household items to start housekeeping for the new bride. Courtesy of Judith Fernandes.

small beaded coin purses, and small cedar baskets for berry picking. These items were tied to a long string of pony beads. The women dressed themselves in shawls, bandanas, and beads. The whole group held onto the long string of beads with the tiny household and kitchen articles tied together. As they neared the house, they all hollered repeatedly, "*Ashxyatúu, uu, uu!*" When I asked my mother translate this for me, she just repeated the phrase. She said it was a time for laughter and joking as they pulled each other along. Figure 3.9 is a drawing of this shower.

The host families met and directed the immediate family to the table exclusively reserved for them. Extended families from both sides formed partnerships with one another, and they remained trading partners for life.

When a child was born to the couple, if it was a boy, the man's side traded first, and the female side hosted. They exchanged gifts like before, but they brought things for the baby and that was why they called the ceremony *X̱tínisha* (diapering the baby). When a girl was born, the woman's side traded. This went on as long as the couple had children. The philosophy in this activity was to unite the families and tribal territory, and to preserve the values of culture, language, and religion.

As mentioned above, the firstborn child is important to the family and especially so when a traditional marriage union had been conducted. Traditional marriages preserved territory, culture, language, and traditions. They united and strengthened people of the same culture. Traditionally arranged marriages were made between the Sahaptins at the Coming Together ceremony. When an arranged marriage was made between ruling families the ceremony was elaborate. If a marriage was made outside the Sahaptin culture, it was usually to facilitate alliance with other tribes.

The Coming Together Dance screened out slaves' children, the children of women from coastal and valley tribes, who could not participate in the dance. The Klikatats practiced head flattening to distinguish kinship and to separate themselves from the slaves whose heads were round. The slaves could marry with the permission of the family or the headman of the village.

MY MOTHER'S STORY / NA'ɨŁASMÍ TɨMNANÁX̱T

This is the story of how my mother, Hoptonix Sawyalilx̱, became the bride of my father, Aylux, from Tap'ashnak̲'it, at age twelve or thirteen.

My mother, Ellen (her English name), was very young and she was easily influenced by her older, mischievous cousin. It was the time of the annual Pawawshtáymat (Coming Together Dance). The dance was held at Umatilla, where the city of that name is presently located. This was where there was a crossing place on the Columbia River that later became a ferry dock to cross from Washington to Oregon. Many people gathered there for this annual dance. The Yuumatálam People who had their permanent village there hosted the gathering. There was a large longhouse built for this event and a "practice" dance was to occur on the night my mother and cousin's family arrived.

My mother told me that the singers and dancers dressed in their everyday clothes to practice that evening. During a formal dance, everyone dresses in their finest clothes. Her family were busy at their camp visiting with friends they had not seen for a long time and were not paying attention to what the young people were doing. My mother and her cousin were watching the preparations for the dance. During the practice dance, the singers began to sing and the young people were brought out on the floor by their Elders to show to the audience the proper way it should be done. The boys were brought out by their uncle or grandfather and the girls were brought out by their aunt or grandmother.

My mother's cousin was a few years older than her and she convinced my mother it would be fun to go out on the dance floor with the cousin representing herself as the Elder. She said they danced up and down for a while when an older man leading a boy came out on the floor to meet them, and the boy put his hand on my mother's shoulder. When this is done during the formal dance, and the female couple does not reject the male couple by turning away, it is interpreted as acceptance of marriage. Then the Medicine Man, holding a staff with an eagle feather tied onto its tip, lays the staff over the boy's hand, and a cheer goes up to announce a selection has been made. My mother thought she was only playing, and she was having fun; she knew it was only a practice dance. She also thought the boy was good looking! All of this was happening while her family were busy visiting relatives. They had no knowledge about what mischief the two girls were up to. However, my father's grandfather was watching, and he approved of the selection.

The traditional dance occurred after that, and my mother was not taken onto the floor to dance by her grandmother. My mother was too young and did not have adequate domestic skills yet. A few weeks passed when an elderly medicine man, Porcupine, came to visit the village at Sih' to have a serious talk with Sawyalílx̱, my mother's grandfather. He brought a message from the village of Táp'ashnaḵ'it, Goldendale Ridge, located near the present town of Bickleton, Washington. When the Medicine Man explained that his mission was to unite the two young village people in marriage—their *ináaw* (young unmarried man) to my family's *tmay* (virgin girl)—to fulfill the traditional law.

My mother said they called her cousin to explain what had happened, and after, the entire family held a private discussion about what should be done. Her grandfather objected to allowing Ellen to marry. He declared she was too young and was not capable enough for domestic life. Her uncle Johnny was a quick-tempered man, and he argued that when X̱apt'íniks went out on that floor to dance, she knew what she was doing.[2] He emphasized that this involved tradition, and that it was important to carry out the agreement.

A large Wedding Trade occurred between the Yuumatálam and the Siɫáma. My father's side exchanged *inawawíksh* (male dowry), including horses and rawhide parfleches filled with dried salmon and deer meat. There were elaborately beaded male costumes made of buckskins and trade cloth, and the much-coveted Canadian blankets that the fur traders brought to this area, as well as robes made of animal skins, with beaded strips across the back of the blanket, an eagle feather war bonnet, and porcupine headgear.

These were exchanged from my mother's side for *tmayíksh* (female dowry) goods, matched in value. There were cedar baskets and five-gallon cornhusk bags filled with many species of dried roots and berries, as well as beaded buckskin dresses and trade cloth dresses decorated with shells and beads. The jewelry was many different-sized strands of wampam beads, highly prized and equivalent to precious jewels of today. Even what the bride and groom wore was given up as part of the dowry, in the trade ceremony called *Pápishx̱wiit* (Wedding Trade).

My mother wore a wedding veil made of dentalium shells woven like a cap and her veil hung down to her waistline in back. It was very heavy. It had gold trade coins on a string of colorful beads that hung over her face to hide her eyes. She said that when she walked, the coins hit against each other and made a sound like the tinkling of bells. Her braids were decorated with dentalium shells that covered about one-third of her long braids. The ends of her braids were covered with otter skins. My father's oldest aunt combed my mother's hair.

My father wore his great-grandfather's *twinúushush* (war bonnet) made of eagle feathers that hung down his back to the ground. He was dressed in buckskin and carried an eagle staff decorated with eagle feathers. His heritage on his paternal side came from Chief Shawaway of the Umatilla tribe. His maternal heritage side came from Latp'áama, whose English name was recorded as Elit Palmer, from the Columbia River band. Latp'áama signed the 1855 treaty for the Yakama. Unfortunately, my father's mother died before his wedding, and the *inawawíksh* goods she had kept for him were traded by her sisters.

Children borne from this type of traditional marriage are highly regarded. My brother Oscar was the first born and his Indian name was Wax̱wín. This was his child name. Later, they put up a big dinner and had a Name Giving ceremony. The people from Umatilla Reservation were invited, and he was given the name Latp'áama, after his paternal great-grandfather. His English name was Oscar Wantux̱ Beavert, after his maternal grandfather Oscar Wanto, our mother's father. Oscar was my mentor while I was growing up.

ADULTERY / PÁCHAPAAT

I asked my mother and an Elder visitor about divorce. They told me about an ancient punishment practiced by the tribe when the man committed adultery: one ear lobe was cut off. When the woman left her family for another man and was declared an adulteress, the tip of her nose was cut off. When I was a teenager, I saw one woman with her nose tip cut off. This practice must have stopped sometime in the mid-nineteenth century because she did not look old, perhaps eighty years old. They said anyone with that type of impairment was shunned by the community. Nobody wanted to marry an adulterer. They quoted the Longhouse religious Prophet. He said the Creator made this law. When adultery is committed by a man or a woman, he or she must be punished. This is Creator's law.

My mother and the visitor refused to discuss this subject any further when I asked if the punishment was performed by a special person. The only thing they stressed was that a child must be made aware of the values of his or her people. Children must be told what is good and what is wrong. That is the reason we have a Whipman, the visitor told me. When the missionaries came, they told the Indian people they could no longer practice this punishment.

SERENADE / ḴLÍWAWYAT

I continued to ponder this subject, and when a visitor came from Colville, a Palouse man who was my mother's paternal uncle, I found him smoking his pipe outside, and asked about this.

There is the Ḵlíwawyat (serenade ritual) when a man or woman can go out and seek another spouse even if he or she is already married. This fun ceremony is really for young unmarried people, but I was told it included married people. I asked Uncle what the difference was between committing adultery and joining in the Ḵlíwawyat ceremony. He said, "Unfortunately, there are marriages that fail. The woman or man cannot produce a child. It is all right to find another wife or husband. Ḵlíwawyat is the only way to go out in public and find someone else. When this happens, it is tragic, but it is accepted by the barren one.

"Let me draw you a picture. [I guess I was looking confused.] One of the purposes of marriage is to bear children and extend your heritage. When this does not happen, it creates anxiety for man, woman, and family.

"The herbal medicine doctor will determine which one is at fault, then it is okay for the other to seek another. A man or woman can get out of bed, go out to join the Ḵlíwawyat, and bring back a different spouse. Nobody complains, and the previous spouse either remains as a servant, or goes away to live with relatives." I was still bothered by this explanation, but this is ancient tradition.

DEATH / TŁ'YÁWIT

Íchi awkłáw iwíi'uysha káatnam ḵḵanáywit miimáwit náktkwanint tł'yáwit. Kúshx̱i náktkwanint imínk átawit anamkú iwyáalakwta.

This is the beginning of a long tradition regarding death. Each portion was historically meaningful and an important part of tradition.

The Sahaptin people anticipate death after midlife. However with modern technology—like cars, trains, and airplanes—we never know when death will occur; we never know if we will meet death from new afflicting diseases. Traditional Indians began gathering material things in preparation for their death after they reached the age of fifty. Listed below are the materials men and women put away. (The glossary includes Ichishkíin funeral terminology.)

PREPARATION OF THE BODY FOR BURIAL / TŁ'YÁWITNAN NÁKTKWANINT

Many modern families ask for a traditional Christian burial ceremony for their relative. Longhouse religion followers, however, practice the old way, and they prepare the body for burial in a different way. This preparation includes the custom of putting away the following items in their own container to be buried with the deceased; the family knows that it is a special collection and that they are not to disturb it.

1. Two large, warm, heavy blankets (Hudson Bay or Pendleton)
2. Several large white tanned buckskins for making either a suit or a dress (shirt or dress will be designed without decoration)
3. An eagle feather to hold in the right hand
4. A shawl that has never been worn (for a woman)
5. String of wampam beads and choker (for a woman); bone breastplate and choker (for a man)
6. Plain leggings and moccasins. Men have long leggings tied to their belt (like trousers), and they wear a "hider" in front (a long strip of cloth or buckskin, one-quarter of a yard wide by one and half yards long) which is looped over the belt in front and back. The women wear short leggings of buckskin or cloth fastened below the knee.
7. Face paint: yellow for women, red for men. This may vary from tribe to tribe, religion to religion. It is best to consult with the Elder in the family before using the paint.
8. White clay was put on the hair (optional; no longer practiced)
9. Three large tule mats: one to put under the casket, and two to wrap around it.
10. Medicine bundle (for male and female shamans) to put in the casket
11. Beaded bag (for a woman); tobacco pouch (for a man)
12. Buckskin or buffalo robe
13. Brass bell (for a woman who was leader or participated in Longhouse religion)
14. Hair and nails. Some people save their hair and nails over the period of their lives. If they did, this must be buried with them.

X̱ÍTWAYMA TŁ'YÁWIT

Anakú iksíks ttáwax̱tma patł'yawyúux̱a, anakú chaw tuun pashúkwaasha tiináwit, ku pawápnaminta, "Míshna míta?" Kwɨnkínknash íchi tímashpa kwɨts'k wapíitat áwyaalakwanisha ttuush nch'i ttáwax̱t míimi laak inícha patún pɨnmiláyk'ay anakú tiichámyaw iwínata. Anakúsh na'íɫas ikúya. Kúx̱ash íɫamayka. Miskilíikitash awyáx̱anya. Apat ku lísx̱aam íkwtɨnk ápax̱wya.

DEATH IN A MODERN FAMILY

When someone dies in a young family, and they have not learned the old ways, they do not know what to do: "What do we do?" The reason I am writing this is perhaps the person put away things for herself or himself for when she or he would go to Mother Earth, like my mom did. She hid her things and we had a hard time finding them. Because at one time the things were stolen.

Na'iɫasaanmí áwacha palaláay patún trunkpa káakɨm pshátani tł'yáwitpayay. Pɨnminkmíyaw átaw patún. Wáawk'a ɨɫáx̱ áwacha. Kwɨnkínk awkɫáw míɫaa ánakpa inícha.

My mom had a lot of things packed full in her trunk for her death. Those that were important to her. She had too much. For her last bundle, she only had a few things. [There is a teaching that you do not take too many things, or things with beadwork with you when you die.]

Úytknik átx̱anax̱a niipt nch'ínch'i ḵ'ɨx̱lí. Tł'aax̱w tun áwata chɨmtí. Paysh áyatma pawáta cháchani, awkú panánata piimínk kw'alálkw'alal. Paysh ɨwínsh iwachá twáti ku inánata pɨmínk pátash.

They must have two large tule mats. Everything must be unused. If the woman was a longhouse leader, she will take her bell. And the man his fetish when he was an Indian doctor.

Chaw tł'aax̱w walptáykt tł'yawitpamá iwá kúsksim. Tunx̱túnx̱ iwá nákwat'uyt anakush áwa sápsikw'at mɨník náx̱shknik káatnamknik.

Funeral songs are not all the same. They are learned through experience at different longhouses by the leaders who sing at funerals. [Some songs were received from spiritual experience.]

According to tradition, dressing the corpse in plain buckskin clothing has been practiced ever since time immemorial.

Maxáx (white clay) was smeared all over the *tł'yáwit* (corpse) the night before burial, then covered with white buckskin to keep the clay pliable. This made it easier to put the corpse on the *k'úsi* (horse) that carried the body to the burial ground. The horse was killed and buried with the deceased.

It was important to put gold coins over the eyes. This practice ceased when white clay and gold were no longer available. Today the clay is mined for toothpaste and other medical use. *Luts'alí* (gold) is mined and unavailable too. Now this ceremony has changed; the horse, clay, and gold are not included.

DEATH SONG / TŁ'YAWITPAMÁ WALPTÁYKT

When a person expires, four verses of a death song are sung by one or two people, depending upon how many know the song, to help the spirit on its way before the body is washed. These ancient songs are passed on by the Elders. They are not sung at social gatherings.

There are special songs for each part of a funeral service: for the Spirit leaving this earth, for dressing the body, for the wake, and for the graveside ceremony. At the dressing, male singers (seven drummers) are seated in a row on the north side of the seating area, facing to the east. The deceased's family brings the funeral bundle and gives it to the man or woman who will do the dressing. The family sits in the first and second rows facing east during the dressing ceremony.

During the wake ceremony at night when the drummers sit down to rest, women chant parables and sing when the deceased is female.

DRESSING CEREMONY / SAPÁTAATPASIT TŁ'YÁWIT

In the hospital the person is cleaned by the nurses; at home the oldest person in the family washes the deceased. She or he is dressed in underclothes and wrapped in a sheet or thin blanket until the dressing service. The Indian people hold the dressing ceremony in public for the benefit of friends and relatives so that they will witness the end of his or her life, and realize that they will never see the deceased alive again.

The body is brought out in public and the family brings out bundles of funeral clothes and items for the dressing. They select a person to do the dressing; usually a man will dress a man, and a woman will dress a woman. Sometimes a woman will do dressing for a male deceased if the family requests it. I believe that the dressing ceremony is the most important part of saying goodbye.

COURTESY

The dressing ceremony is not a staged performance; it is a serious way to pay respect to the deceased for the last time and to offer condolence to the family too. Friends of the family are allowed to sit with the deceased's family. If the dressing takes place in a funeral home, Indian folks do not usually sit in the reserved area because the seating arrangement is facing toward the south; the Indian traditional way is to sit facing east.

When the Medicine Man or Woman comes out to dress the corpse, it is important to sit in silent reverence. Those who must go outside or to the restroom do so quietly. Recently, I have observed people hugging and crying on the shoulders of the grieving person, which is not acceptable. There is a proper way to show respect during grieving time.

Friends and relatives of the deceased appreciate a handshake in the traditional way. It is important to remember how to shake hands. It is courteous to shake hands in the traditional way. Take the right hand and pull gently downward once, while you nod your head in a sympathetic manner, and let go. Show your sympathy by allowing some space between you and the person you are shaking hands with. Do not pump their arm like when you greet a friend during happy times. Do not cry and hug or hang on. This only adds to their grief.

After the dressing, the men are called forward first to view the body. They pass in front of the immediate family and shake their hands. After the men, the women line up and go around.

Regardless of how distressed you feel, do not cry on top of the casket when you observe the deceased. Take a quick glance, turn completely around counterclockwise, raise your right hand at shoulder level, palms towards your left, take it down, and walk away and go back to your seat. This is your goodbye, or you can interpret it as meaning, "It is finished."

People prefer to attend the dressing service when they cannot go to the funeral services. It is appreciated when everyone can stay through the entire dressing service until the body is loaded for transport. Sometimes people have to go back to work and cannot stay for the entire ceremony. Modern times dictate our own Indian ways today.

When there are flowers, there are flower carriers, usually women, who are responsible for the care of the flowers when transporting the body from the mortuary to the longhouse and then to the grave. They carry flowers behind the casket to the hearse; follow the casket into the longhouse and then walk around the casket to the right, and arrange the flowers on the floor, and later carry them out of the longhouse. After the burial they place flowers on the grave.

Throughout the night during the wake ceremony at traditional Native funerals, traditional songs, rituals, and dancing are practiced. These are different from Christian or military funerals. Each longhouse performs the wake in the manner they were taught by their Elders. They have their own songs and ways of conducting the ceremony. Often there is conflict when someone from another area does something that is not in accord with the local ways.

NOTE: The Silama bring the deceased's family to stand by the casket (or body), and the Elder sings the prophet song. This is to help the spirit of the deceased to leave, and for the family to let go.

Áwnash íchi sɨ́nwisha tł'yáwitnan náktkwanintki, anakúsh iwá miimawítki náktkwanint.

I am going to talk about taking care of a corpse, in a traditional manner.

Íkuuk tł'yáwii tíinnan panánax̱a tł'yawitpamáyaw, pashtɨnwít panáktkwaninta. Kpaylimá iwá tamánwit pashtɨnmí, háaynam íkush kúta. Ku míimi tíinma chaw íkush pakúx̱ana. Áwtya paníchx̱ana tł'aax̱w tł'yawitmí tun awkuníik wáwnakwshashpa. Chaw tun patamáatanix̱ana.

Nowadays a body is taken to the mortuary and they take care of it in the white person's way. This is a modern way and the regulations require it. A long time ago the Indian people did not do this. They buried their dead with all body parts left whole.

Niimípa tímanii tiichámpa páshtɨnma naktkwaninłáma patmáakɨnx̱a tíinmaman. Ku panáktkwaninta wáwnakwshashnan kushkúsh, anakúsh tíinmapat áwatł'awita. Kútya íchi tiinwítki iwá páyu áwtnii kútkut. Háaynam wáta wapsúx̱ ikushpáynk sápsikw'ani nch'inch'imamíki. Anakú áwa ɨt'úk sápsikw'at. Wíyat'ísh.

On our Indian reservations the morticians respect the Indians. They do their work the way the Indian family instructs them to do it. But the Indian traditional way is very complicated. The person who handles the body must be tutored by the ancient people. Because the teaching is tedious and long.

Anakú páwiyaalakwta wak̲’íshwitin tíinnan; anakú tł’aax̲w háashwit ku tɨmná áx̲awshta, íx̲wiyakut wak̲’íshwit awkuníik átx̲anax̲a mɨ́taat łkw’íyaw. Kushkínk pasápsikw’anx̲a wapatwinłáan wáwnakshashnan, “Pina’atł’awyáshataam kunam kpaylk áwapatwinta wáwnakwshashnan kunam íkw’ak itmáakta.” Páyshnam yalmílk áwapatwinta, láaknam ímktya wiyáwk̲ta.

When life ceases and the person’s breath and heartbeat stops, the Elders say that the Spirit continues to exist for three days. That is the reason the Indian Body Handler must be careful. “Ask for protection from the Creator before you touch the deceased body. Then the Spirit will respect you.” But when you are careless you will endanger yourself.

Náx̲shk’a tnúwit iwá nch’inch’imamíknik. Cháwnam wáypshaninta tkwátat yalmílk sts’átpá anakú tł’yáwii ilá’ɨshata ts’áapa.

There is another warning from the Elders. Do not walk around juggling food at night when there is a corpse lying closely nearby.

Láaknam x̲áwapawx̲ita kúts’k tiichámyaw. Cháwnam tk̲áwɨnpta ku shapáynakta, anakú tł’yáwit míimi iwɨ́npa kuunák. Anamkú ánuk̲’ta íkushnananak, payúwitaam.

You might accidentally drop a piece of food on the ground. Do not grab it and put it in your mouth, because the dead person already took it. When you swallow that kind of food, you’ll get sick.

Úyknik iwá sápsikw’at. Áwntaam myánashmaman, chaw pałk̲’íwita ámchnik sts’átpa, anakú kwmak lawiishk̲’íshishma pawyáninx̲a sts’átpa pawak̲’ítsha wáwnakwshash páx̲witay, anakú myánashma pawá ts’i’íix̲ íkushyuk.

The lesson continues further. Tell the children, do not play outside at night, because those black shadows are wandering around at night looking for a body to steal, and children are easy to possess.

Lawiishk̲’íshishx̲i iwɨ́npx̲a nch’imamí wáwnakwshash. Paysh palaláay itx̲ánata túkin láamki ku laak ix̲átamawshpta táa’am łamtɨ́x̲.

The shadow will also take a mature body. Maybe he becomes unconscious from drinking alcohol or else he falls down and temporarily blacks out.

Anakú pawɨ́npanita wáwnakwshash, kw'ɨnk tíin itáx̱shita túnx̱k'a. Awkú itx̱ánata anakúsh lawiishḵ'íshish anakú iwachá wáḵ'ish. Áykɨnx̱aash tíinmaman táymuntyaw shímikin, "Anakú itáx̱shiya, kuumánk iwá anakúsh tunx̱ tiin."

When they take possession of the body [during the blackout], that person wakes up different. Then he becomes like the shadow when it was alive. I hear people talking about someone, "When he woke up, since then he is like a different person."

SHAPÁTATPAASIT

Ttuush tiin pápanichx̱a tunx̱. Náx̱shpa laak łamtɨ́x̱ tł'yawyinmí áwata tináynaktkan, ku tł'anx̱ náx̱shpa anáttkan. Páyu átaw iwá íkwak. Anakú áwtni tax̱shiłáináchikx̱ana isíkw'at, "Íkushpam kúta, anakú Tamanwiłá iwiyánawita kupam kuuk áwshtaymata. Kwmak tináynatknik patútita. Kwmak anáttknik pimásapawiisklikta ku pawiyáwshtaymata." Awkú úyknik iwá yáwatashki sɨ́nwit. Walptáyktki nicht tiichámyaw, ku sapátkwlikt łíimki, ku nit łałx̱.

DRESSING SERVICE

People bury their dead in different ways. Some people bury the body facing toward the west, and others to the east. This is important. As the Prophet told them, "The dead will be prepared in this way to receive the Creator when he comes. Those facing the east will rise up. Those facing west will turn counterclockwise and meet him." Further teaching involves how to bury the body wrapped in tule mat, and the giving of dirt with special sacred songs.

Áwa ayatmí sápsikw'at myánashmaman túkin pasapátaatpasita. Plash lɨmɨ́slɨmɨs tł'aax̱w táatpas, łḵ'am ku nyach. Chaw tun kwnák chalútimat. Łpápa nɨwítknik laxs x̱wayamanmí wáptas. Pɨnmínk ikks patún, kw'alálkw'alal uu pátash, sápk'ukt ayatmamí. Ikwł iwá wát'uytx̱aw patún, ku ánaknam áshapatkw'likta shátayki, kushx̱i áyatnan.

It is the woman's responsibility to teach the family how to dress the body. White buckskin for all clothing, moccasins, and pants or leggings. No beadwork. On the right hand, one golden eagle tail feather. You may include incidental things like a brass bell, fetish, or a bag for the woman. Those are most important, then you may include buckskin wraps or blankets for the woman.

Páyshnam apx̱winúusha íchi iwá áwtik'a. Chaw. Íkuuk pashtɨnwítin páshapalaaksha átaw tiináwit ttúush-maman tíinmaman. Íkuuk tɬ'aax̱w mish iwá shapyáwit.

You might think this information is trivial, however you do not know how much modern life has caused changes in lifestyle for many Indian people. Today there are all kinds of problems.

Cháwnam náx̱tita, haay ix̱átamaynakta wáwnakwshash tiichámyaw. Náx̱titaam anamkú áshta káatnamyaw nichtnaḵ'ítpa.

Do not cry until after the body is interred. You cry when you go back to the longhouse after the burial.

PÁPAWɨNPANIT ɨPÁP

AFTER THE BURIAL CEREMONY

Anakú paníchtnaḵ'ix̱a tɬ'yáwitnan, tɬ'aax̱w shin itúx̱ta káatnamyaw. Awkɬáw tɬ'yawyáshanima papa'iwáx̱ita ámchnik. Haay tɬ'áax̱w chɨmyanashyíima pawyánawita yáwatashknik.

After the funeral, everybody returns to the longhouse [except for the people that were left behind at the cemetery]. The immediate family waits outside until their whole family has arrived from the cemetery.

Wishtaymaɬá pawaníksha, anakwmák pa'iwáx̱isha tɬ'yawyáshanimaman asht káatnampa. Pima'its'wáykta, pa'áwx̱anaykta kkúuksim náakni. Awínshma niwítknik ku áyatma waḵatsálknik. Yats'áam pa'iwáx̱ita. Chaw shin ityátyatta, uu ináx̱tita. Awkɬáwnam shíx̱ki px̱wítki a'iwáx̱ita.

Those people waiting inside the longhouse are called receivers. They will prepare themselves by lining up on both sides. Men on the right side of the longhouse, and women on the left. They stay quiet while waiting. No one will joke around or cry. You will wait in reverence.

Tł’yawyáshanima pimá’ ikwstɨmita íkush. Awínshma pima’its’wáykta. Wyánch’i iwyáwat’uyta. Pátwanata palaxsíksiin, ku ának myánashma. Kúshx̱i áyatma. Iwyáwat’uyta wyánch’i, ku palaxsíks, ku myánashma.

The immediate family prepares in this way. Men will arrange themselves in a proper way. An Elder [sometimes an uncle] will lead, walking in front of the line. The younger ones will follow the widow(er), and the children are last. It is the same way with women. The Elder is at the head of the line, then next comes the widow(er), and then the children will come afterward.

Anakú pa’áshɨmta, pawyánknikɨmta awinshmamíknikx̱ush. Tkwápchayktaam ɨpáp, kunam shapálak’itita kwnak imínk átawish pɨnmyúuk. Wapíitatnam ánisha pimyúuk.

When the family of the deceased enters, they will circle the longhouse beginning on the man’s side first. You will extend your hand, and shake hands. Through the handshake is how you are sending your sympathy and love across to them.

Anam áwɨnpanita ɨpáp, cháwnam náx̱tita x̱wíimichnik pɨnmipáynk. Chaw íkw’ak iwá tiináwit.

When you shake hands with those who were left behind at the funeral, you do not cry over him or her. That is not the Indian way.

Íkuuknash átk’inx̱a ttuush tiin awkú pawáx̱pwax̱psha ku panáx̱tisha x̱wíimichnik tł’yawyashanimamípa. Cháwnam áwax̱pta. Íkw’aknam awkú wáa’aw payú áshapapx̱wisha. Kúshx̱i palaxsíks iwá cháwx̱i ímałaki. Tł’yawyinmí íx̱wi áwach’aksha ɨlúy wáwnakwshashpa palaxsiksmípa.

Nowadays I see some people hugging and hanging on, and they cry over the mourners. Do not hug them. This gives them more grief. Also, the widow(er) is not yet cleansed. The deceased still has the physical attachment on the body of the widow(er).

Míima áwacha sápsikw'at, "Piná'awtnanitaam wak̲'íshwit ku káwnakwshash, imk palaxsíks; cháwnam átkwatata pɨłx̲ú nikwɨ́tnan mɨ́taat álx̲ayx̲ anamkú tx̲ánata tł'yáwyashani."

There is a traditional rule for the widow(er), "Respect your life and soul; do not eat raw meat for three months after your spouse dies.

K'áawpam ayíkta. Kupam amts'íx̲wata anakwiiník pánakpniyanita táatpastaatpas, kapú, ku łk'am uu k̲aylí. Ku Sɨnwiłá isɨ́nwita "Íchipam tł'aax̲wsímk'a áyknanita wánikt ku ák̲'inanita patún." Kúukpam náx̲tita.

You go sit together, and listen to the Crier announce and show the deceased's old clothing, coat, moccasins, and shoes. The Crier says, "This is the last time we will speak their name and see their clothes." This is when you cry.

Tiix̲wałá ichápkwta walákw'iki patún táatpas, kapú, ták̲maał, ánam íkwɨn áshuukx̲ana táatpasityaw. Páchawiluukanita laxsláxs patún ku tiix̲wałáyin pa'ititámanita tł'yáwitnan wyanínt ku shíx̲ki tɨmnáki páx̲twayt. Ának íkwɨn nch'íki inátx̲anata, "Áwna tł'áax̲wk'a sɨ́nwisha pɨnmikínk, áyknanisha piinák waníkt. Aw iwá cháawk'a tmíinwa."

The Crier opens a bundle of clothes often worn by the dead one, perhaps ones from when you met or visited with him or her. The Crier talks about the deceased's personality and occupation. Then he loudly announces the name and declares it is the last time you will hear this name, the person is gone forever. [This is to alleviate the pain of loss, so that you don't miss him or her so much, but remember with love.]

Kúuknam imínk páyupx̲wit shapá'atta kunam náx̲tita. Chawnam tɨmnanch'íwita. Páyshnam chaw náx̲tita, íkw'aknam ímktya pinánita shapyáwit. Áwnam awkú nax̲titwyáninta kunam payúwita. Kúshx̲inam awkú ix̲aashyúuta tł'yáwitnɨm.

You let your sorrow out when you cry. Do not hold in your emotions. If you do not cry, you will cause trouble for yourself. You must cry and release, or you will become sick. And the dead one will want to keep you near.

Íkw'akat iwá nch'i-íi, tawtnúk imyúuk, anamkú tł'aax̱w shapá'atta páyu px̱wit kúuk. Páyshnam tɨmnanch'íwita íkw'aknam ímktya piná'aniyanita shapyáwit. Áwnam awkú nax̱titwyáninta kunam payúwita tł'áax̱wki túkin.

This is BIG medicine when you allow yourself to express your grief at that time. When you hold back your grief, then you are harming yourself. When you go around grieving here and there, soon you'll suffer with all kinds of sickness.

Anakú ix̱áwshx̱ta náx̱tit, tł'áax̱wshin ishmát'ata. Ának papatúkta tkwátat. Ḵaaw palaxsíks itkwátata, chaw itkwatatwíita tíinmaman. Pɨlksá wíyat itkwátata, áchaash chák'ɨnki. Chaw itk'itk'ita yalmílk. Chaw itkwáta płx̱u tilíwalyi tkwátat, anamáal wáwnakwshaash áwata tł'yawitmí płx̱u.

After everyone stops crying, they wash their faces. The food is set for the dinner. The widow(er)s must eat far away from the others. They must cover their eyes [with dark glasses or a bandana] and not look around. They should not eat fresh meat for at least three months, as long as the body in the ground is fresh. [This is the beginning of widowhood, and isolation for one year.]

Tmáaktapam waḵ'íshwit, átaw iwá. Shíx̱nam imínk átawitma náktwaninta. Pápa'atawitapam. Awkłáwna lísx̱am wa níyii niimí waḵ'íshwit, cháwna tł'yáwita kuna kw'áx̱i táx̱shita, chaw. Tamánwitkina wa íchna tiichámpa, chaw áwtik'a. Wáshna níyii kútkut náktkwanint tł'áax̱wnan tuun waḵ'íshwityiinan.

Respect your life. It is valuable. Take care of your loved ones, love one another. We are given life only once. We cannot die and come back to life again later, no. We were created and put here on this land for a reason. We were given life to dwell here and take care of everything that has life. [Indians believe animate and inanimate all have life.]

Ttúushma panátx̱anax̱ana, "Páyshna piná'ɨshnawayta wáawk'a kunam áshapapx̱wipx̱wita tł'yáwyiinan, kunam ix̱aashtyúuta." Tł'áax̱wnam tun lapaalakwá átanshkanita. Kunam áwimałakanita pinmínk ɨlúy nisháyktpa.

Some people used to say, "If you grieve and feel sorry for yourself, the spirit [of the dead person] will hold back from its journey and haunt you." Burn all of the used clothing. Clean and wash all fingerprints off in the house [where he or she lived].

Íchiish kuts'k tun ínch'a íkks-maman ttáwaxtmaman áwiya-laakwanita. Cháwpam px̱wíta tx̱nawtyúushamatash. Áwtyamatash kuts'k túkin tíix̱washa, ash tun inách'a na'íłasaanɨm isápsikw'ana, ku ttúush sapúukasit Nch'ínch'imaman ash kush áykɨnx̱ana.

These are a few bits of information I leave for the young generation. I do not want you to think that I am preaching to you. I am only sharing information my mother taught me, and in addition what I heard the Old People used to say.

MY MOTHER'S FUNERAL / NA'IŁASMÍ NICHT

A person told me that several Yakama people gossiped about how pitifully *na'íłas* (my mother) was buried. They said, "Virginia Beavert barely clothed her mother. She turned away contributions from the relatives." They did not know my mother put her request on paper. She directed her own funeral. She asked me to put on her body only the things she put together herself. They were put away in a small padlocked wooden box which contained a plain white buckskin dress, a pair of tanned buckskin moccasins, a shawl, a beaded bag, a bone necklace, a plain belt, and a *patł'aap'á* (basket hat).

She told me not to accept blankets or other items from any of her cousins, except from Woodrow Bill, her favorite nephew. He brought a light shawl, the kind women wear for every day. We covered the closed casket with it. I also put her solid gold watch on a solid gold chain inside the casket, including the *kw'alálkw'alal* (brass bell) she used when she prayed. I put a *x̱wayamá wáptas* (eagle tail feather) in her right hand held across her chest. I dressed her myself. Barbara, the wife of my mother's grandson, Ronnie, combed and put a *wápshash* (braid) in her hair like she had when she moved in with us for a while. My mother was bathed and dressed in her new Sunday *tł'piip* (wing dress) on Sunday morning, and on Monday, we put the buckskin over her wing dress and she was transported to where her family had the wake that night. My mother also requested a special person to conduct the longhouse ceremony during her funeral. I went to his home to tell him what she said, and he selected the drummers who would assist.

When certain people tried to take over the funeral, I stood firm and carried out my mother's personal requests. I realized there would be bad feelings, so when I was challenged by a family member, I had her listen to my mother's voice on a cassette player telling me what she wanted me to do. The woman listened and left quietly.

Many times young people ask me for advice when they have a death in their family. They do not have the experience, nor have they witnessed one. I do not take over, but I tell them to start by consulting close relatives, or talk to a leader in the longhouse; to talk to knowledgeable people they can trust to guide them. I tell them to take care of everything themselves, and not to let anyone come into their home and disturb or remove their loved one's belongings. Sometimes this happens too, if you are not careful.

The *k̲'ɨx̲lí,* tule mat, is a vitally important item to include at a traditional funeral. The Elders said that the earth and *k̲'ɨx̲lí* will glow when the *k̲'ɨx̲lí* is put into the ground wrapped around the body. The *patł'aapá* (basket hat) and the bell are also important for women who were active in gathering the longhouse traditional foods, and for the leader of the ceremonial food gatherers.

ROLE OF STORYTELLING IN MOURNING / NCH'ÍNCH'IMA WATIŁÁMA

The Elder Indian woman has one important role dependent upon her talent as a storyteller. When a parent dies and the children are orphaned, or when the head of the family dies and leaves a spouse and several children, this is when the old Storyteller begins her work.

She will take her bedding, one cup, a spoon, and a dish and tie them up into a bundle and move in with the family left behind. Her presence is always welcome. She will entertain the children by telling them amusing legends or stories to keep them from mourning too much. She playfully pantomimes the animal stories by acting out their antics. These stories do not emphasize punishment, but are stories like "Spring Flower Girls."

She will counsel the remaining spouse about observing widowhood taboos. This is a crucial time of life, because when one does not observe the rules, he or she can become blind or afflicted.

PALASÍKS PÁ'ANIT

Łwínsh itł'yáwaya ku mɨtáatipa łkw'ípa itáx̲shya. Pápashapatux̲ma tíix̲watay tíinmaman. Íkush Nch'ínch'ima panátx̲anax̲a:

WIDOW-MAKING CEREMONY

A man [a Prophet] long ago died and three days later awoke. [This was in the 1800s.] He brought back a message for the people and this is the message:

"Nch'íi iwámssh shapyáwit tiinmamíyaw ku shíx̱pam papanaknúwita, pápa'atawitapam. Átmaaktapam tł'áax̱wnan tuun íchna tiichámpa anakw'ɨ́nk iwá tamánwiyii imik'aláy shíx̱witay. Naknúwitapam tiináwit, níchta tɨmnápa."

"Be aware, much trouble is coming to you. Take care of each other; love each other and respect what is here on Earth, put here for your benefit. Respect your traditions and keep them in your heart."

Kwɨnkínk tiin itwánaniinishamsh kuumánk ku ináktwaninx̱a pɨnmínk tiináwit, íchi anakwɨ́nknam átḵ'ix̱sha shúkwaat. Kwyáam, ɨt'úk iwá. Iksíks ttáwax̱t ipx̱winúusha íkush. Ashkú ínch'ax̱i chaw wa kuumánk kush pamíshpamish ásapuukasyanita tiimnanáx̱t.

This is the reason the Indian people carry on their traditional ways. True, it is difficult for the new generation to do it the proper way. I, too, am not from the old era, but I will do my best to translate [these teachings] from the old way.

Anakú ɨwínsh uu áyat itx̱ánata palaxsíks, anakwmák pawachá ḵw'iit shúkii wíyat'ish panisháatuna ku áwacha myánashma, Anakw'ɨ́nk itł'yáwya kwɨnmínk x̱ɨ́twaymapat áwanita palaxsíks wyáalakwiinan.

When a man or woman became widowed, and they were known by everyone to have been married a long time, to have established a home and had children, then the family of the person who died came to the home to the widow-making ceremony.

Úytpat áwimałakanita ɨníit. Tł'áax̱w tun ɨluyłimápat átanshkanita, táatpas, smáas, sapakw'stikáwaas, anatún napwák pakúx̱ana.

First they come and clean the house. They will gather all the clothes and material things, clothes, bedding, and towels; everything the deceased touched around the home was burned.

Anakw'ɨ́nk áwa kuukitpamápa lawaax̱tpamápa áwa níchii mɨnán íx̱wiyay shapanaknúwitay.

The things in the kitchen and living room are stored to give away later.

Ák'aatnanitapat pnupamá. Pátun áykawaas, tkwatatpamá ánichanita íx̱wiyay wínitay. Ánitapat tsmɨ́ti pnupamá ku chmáakw íitpaas ku smaas.

They will remove the old bed and bedding, and store the rest of the furniture. They replace the bed with new, dark-colored sheets and blankets.

Palaxsíksnanpat ánita chmuk achaashpamá, ttúushmapat áchak'ɨnkanita áchaash chmuk chátł'umx̱shki. Chaw yalmílk itk'ítk'ita anakú wáwnakwshash ik̲átamaynakshata tiichámpa.

They will give the widow(er) dark glasses or some people will tie a black bandana over their eyes so that he or she does not carelessly look upon people since the body of the spouse is now in the ground.

Anakú tł'áax̱w tun áwata ímałaki, kuuk Nch'inch'ima tł'yawyiinmí áwinamta ɨníityaw kupat awítma áshapa'aykta páchupa ku patwáwata. Anakú panáwnak̲'itpa, kúukpat palaxsíksnan áshax̱tł'kanita tútanik ku áshapataatpasita chmuk táatpas ku áchak'ɨnkanita áchaash.

After the home is cleaned, the Elder relatives of the deceased's in-laws will have the widow(er) sit in the center and they all keen. After they finish keening, one Elder will cut the hair. Then they will dress him or her in black clothing and partially cover the eyes with a bandana.

Ának kuuk nch'ínch'ima pápapshx̱wiita. Áwtya kwlaa pátun chaw anakúsh pakúya papshx̱wíitpa. Patkwáta. Ánitapat palaxsíksnan k̲aaw tikáy ku ápatukanita wíyat tíinaknik. Anamáal íkush iwáta.

After, the Elders will have a small trade [like they did at the Wedding Trade], but they trade just a few things, to show that the home of the deceased was known by everyone and it was an honorable marriage.

Anakú lulukłá myálas ánut'atwita, ánichtapat nax̱sh ayatmíyaw ánakw'ɨnk ishapálulukɨsha pɨnmínk myálas, kwiiník panaknúwita nax̱sh anwíkt. Kúshx̱i máyknch'i myánashma pawínata x̱ɨtwatmamíyaw.

When an infant becomes orphaned, he or she is fostered out to a woman suckling her own child. This woman will look after the baby for one year. The older children will go to close relatives to live.

Anakú ának̲'ita piná'iwyatt anwíkt, pnáchmapat áwix̲wch'kta chmuk táatpas, útpaas, ku patún; kupat átx̲taymaniita ḵayx̲ḵáyx̲ki patúkin. Chmaakw patúnpat átawsaypanita wyanawiłamíyaw náktux̲tay. Íkw'ak áwa wyának̲'it palaxsíks, wanak̲'itpa áwiyatł'x̲a.

When the year of confinement is complete, the in-laws come again to remove the black clothes, bedding, and household items and replace them with light-colored ones. The other dark-colored items are distributed to the people who come to witness this happy occasion. It is a day of celebration, the end of grieving, and a new beginning on a Monday (*Wának̲'it*).

Paysh nch'ínch'ima patmíyuta, kúukpat áshapá'aykanita awít. Kwiiník awkú panaknúuwita. Miyánashma páshapattawax̲anita. Kúshx̲i ínpalax̲sika awkú i'atawita, chaw ishapáwaynata. Íkush iwachá míimi naknúwit nisháykt ku tamanwit tiinmamí.

When the Elders decide [it was time], they bring a substitute for the deceased, to take care of the family and take up the overall responsibilities. The ex-widow(er) must not reject them but must love and respect the new spouse. That's how the Indian people kept the home and old ways together.

There are strict rules to follow during the mourning period; the remaining spouse is isolated from participating in social affairs for one year or more. This is important.

After a year of mourning, a ceremony to mark this time occurs. Clean light-colored clothing is provided, everything dark is replaced, and the bereaved is able to participate in social affairs again, and is eligible to remarry. In the "old days" the brother, sister, or cousin next in age would move in and take up the deceased's responsibilities. This has been banned by law, unless there is a formal traditional marriage. This practice is followed by very few families now.

The third union in marriage is the substitution of a young woman or an older woman as a substitute wife for the surviving spouse of her deceased sister or first cousin. They usually chose a childbearing woman to continue the growth of the heritage; however, I was told by an Elder that sometimes when the widower was a young man, an old woman was substituted. The young man took the old woman and they lived together as man and wife and looked after the children that were left behind. The children could then inherit from the old woman, as well as the father.

MY LESSON ABOUT WIDOW-MAKING

Monday morning when it was still dark outside, my mother woke me up and told me to get ready to help her pack things to the car. She said I was excused from school. This was my first experience observing the Widow-Making ceremony.

The elders from the Palouse side of my mother's family gathered outside the home where my Uncle Allison and his wife lived. The prior week we had buried her at Celilo.

On the way I asked mom why we could not do the ceremony on Saturday or Sunday. She told me the Prophet, long ago, brought the message to tell the people when they carried out the burial and widow-making tradition to do it on Monday, *Wanak̲'it*, because it meant "the end of life and the beginning of a new experience, for both the living and the dead."

We waited until the in-laws of Allison invited us inside. I noticed the house was cleaned and the only piece of furniture was one chair where my Uncle Allison sat. We had brought bundles for the ceremony; when we entered we placed them by the door. I noticed then that everyone was sitting in a circle and keening. The mother-in-law and her helper began to remove the widower's clothing and dress him in black. She cut his long braids off to shoulder length, covered his eyes part way with a black bandana, and gave him dark glasses. (These were to wear when he did business.) The bundles we brought were taken away by the mother-in-law. A pan of water with a washcloth and towel were passed around for everyone to wash off their tears.

On the way home, Mom answered all my questions. She explained that everything had been sorted in the house, the old, used clothing burned, and the usable items stored for the giveaway next year when the widower's black clothes would be replaced. During the year of mourning, my uncle could not hunt or fish because he must follow the Prophet's teachings to protect his children and himself. My mother told me, "He cannot touch living things, including his children. Your uncle cannot go to powwows or participate in public affairs, except his job. He must wear dark glasses wherever he goes. And for three months he must not eat fresh meat of any kind while his wife's body is still fresh in the ground."

When the male spouse dies, the wife must observe the same taboos. For the year she is in mourning she cannot dig roots in the hills, go to the mountains to pick berries, or go to the orchard to pick fruit; she also cannot eat fresh meat for three months.

My mother explained to me: "One year from now, Monday at sunrise, we will have another private ceremony at your uncle's home. Then they will remove the dark clothes and replace them with light-colored clothing. If the in-laws decide to present him with a substitute wife, he cannot refuse their offer; this is called *awít shapáanit*.

At the second ceremony, the stored furniture, artifacts, and materials are taken to the longhouse to complete the cycle started one year ago. Here things are given away to friends and relatives as keepsakes to everyone invited to dinner to visit with the widower. Also it is the place and time where he introduces his *awít* (sister of his passed-away wife). He will say: "*Íchiish wa ínmawit*, this is my wife's sister."

The dinner with Uncle Allison was electric with happiness and excitement, but we could not linger. The dinner must conclude before three o'clock because this is the teaching of the Prophet. These customs are still practiced by Sahaptin people. This was my first lesson about widow making.

TABOOS FOR WIDOWHOOD

1. Of utmost importance: Widows and widowers cannot eat fresh flesh foods for the first ninety days, while their spouse's body deteriorates in the ground.
2. They must keep their eyes covered with dark glasses or partially covered with a bandana when in public, especially while at work.
3. They must stay away from powwows, bone games, or other social affairs.
4. They may not touch children. Women do not nurse their infant nor touch a child as it is considered unhealthy for the child.
5. Men cannot hunt or fish. They must stay away from the environment where wildlife exists.
6. Women do not dig roots or pick berries or other fruits. They may not walk around the hills and mountains where food grows.

With regards to the last two, it is claimed that when a widow or widower walks on the earth where wildlife roam and plants grow, they contaminate the fertile conditions of the ground. It is believed that animals will not reproduce the following year(s) and plant areas will dry up.

Átaw iwá ánamku wapáwx̱ita imínk átaw am, ásham. Tł'yáwityaw. Chaw túyay iwá sap'ináwitay imínk ɨshnawáy px̱wit.

When you let go of your beloved to death, your husband, wife, there is no way to measure your grief.

Tiinmamí áwa ḵ'tɨt tamánwit amashkú imínk ásham uu am tł'yáwita. Palaxsíksnam tx̱ánata, kúuknam imínk waḵ'íshwit watwáa naknúwita. Ímktyaam pinátmaakta chaw ánach'ax̱i túkin. Kúuknam piná'iwyaatta tiinmamíknik.

The people have a strong belief about death when a wife or husband dies. You will become a widow. You must carefully take care of yourself. It is the respect for self—not anything else. That is when you isolate yourself away from the people.

SUICIDE / PINÁ'ITŁ'YAWIT

Íkuuk iwá px̱wípx̱wit tímaniipa tiichámpa anakú myánashma pimá'itł'yawisha. Anakúsh mish "Pima'anákwsha." Chaw pawíipx̱wisha, íkw'ak ísatsim awkú patł'yáwita ku chaw míshkin kw'áx̱i patúx̱nɨmta.

There is concern on Indian reservations about the young people committing suicide. They "throw themselves away." They do not realize that when they die, they will not return.

Tł'ápx̱i tun áwtik'a tx̱ánat—ku pasx̱íx̱sha kwɨnkínk ku pimá'itł'yawisha. Chaw wípx̱winii ánach'a túkin, uu shimíkin –laak piimínk myánashma, uu túuman átawitma páyu áshapapx̱wisha íkushkink kútki. Chaw ipx̱wísha, "Láaknash ɨshnawáy ákusha inmí átawitmaman."

It might be a simple thing that happens at home—and they are angry about that so they kill themselves, to retaliate. Again, they are not thinking about anything else or anyone else—about perhaps their children, or whomever they hurt [their loved ones]. They don't think, "I will hurt those I love."

Anamkú piná'itł'yawita íkw'akatakut iwá chilwítit. Nch'ínch'ima patx̱náwɨtax̱ana íkush.

They say it is a sin to kill yourself. This is what the Elders would preach.

Míimi anakú íkush shin íkúx̱ana, chaw iwachá níchii walptáyktki. Awkláwpat xɨ́twayma átamaynakx̱ana tiichámyaw awkushyúuk, chaw sapátaatpasyi. Chawakút paníchx̱ana wáashatki. Awkłáw pashapátkw'likx̱ana lapaalakwá shátayki, ku lapaalakwá ḵ'ɨx̱líki pashapách'ɨmikx̱ana. Ku wyátpa x̱ɨtwaymamíknik paníchx̱ana yáwatashpa. Chaw pawalptaykúux̱ana. Chaw patwáwax̱ana.

A long time ago, when someone committed suicide he or she was not put away with ceremony. Only the parents or the relatives put the body in the ground, dressed in the clothes the person wore at the time it happened. They wouldn't bury them in the longhouse way. They would roll them up in an old blanket, and wrap them in an old tule mat. And they would bury them separate from relatives at the graveyard. They would not sing for them. They would not keen.

Cháwpat tíinma áwyanawyuux̱ana. Awkłáw pmaksá chɨmmyanashyíima uu xɨ́twaymapat ánichx̱ana.

Nobody came to grieve for that person, only the immediate family was involved.

Páyu ɨt'úk iwá anamkú áwatawisha kuunák tł'yáwyiinan, kunam íkush ákuta, anakúshnam awkú áwałata imínk átawit.

It is very difficult when you love the person who did himself in, and it seems like you do not care when you have to treat him this way.

Anakúyat iwá tamánwit. Tamanwiłánɨmna iníya waḵ'íshwit ku awkłáw pɨlksánɨmna iwánaḵ'yanita anakú niimí kútkut wiyátł'ux̱ta. Nch'i iwá wiyákwshtikt anamkú imknínk áwanaḵ'ita kunam piná'itł'yawita. Cháwmash awkú mún míin wínata imínk waḵ'íshwit, awkwnákmash íchna tiichámpa wiyáninta sts'áatpa.

Because that is the law. The Creator gave us life, and only he decides when our work and life are finished on this earth. It is a sin when you decide to end your life and commit suicide. Your spirit will remain here on Earth and wander in the dark.

Nch'ínch'ima panátx̱anax̱ana káatnampa pachwáywitpa, "Íkw'ak iwá nch'ítx̱aw wiyákwshtikt anamkú (imknínk) piná'itł'yawita." Íkushnash nakáłasaan áykɨnx̱ana sɨ́nwityaw.

The Elders used to talk in the longhouse during Sunday service, "When you take your own life, by committing suicide, it's one of the worst sins, breaking God's law." This is also what I heard my grandmother say.

Tamanwiłánɨmna iníya waḵ'íshwit ku awkłáw pɨlksánɨmna iwánaḵ'yanita anakú niimí kútkut wiyátł'ux̱ta. Nch'i iwá wiyákwshtikt anamkú imknínk áwanaḵ'ita kunam piná'itł'yawita. Cháwmash awkú míin wínata imínk waḵ'íshwit, awkwnákmash íchna tiichámpa wiyáninta sts'áatpa.

The Creator gave us life, and only he decides when our work is finished on earth and life is taken away. It is a sin when you decide to end your life and commit suicide. Your spirit will remain here on earth and wander in the dark.

Nch'ínch'ima panátx̱anax̱a: áwmash áwku awkúnak íchna tiichámpa, wyáninta imínk waḵ'íshwit. Awkuníiknam awkú wáta shapyáwyi.

The Elders say: your spirit will wander here on this Earth, your soul will remain here forever. It does not solve your problem.

Aw míshkin px̱wit íkush, iwátax̱nay tɨx̱taymaní. Míshkin íkksma ttáwax̱tma pacháx̱ɨlptax̱nay piimínk mishyú ku tɨmná, ku mts'íx̱watax̱nay míimanan sapsikw'átnan.

If there were some way for this pattern of thought to be changed; the younger generation would listen and absorb the old teachings that made its ancestors strong and able to survive for generations.

Amashkú waḵ'íshwit wiyátł'ux̱ta, cháwnam awkú míshkin wiyatux̱ta.

When your life ends there is no way for it to return.

A person cannot realize how suicide affects their loved ones, especially the children. One evening I was checking on a suspicious activity at the community center and found an elderly woman and five boys and girls of various ages seated quietly on the floor around a plain wooden casket resting on an old worn blanket.

I asked if I should call the relatives and inform them for her. The Elder replied that there was no one to inform. This was her family she had gathered together, and it was her grandson who was in the casket. He had committed suicide. She told me they planned to bury him the next morning. I worried about them although I did not know who they were.

My mother told me the Elder was following the Prophet's protocol regarding suicide. I wanted to ask Human Services to help them but she told me not to interfere.

SWEATHOUSE / X̱WYACH

MY PERSONAL EXPERIENCE / INMÍNKSIM TX̱ÁNAT

X̱WYAKT MYÁNASHKNIK

Áwx̱ashat shapátwaani tíix̱wat anísha chɨ́nik, anakú paláamsha Ichishkíin sɨnwiɫáma. Awkɫáw paysh mɨ́ɫman pawíwanikta inmí tímash íx̱wi, ku laak tún átx̱atamaynakta tɨmnáyaw tiináwit px̱wit kuna niimanách'a pap'íx̱ta.

Ashkú wachá iksíks ttawáx̱t kush nakáɫasnɨm ishapaɫḵ'íwix̱ana ámchnik. Kush pamún isapákw'stikx̱ana yátɫ'pit síilki kush maɫáa isapátaatpasix̱ana.

Íkushnash wachá maal – cháwnash awkú shúkwaasha mɨɫ anwíkt. Kush awkú na'íɫasnɨm inásha x̱wyáchyaw kush itwá'awḵanina isapákw'stikaanya ɨlúy. Ishapáx̱wtɨtx̱wtɨtnash wáwnakwshashpa kush ɨna: "Íkushnam aw chɨ́nik ɫkw'íknik piná'imaɫakta x̱wyáchpa. Táaminwanam maɫáa pinanaknúwita."

SWEATING AS A CHILD

I guess I will be mixing languages in this writing, because Ichishkíin speakers are disappearing. Perhaps someone will read my writing later, and he or she will learn something valuable about our Indian values and language, and will remember us Elders.

When I was a little girl, my grandmother's mother, X̱ax̱ísh, would let me play outside. And then she would bring me inside and clean me with a wet cloth and put a clean dress on me.

This lasted for a while until my mother took me to the sweat lodge. I do not remember how old I was that time. My mother rubbed my body vigorously to scrub the dirt off me, while she was telling me, "This is the way you must keep yourself clean."

Ashkú uyt na'íłasnɨm inákx̱wyaka, wacháx̱ashx̱ashat mɨtł'ítł'ksim łḵ'iwitpamáknik, ku ɨlúysim.

When my mother first took me to sweat, I must have been all dirty and muddy from playing close to the water.

Anakú iláx̱uyx̱na x̱wyách, kush wáwnakwshash láatlana, kúuknash itwá'awḵanina kush isháppx̱wtɨtkanya ɨlúy ɨpáx̱knik.

When the air heated up inside the sweat lodge, my body began to sweat; she rolled me around and rubbed the grime from my skin.

Nax̱sh x̱wiimichnikpamá ɨlúy ináwnaḵ'ix̱ana, kush ishapápuxpuxɨnx̱ana anakwnák ɨlúy iwíik'ukɨnx̱a wáwnakwshashpa; k'úpkw'p, k'áshinu, tánwat, ḵ'ux̱ł, ku wɨx̱ápa.

Once the topmost layer was finished, then she blew on me where the dirt was layered on my body: on my back, elbows, neck, knees, and feet.

Kush ánach'ax̱i ishapáx̱wɨtɨtkanix̱ana ɨlúy, iwyáshapapuxsha. Háaynash tł'aax̱w ínawnaḵ'ix̱ana kush awkú átx̱ana kush x̱átik'aliix̱ana tł'áap k'pɨs chíishyaw. Małáak'a!

Then she rubbed more grime off again, as she blew on me. When she had finished, I went out of the sweathouse and jumped into the shallow cold water. Clean!

Winaniitpamá watámtash winátshama wiináttknik ku iwachá páyu k'pɨs. Ilát'ilkx̱ana ánmiki. Małáa iwachá chíish.

Our swimming lake came out of the spring and it was very cold. It steamed in winter. The water was pure.

Amíismaman, náx̱shpa anwíktpa, ánmiki anakú iwitx̱úupshana ámchnik, kupat wawyałánɨm ishapáx̱atiḵ'aliina chíishyaw.

One year, in winter when there was a blizzard, the Whipman cut a hole in the ice and made the boys jump into the icy water.

Íkw'ak tawnáapak'a pa'ányanitax̱nay ḵw'ɨłtɨ́p wáwnakwshash ku waḵ'íshwit. Íkush ttúush tíinma pakúx̱ana.

This would supposedly make their bodies and spirit strong. This is how some people would do this.

Inách'ax̱iish lɨ́sx̱aam íkush pakúya. Nakáłasiin páyu pasx̱ɨx̱núuna, kush cháwk'a íkush pakúya. Ka'áwtyash awkú winaníix̱ana k'pɨ́ski chíishki kpáyliyaw, kush dáktanɨm ishapáx̱awshx̱a, ashkú tɨmnáki wíi'uyna payúya.

Once this was done to me too. My mother's mother became very angry with them, and they did not do that anymore. But I always bathed with cold water anyway, until the doctor made me stop, when I developed heart trouble.

Íkw'ak áwacha miimawít tx̱ánat íkush. Ku aw páshtɨnma pa'anyúusha tamánwit ikushyúukk'a.

That describes the traditional way to sweat, but the white people have a law even for that.

K'ttáaspa tíinmaman pá'wyalɨlkanya x̱wyách. Tawnáapak'a tkwalánan ku pátatnan wánapaynk pa'íchayshana, ku wásku iláx̱yawishana.

At Kittitas County [at Ellensburg], the police destroyed the Indian sweat lodges because they claimed taking sweat baths spoiled the fish and trees along the river, and dried up the grasses.

Ku tɨ́knik'a tł'aax̱w shimín kwnak íkuuk pɨ́shaat, iwsh, ku chílwit tawtnúk ipawíitwasha wánayaw, ku íchaysha chíishnan ku túx̱ɨnan. Kwɨnḵínkna awkú íkuuk payúwisha.

And there, in contrast, everyone's feces, urine, and bad chemicals mix into the rivers and merge with water and the air. This is why we get sick today.

Íkuuk músmustsɨn itináx̱yawksha chiitpamánan wináttnan pɨ́t'x̱anukpa, pa'íx̱yawksha chiitpamá chiish.

Now the cattle in the mountains are tromping the springs and drying up the drinking water.

SÍPA NIIMÍ X̱WYAKÁWAAS

OUR SWEATLODGE SETTING AT SIH'

Tł'áax̱wpa, wanapáynk, uu anamɨnán iwá chíish, tiinmamí áwacha x̱wyach.

All along the waterways, or where there was water [from a stream, river, or spring], the Indians had a sweat lodge.

Kwnák patk̲’íx̲na tímani tiichám pasáp’awya, tɬ’ápx̲i chaw páshwini túyay tamaníktay.

That was the reason most of the Yakama Indians selected land near the river for their allotment, although it was not good for farming.

Sípatash wachá niimí nisháykt. Tɬ’áax̲wnatash wachá tun kwnak. Wacháatash tkwátat tamaníksh ku tmaanít: ápɨls, chílish, paas, plams, píchish ku ápɨlkats. Nakáɬas itamaníkx̲ana skwáasis ku st’ɨx̲swáakuɬ. Úyknik ittáwax̲shana tiin tkwátat; tmɨsh, pínush, chcháya, tɬ’áax̲w tun tmaanít. Chaw míshkin tɬ’áax̲w wíwaniktay.

Our homesite was at Sih’. We had everything there. We had a garden and fruit: apples, cherries, pears, plums, peaches, and apricots. My grandmother planted squash and corn. To supplement that we had Indian food: chokecherries, currants, serviceberry, all kinds of fruits. Too many to name.

Ksksátash wachá átaw. Nakáɬas ítwax̲ana wáptuki twáshani k’úpkw’p mɨt’ulaanmíyaw ánmiki. Páyu shix̲!

We prized mushrooms. My grandmother would mix them with boiled potatoes and the dried spine of the chum salmon in the winter. It was delicious. [This is the last food we ate in the wintertime, when we were out of everything else. She would string and dry the mushrooms, the salmon was dried, and we always had potatoes in a root cellar.]

Kwnak iwachá k’pɨs wiinátt. Iwachá áwtni. Iwíip’ɨnkshayka x̲wɨ́shyaw ku kwnáktash wachá x̲wyach, álaytpa anakwnák iwíikkɨmshayka watámyaw. Iwachá haawláak kwnak, anakúshnam íchi íkuuk áshta tálx̲yaw nch’i tanamutɨmpamáyaw.

There was a cold spring there. It was sacred. It flowed out into a canyon and that is where we had our sweathouse, at the bank where the creek flowed down into a lake. It was holy there, just like when you go inside a cavernous cathedral.

Kwnáknash łk̲'íwix̲ana ilksá. Wacháash mɨtáat waachitłáma k'usík'usima, Yáka; Káysa; ku Shap. Lch'íilch'i pawachá. Cháwnash áshukwaasha mɨnán Nakáłas iwɨ́npa íkwmak. Anakú X̲ax̲ísh itł'iyáwya, tł'áax̲w pa'itlyáwya, pat átwanana.

I played there by myself. I had three caretaker dogs: Yáka [Black Bear], Kaiser [a German shepherd dog], and Shep [a sheep-herding dog]. They were large dogs. I do not know where my grandmother got those pets, but when she died, they all died too. It was just like they followed my grandmother.

Lɨ́sx̲aamnash x̲átamaliina watámyaw, kush chaw áshukwaashana shɨmnátit. Ashkú yáwinaynaka ɨmítichan, k'usík'usima patłúpwilachaliina kush tł'áax̲wma pacháwinata, kush pachápyuka. Nakáłasnɨmnash kw'áx̲i ɨyáx̲na, lá'ɨsha nash paláay ts'aa x̲wyáchpa, ash kwnak k'usík'usima pawɨx̲ína. Ilátk'ishanayakut íkwɨn. Kuumánk áwacha átaw k'úłima. Cháwnam mun áwawk'iinitax̲nay.

Once I fell into the lake, and I did not know how to swim. And when I went underwater, the dogs jumped in and they all pulled me out, they pulled me out of the water. My grandmother found me. I was lying unconscious by the sweathouse, where the dogs put me. She was watching that. After that, those were highly regarded dogs. You could never chastise them.

Íkuuk tł'áax̲w tun ix̲yáwsha kwnak Sípa. Cháwk'a iwá winátt, ku anakwnák iwachá watám, iwá káakɨm chak̲chák̲t ku k̲wɨtk̲wɨ́t.

Now everything is drying up at Sih'. There is no spring, and where there was a lake is full of rosebushes and brambles.

Inmí páshtɨn wamshiłá ishákw'ɨtka tł'áax̲w nisháyaasnan; ku tawt-núkyiki chíishki ishapawanan-úusha tamaníksh, ku aw íkuuk tł'aax̲w tun tkwátat iłamáya wanapáynk anakwnák ínx̲twayma patmaaníx̲ana.

My non-Native renter plowed up where we used to live; then he sprayed the plants with weedkiller. Now, everything that was edible there has disappeared, where our relatives would come to gather the wild fruits.

Wacháatash nɨx̱anásh wánapa, kwnink patáwsaypx̱ana núsux̱. Kútash wachá tł'aax̱w tun tunx̱túnx̱ tkwalá; kwɨnkínknatash wyá'anwikx̱ana. Táaminwa nch'ínch'ima pax̱áashwishana tkwátatyaw, kúshx̱i áwacha tł'i'íish kumyúuk anakwmák pawachá shapyáwyi piimipáynk nisháyktpa.

We had a fish weir at the [Yakima] River, where we caught salmon. We had all kinds of fish; that is how we wintered over. The Elders always asked for food, and it was generously given to them, those who were disabled and did not have these foods available at their home.

TAMÁNWIT X̱WYACHPAMÁ

THE IMPORTANCE OF THE SWEATHOUSE

Iwá napwinanmí, ayatmamí ku awinshmamí, tx̱ánat x̱wyáchpa. Iwá walím ímałakt wáwnakwshash; ku nax̱sh iwá láx̱pit; ku nax̱sh iwá piná'imałakt anamkú wa tł'yawyáshani; ku nax̱sh iwá sápsikw'at myánashnan.

There are different ways practiced by the Indian women and men in the sweathouse. One is simply cleaning the body; and one is healing; and one is cleansing yourself after a death in your family or before you do something important; and one is to teach the children.

Áwa átaw tawtnúk anakw'ɨnk áwa chcháanwyi. Íkw'ak iwá páshwini átawyay túyaay tx̱ánatay. Palaláay tun pápa'iyushɨnx̱a íkwɨn. Íkw'ak awkú kuuk pawánpx̱a uu pasapúukasix̱a anatúnpat ásapsikw'ana, wyánch'ima.

The sweat where you use sacred medicine, that kind is kept secret. It is treasured for use for important things, in important ways. They pay a lot for this teaching [on how to identify, gather, prepare, and use these medicines]. That is what the Elder teaches them.

X̱wyáchpa iwá áwtni wapíitat anamkú ímktya pinátmaakta kunam aníta laxs px̱wit, kúuknam iyáx̱ta wapíitat.

In the sweathouse there is valued help when you respect yourself and you make one mind, then you will find help.

The sweathouse heals you. It heals a lot of things. Those who mourn for their husband or wife will feel better after they have sweated for five days beginning right after the funeral. With death, the spirit stays three days and wanders, because he or she may not understand his situation. When a couple lives together for a long time, and they love each other very much, they become spiritually connected into one person. The bereaved must be released from that attachment before there is peace, both for the one who has passed and for the one who remains. The sweat will release that tie so that he can go on his journey and she can go on with her life.

PREPARING THE SWEATHOUSE / ÁNIT X̱WYACH

Usually the men build the sweathouse; I have never built a sweathouse. It is located usually where there is fresh running water. The circumference of old sweathouses accommodated no more than ten people: eight or fewer participants, plus the leader, and the fireman who also took care of the door after everyone entered.

Today, Indian reservation housing is often located away from the river, so sweathouses built in these areas rely on improvised outdoor showers for rinsing off. The modern walk-in sweathouse is enlarged with elevated seating inside. I recently saw a picture showing a luxurious interior with a bench padded with soft pillows—very different from what I knew growing up.

The wood, stones, earth, and plants used in the sweathouse are all treated and collected in special ways.

> Wood: The Wood Chopper is special. He performs a ritual before he collects wood. He turns toward the east, and clears his mind of personal thoughts. He thanks the Creator for another new day and for everything that was created to benefit mankind. He asks the Creator to bless the wood he is preparing to cut for the healing ceremony at the sweathouse. At home too, special wood is used for the sweathouse. It is dry wood, so it does not spark or pop; the kind of wood that is never burned in the fireplace for heat.
>
> Stones: Stones are volcanic and are collected at the mountains where they are found exposed from erosion. They are seasoned by volcanic processes and the elements so they will not crack or break in the heat. I used to go with my mother to Mount Hood to get our rocks. She would smoke and pray, then tell me what sizes to pick out. I would gather them and pile them in one place; then she would see if I had enough, and we would carry them to the car and transport them in a heavy wooden box. These rocks were for her sweathouse. When she died, we burned the sweathouse and buried the rocks.
>
> Earth: The sweathouse floor is lined with clean packed dirt and boughs of cedar or fir. Nowadays, blankets are used to cover the sweat lodge. Every so

> often, the sweathouse is cleaned: new earth is brought in for the floor and all the bedding or boughs where people sit are removed and replaced with new.
>
> Plants: Soap vine, rosebush, alder, white and red willow, yarrow, sage plants, and bark from trees were all used as medicinal remedies for healing in the sweathouses. The water the leader sprinkles on the rocks is mixed with medicinal herbs.

Parts of trees and plants were put to many uses both inside and outside the sweathouse. *Psúni* (alder) bark was used by the men for hair rinse. *Tamsháashu* (rosewood) was boiled and set aside for body rinse. *Shchápa* (rose hips) have lots of vitamin C. They are used by women to rinse their skin, and also for tea. Fresh yarrow leaves were rubbed over the body to ward off muscle pain and rubbed on the chest for cold, and women dry the yarrow blossoms and use it in sachets. Red willow and white willow (*tax̱sh,* willow) were both used for severe viral ailments, especially influenza, as willow contains the pure ingredients that are made into aspirin.[3] *Pshx̱u* (sage) is used fresh to invigorate the body's circulation and people beat themselves with bunches of fresh sage inside the sweat. Although this is not a plant, another thing that men used for scent was a *x̱ínu* (dried beaver testicle), tied onto their hair at the nape of the neck. The musky scent is said to entice women.

My grandmother used *aláala* (devil's club) for arthritis. She would bundle a handful of fresh plants and beat herself where her body parts ached: her knees, shoulder, and back. The devil's club needles have a sting like yellow jackets; be careful when you handle it.

It appears as though the place where I grew up resembled a pharmacy. This has changed because of farming practices. The plants are all gone where I used to live. The sacred spring and lake have dried up and are now covered by tall foreign thistles. I do not know all about the medicines. I only know just a little bit, and I am never careless about their use.

Áykɨnx̱anaash nch'ínch'i áyatmaman sɨ́nwityaw ikwɨnkínk, panátx̱anax̱a, "Cháwnam yalmílk ásapsikw'ata. Ttuush áyatma pawá kiłáa, áwnam awkú pa'íchaychaynanita tawtnúk, chaw patmáakta."

I heard the Elder women talk about it, and they say, "Do not be careless about teaching this. Some women are not careful, and you will ruin the use of your medicine, since they will not respect it."

Pina'iix̱tpamá iwachá tamḵ'ikskúla, suup. Iwáltawix̱ana pátatpa ts'aa wiináttyaw uu wánapa, anakwnák iwachá mɨtíit tiichám. Íkuuk aw cháwk'a iwá anakú cháwk'a tun iwá winátt. Ix̱yáawna kwnak, ashkwnák ink ttáwax̱na, Sípa.

Tamḵ'ikskúla, soap, is for cleaning yourself [used by men and women]. It hangs down in the trees by the river or spring, where there is damp ground. It dried up there where I grew up, at Sih'.

Awkɬáwnash nakáɬasnɨm isíkw'ana tiinmamí pina'imaɬaktpamá wawnakwshashpamá, anakw'ɨ́nk pashtɨnwít sɨnwítki pawaníkɨnx̱a 'soap.' Átawnash wachá tamḵ'ikskúla.

All my grandmother showed me was about the Indian way of washing our bodies, that is what is called *soap* in English. I liked that herb called soap vine.

Anamkú áwap'ikta, awkú iwíip'ushɨmita. Ɨwít itíwasha, ku itx̱ánax̱a mɨx̱ɨ́shpyat.

When you crush it in your hand, it foams up. It smells good, and the color turns green.

Tɬ'áax̱wpanam túpan piná'iix̱ta, kunam pinayax̱ikáshata tam-sháashuki, kunam kw'áx̱i áshta x̱wyáchyaw. Íkushnam kúta mítaam.

Wash yourself all over your body with the foam soap, then douse yourself with rose hip water, and go back into the sweat lodge. Do this three times.

Chaw iwá túyay ɨwínshay. Awtyá iwá íḵwikt imínk wáwnakwshashyay.

This is not man medicine. It is to perfume your body.

When you come out from the sweathouse for the last time, that is when you dip yourself into the water. That is what we girls used to do at the Mission.

Íkushx̱itash pasápsikw'ana iix̱t ɨtɨ́t táx̱shki. Anakúshna íix̱ɨnx̱a 'toothbrushki' íkuuk. Tɨ́knik'anam tax̱shnmí psáki íkush kútya.

This is how the Elders instructed us to brush our teeth. It is like we brush our teeth with a toothbrush, except we used willow bark.

Íkw'aktyaatash pt'ilímaman pasápsikw'ashana. Kútya ayatmamí áwa nɨmnɨwíit úyknik shúkwaat tawtnúknan.

Those were lessons for girls only. The women had far advanced knowledge about herbal medicines.

Tawtnúkx̱i iwá tamsháashu. Íx̱wi pimayax̱ikáshax̱a x̱wyáchpa kunkínk. Úyknik áwacha shúkwaani; kush chaw áshukwaasha kúunak, tunx̱túnx̱ tawtnúknan. Tamsháashu iwá tawtnúk, shíx̱nam inaknúyanita ɨpáx̱ ku wáwnakwshash. Anamkú wáta tɬ'yawyáshani, kwnɨ́mknam ímałakanita wáwnakwshash kunam chaw wáta shapyáwyi, ku cháwnam íhananuykta tɬ'yáwyinɨm.

Rosebush is also a medicine, still used to wash yourself in the sweathouse. They had some other medicines, and I do not know about them, there are so many. Rose was always recognized as a medicine. It will take good care of your skin and your body. If you become widowed, it will wash your body clean, and you will not be bothered, the spirit of your loved one will not trouble you.

Cháwnash nɨ́mnɨwit ínch'a átk̠'ɨx̱na shúkwaat ayatmamíki pɬáx̱ki. Tɬ'ápx̱iish pasapsikw'ayát'ana, kush áwna, cháwnash átk̠'ix̱sha íkuunak shúkwaat. Kush Na'íłasaanɨm ɨna, "Ii, ánam áwku imksá łmamáwita, chaw tun ɨwínsh." Kush íkwɨn áwna, "Áwx̱ashat awkúsh wáta."

I was not interested in learning about herbs used to get a man. Although many times my Elders wanted to teach me that culture, I refused to learn it. My mother was worried about it, and she told me "You will grow old without a man." I told her, "If that's the way it has to be, okay."

PARTICIPATING IN A SWEAT / X̱WYAKT

There is distinct protocol for the sweathouse. You must enter in a specific way, counterclockwise. The leader goes in first, then you line up in the way the leader or doorman directs you. Everyone crawls inside. The leader goes first over to the farthest side where he will conduct the services. The fireman's responsibility is to heat the rocks and bring them inside the sweathouse. He may also serve as the doorman. The leader has a bucket of water where he sits. He controls the heat inside.

When everyone is inside, the door is closed and no one can leave until the leader gives the signal, finishing one cycle. The number of times you enter and leave the sweathouse depends on what type of sweat it is: regular, mourning, healing. Sometimes people go in three times, maybe five times: it depends on a number of things. The steam is very hot, and older people and young children cannot stay inside very long. Men who are going to go hunting and fishing, and the women food gatherers, they go in three or five times and rinse off. The participants must stay inside until the prayers are completed. When the doorman opens the door, everyone goes out to rinse their body and rest. There are different ways practiced by others.

PINA'ITS'WÁYKT ASHT X̲WYÁCHPA

HOW TO CONDUCT YOURSELF IN THE SWEATHOUSE

Íkuuk anakú wyátunx̲isha tiinmamí px̲wit, cháwk'ana apx̲winúusha wak̲'íshwityi iwá tł'aax̲w tun íchna tiichámpa.

Now that the majority of the living Indian people's lifestyle is changing, they tend to forget the ancient belief that other things on this land have life.

Paláayna apx̲winúusha anatúun ák̲'inusha. Tiináwitki áchaashki iwá námunt tł'áax̲wnan tuun anatún iwá hawláak tamánwyi íchna tiichámpa.

We no longer pay attention to what we see. The Indian eyes see life in everything on this earth that has life and claim them as relatives.

Kwɨnkínk x̲wyach iwá anakúsh náx̲shpak'a tiichámpa ku kwnák-nam pa'ashtwíita imínk x̲ɨ́twayma, anakuumínk áwyaninx̲a wak̲'íshwit.

To illustrate this thought—the sweathouse is a different land, and when you enter the sweat, the spirit of our relatives, who walk this earth, goes inside with you.

Pa'áshtwanashaam kunam pimanách'ax̲i áwatł'awiyax̲a wapíi-tatyaw. Íkwłnam pawapíitax̲a ímx̲twayma.

They come to assist you when you ask. That is how your relatives help you.

Cháwnam áwap'aalakta anakú nakwat'uyłá iwánpita, ku iwíwanikta.

Do not challenge the leader in the sweat, when he sings and calls the spirit animals to come inside the sweat lodge.

Kwyaam paysh, cháwnam tuun ák̲'inuta, kútya wak̲'íshwit áwata hawláak kupam pa'áshuuta.

When the ceremony is carried out correctly, you may not see them, because spirits are invisible, but they will come inside to you.

Páyshnam ákwyaamta, kunam áshukwaata.

If you believe it, you will know them.

Sts'aat iwá asht x̲wyáchpa. Cháwnam tuun ák̲'inuta, kunam lɨmk̲'íita. Chaw ttúush tiin itk'ítk'inx̲a asht x̲wyáchpa.

It is dark inside the sweathouse. You cannot see anything. Some people do not close their eyes inside the sweat lodge.

Íkushnash ink wachá sápsikw'ani. Lɨmk̲'íinam x̲wyákta.

I was taught to keep my eyes closed inside when I sweat.

Tł'áax̲w iwá átaw páyshnam ákwyaamsha tiinwítki pinánaktkwanínt. Íkushkink miimáma tíinma pa'iyáx̲ɨnx̲ana x̲túwit.

All is sacred if you believe the Indian way of caring for yourself. This is the way the old people found strength to live.

Małáaki wáwnakwshashki ku px̲wítki pawak̲ítatax̲ana shúkwaat.

With a clean body and mind they went to search for knowledge.

Anatúyin pásamx̲nax̲ana ku pánix̲ana kútkut íkw'ak íkwɨnkink wapíitat awachá íchna tiichámpa.

Whatever kind of Spirit [animate or inanimate] responds to the power seeker, the individual becomes endowed with a specific task to help the people and the land.

Íkuukna chaw shínɨm ikwyáamnanisha íkwtɨnk x̲túwit anakú cháwk'a shin iwá íkush. Awkłáw tanamútɨmtkisim iwá wapíitat. Ka'áwtya awkú íkw'ak iwá átaw.

Today nobody believes in that kind of power, when there is no longer anyone left with that kind of endowment. Therefore many people depend upon Christianity for strength. Perhaps that is just as well for some people.

Twátima pawachá tunx̱. Piimikínk iyax̱tpamáki payúwitnan panáttx̱ana.

Indian medicine doctors were different. They did their healing with the strength they found in the wild.

Haay pinásɨnwyanix̱ana, ku áwatɨnx̱ama x̱túwit, anakwnák i'yáx̱na. Awkú iwɨ́npx̱ana ku its'úux̱ɨnx̱ana ku inátx̱ana payúwitnan.

It was necessary [for an Indian doctor] to call forth the power from where he found it before he could continue the healing. Then he would take the sickness out of the body with his hand, or he would suck it out.

Kúshx̱i itamáshwikɨnx̱ana íkushx̱inam tx̱ánana; "Íkush iwá ḵ'ínupa, kwnɨ́mknam íkush ipx̱winúuna."

The Indian doctor would interpret what happened to you [from his vision], "This is the way he looks, and that's how you acquired your sickness." [The Indian doctor would get a vision when another person with power had caused his patient's sickness. He would describe the other person, and mimic the words that were spoken to cause the illness on the patient.]

Anakú x̱tu áwacha shúkwaat, pa'ítł'yawix̱ana px̱wítki, ánam ku átawit páyupayu ákwiinita.

When the Indian doctor had a strong power, he could kill another person with it, if you injure someone he loves.

Ttúushma twátima páwacha watwinłá waḵ'íshwitnan. Páyshnam wiyáwḵa mɨnán, kumash waḵ'íshwit wiyápaana wáwnakwshash, kunam payúya kwɨnkínk.

Some Indian medicine men were Spirit Trackers. When you were in an accident, and your spirit separated from your body, you became ill.

Iwatwínanitaam twátinɨm, kunam iyáx̱anita, kunam ítux̱ta imínk wyáłamayki waḵ'íshwit imyúuk wáwnakwshashyaw.

He would seek your spirit, find it, and return it to your body.

Paysh íkwtɨnkmamannam awkú íkw'ak ax̱wyaktwíix̱a anamkú áshta x̱wyáchyaw. Kushkínknam táaminwa pinanaknúwita.	Those are the kind of people you might sit with in the sweat lodge. That is why it is important for you to be cautious around the people you sweat with.
Chaw iwá łk̲'íwit tiináwit; iwá miimáknik tamánwit.	Indian tradition is not taken lightly by Indian people; it is ancient law.

WOMEN'S PRACTICES / AYATMAMÍ TX̱ÁNAT

The women sweat separately from the men, and they use their own female herbs. Also, women do not sing in the sweathouse, they just talk. Each one gives thanks to Grandfather Sweat, and talks about their problem. This is how it was for me. I notice that in more recent sweats, the woman leader will sing.

The only experience I can relate about male sweat is when the Medicine Man asks for my help when he is conducting a healing ceremony, because in the past, I have been Water Woman in the Native American Church.

The women from our land do not sweat together with men. Women do their things separately, especially with their medicine and perfumes for different uses. Just for cleaning their body they use an ordinary medicine, only for perfuming themselves. Some of them will mix it with the water and then when the leader puts that water on the rocks, the steam perfumes those who are in the sweat.

Kútya úyknik áwa átaw tawtnúk anakw'ínk áwa chcháanwyi. Íkw'ak iwá páshwini átawyay túyaay tx̱ánatay. Palaláay tun pápa'iyushɨnx̱a íkwɨn. Íkw'ak awkú kuuk pawánpx̱a uu pasapúukasix̱a anatún pat ásapsikw'ana, wyánch'ima.	But the other sweat, where you use sacred medicine, that kind is kept secret. It is treasured for use for important things, in important ways. They pay a lot for this teaching [how to identify, gather, prepare and use these medicines]. That is what the Elder teaches them.

When I was little I never paid any attention to the naked women walking around at the sweat lodge. I was running around there naked myself, and they ignored me too. Later I noticed the women were naked, but they held one hand between their legs, over their pubic area.

Ashkú áshapnya na'íɬasnan íkwɨnkink, kush i'ína: "Tɬ'ápx̱inam áyatmasim wáta kunam táaminwa pinásapak'ɨlkta. Cháwnam shiin awisíkw'ata imínk páshwini."

I wondered about what I saw, and I went to my mother and asked her about it. She said, "Although there might only be naked women bathing together, always hide your 'private' part. Do not ever show your treasure to anyone." [This is the olden way some of us Indian girls were raised. Those were the days when virgin girls were treasured. They were worth a lot in wedding exchange, the girl's dowry for the boy's dowry.]

PRAYER / PINÁ'ATŁ'AWIT

Thus the Elders taught me when I was still young: no one can ask for help for you; you yourself must talk to the Grandfather and explain your problem. That is God's law. Everything—the fire, the rocks, the water, the land—it is all connected. You talk to them just like you talk to your mother or your father when you ask for something. Speak for yourself.

Prayer is personal. It concerns your private thoughts about what you believe. In my childhood I saw a miracle. I heard a story about a man who broke God's law by working on Sunday when he was expected to worship. This man was the Prophet's younger brother. He did not believe in the words the Prophet was teaching that day, words about observing the Holy Day in prayer and not work. The man left the Longhouse and cut down a tree for firewood. He sawed blocks partway along its trunk. He went home to eat lunch and when he came back, the tree had stood back up. The man became a believer of the Longhouse church the rest of his life.

That tree was alive when I was a child. I would go there and look at the scars left by the saw, and remember the words my grandmother recited every morning before sunrise. "Those things God created on this earth are alive. They are worshiping God on Sunday. This is the teaching from our Prophets. Do not pick a flower, break a limb of the willow tree, or step on an ant on Sunday. They are worshiping and thanking the Creator for their life." I was careful when I walked around on Sunday.

Prayer—it does not matter how you do it, as long as you believe in where your help is coming from. The Indian people believe in one God, the Creator.

So when we pray, we address our Creator because we know he hears our prayer. The petitioner will state his problem and humble himself, and ask the Creator to take pity and hear his prayer. He prays for himself, because he, alone, is responsible for his discretions, and nobody or nothing can forgive him except God. The prayer must come from the heart.

When the Shakers call a meeting to help a sick person, they say: "We are going to help so and so at a meeting tonight." They do not say we are going to pray for someone.

The Indian people do not worship the Prophets who were sent back from the dead. They treat them with respect, the same as they treat the Medicine Man or Woman, all God's creations. They listen to the messages that were brought back, and the songs. The Longhouse people sing those songs during the Sunday services. The words in the songs cite these teachings. The Elders say the songs are not written, and they are not interpreted. The only way to know the words is through the spoken language.

There were Prophets among different tribes and bands that spoke their own languages or dialects during the historic times. Nobody knows when the Longhouse culture came into existence.

Praying in the sweathouse is also personal. I go inside the sweathouse and I sit on the leader's right side. After everyone is inside and the door is closed, I thank the Creator for Grandmother Water. This reverence must continue throughout the service while the Medicine Man or Woman continues calling each Spirit of the Earth inside to help in the healing.

The participants talk to Grandfather Sweat, and become connected to Mother Earth, the Rocks, Grandmother Water, and the Steam, the Spirit of the Sweat. They are all composed into one. They hear your request.

When you go in, the leader will talk to you about spirituality, your environment, things you were born to respect. You are asked to pray for yourself; the others can pray with you, but not for you. The leaders and those praying are addressing all that is there, the rocks, the water, the earth, the steam. Those rocks and earth are called the Old Man. People believe it represents something male. The water is a woman, and she provides the steam.

There is no routine way to give thanks for all things we are thankful for. When you address the Creator it is direct. You thank him for your life, for another day for you to live, for health, your loved ones, and all those things that are important to you. You ask for his blessing for what you are about to do. You thank him for creating the sweat for the benefit of all the people. You will talk to Grandfather Sweat, and address him too. Thank him for being there for you to help you to accomplish the important things you need to do, and also during your troubled days. When you are praying for someone else, tell him someone needs help. That person needing help will pray for himself, and you can assist by singing along or providing support with your prayer. Of course, it is much easier for a fluent speaker to talk to God, and to Grandfather Sweat, and Grandmother Water, but I suppose a memorized prayer could assist those who do not speak their Native language.

REACHING VETERANS THROUGH SWEATING / WAPÍITAT SHAPYÁWYI SÚLTSASMAMAN

Several years ago, the Yakama Warriors, a local veteran's organization, asked me to participate in the Healing Gathering for Veterans at Camp Chaparral. The camp was a summer recreation and learning center for youth. It could accommodate many people with provisions for meals and housing. I was asked to participate because I am a veteran of World War II. I was a wireless radio operator in the U.S. Air Force. I did not go overseas, although I was offered a position in Germany after the surrender in Europe, but I was needed on my job where I was stationed. It was a training base for the B-29's that bombed Japan. I was honorably discharged November 28, 1945.

At the first session of the gathering, I met an Elder from the Níimipuu, Nez Perce Tribe. He was the spiritual leader and conducted the gathering with Longhouse songs and teachings.

I was assigned to the women veterans. The women veterans came from all walks of life and from all over the United States. They were traumatized during war. Most of them were army nurses who had served in the South Pacific. Those who were not nurses had lost their loved ones and lived alone.

This was a difficult assignment. It was difficult for all of the participating veterans during our morning session before we broke up into groups. They could not talk about their problems. I asked the Elder to give me permission to make a Talking Stick. The Talking Stick is passed around the circle and the person holding it must speak. The stick is created with reverence. It is sixteen inches tall, small enough to hold in your hand, and it has an eagle feather tied at the tip.

The Talking Stick assisted the veterans to open up and talk about their problems. They described their experiences that brought nightmares, causing some of them to drink and use drugs to help them ease the pain. They cried as they talked.

There were three large sweathouses by the creek. The mountain water was icy cold. The women were assigned to three groups, each with a leader; mine had the fewest women because I was closest to the creek.

The fireman had the rocks inside the sweathouse, and all we had to do was enter. I assigned one woman to take care of the door and told her to open and shut the door when I gave the signal.

We heard singing at the other sweat. I told them I did not sing, and that I would explain about the meaning behind why we were inside this sweathouse. I explained that they were to talk to the Old Man, to the Rocks, and ask for healing. They did not have to pray, all they had to do was talk about their problem, cry if they wanted to, and open their heart and let it all out of their system. There would be time for each person to communicate, and if someone could not talk then, she would have time later during the week.

I explained when we came out to rinse our bodies, the meaning behind that was to cleanse our spirit and give us strength to face each day. They went inside the sweat three times each day and plunged into the icy cold water after each session. They told me that they were relaxed and able to sleep after the second day. I do not know how the other sweathouse turned out, but mine began to fill up with more women. We were packed inside like sardines.

The women and men both participated in the Talking Circle, and they appeared more relaxed and able to talk without breaking down.

TEACHING OUR CHILDREN, A FUNNY STORY / SÁPSIKW'AT MYÁNASHMAMAN

Children learn about the sweathouse when they are able to understand the Elders. My little brother Rudolph Valentino Saluskin was tutored by an uncle, along with his cousins William (Bill) Yallup and Joe (Jay) Pinkham. When they were too young for school, they were learning about hunting and fishing, and about the sweathouse.

Rudy's dad, Alex Saluskin, made him a portable sweathouse, large enough for children. A portable sweathouse is not attached to the ground like the regular type. The bottom is a circular frame made of willow or chokecherry branches tied together. The top is a dome high enough to cover people. The dome is composed of long branches from the same type of wood as the permanent round sweathouse. The branches are bent over, woven back and forth, and tied to the circle. It must be strong enough to hold the covers that hold in the steam. The cover is porous, made with blankets or quilts. *Never cover a sweathouse with plastic!*

We lived within the city limits and Rudy had four non-Native friends. They were his dearest friends and they did everything together. One day Rudy prepared a sweat. Three of the boys knew how to sweat already and they wanted to teach the fourth friend, Sylvester. Rudy used to sweat hot, meaning he poured the water on the rocks often, which created more heat because steam did not have time to evaporate. Sylvester was not sure he wanted to learn this culture.

They finally coaxed him inside, and put him in the middle. Sylvester was told he could not go outside until it was the proper time. Rudy began the ceremony and poured a lot of water on the hot rocks, and Sylvester begged to go out. The boys told him, "No, you cannot." More water was poured on the rocks and the steam began to thicken, then Sylvester jumped up and ran away down the alley carrying the sweathouse on top of his head. The boys were left sitting naked in the open, watching their friend taking off.

I laughed until I nearly fell down. I told our parents when they came home, and I thought Alex would have a heart attack, he laughed so hard. My mother said, "Do not laugh. They are just little boys. Later, when they grow up they will do great things." They later became the Toppenish Wildcats from Toppenish High School, the best basketball team in the Yakima Valley at that time, and the biggest rival to Wapato High School.

NOTES

1 These serenade songs are located at the McWhorter Archive, at the Washington State University Libraries in Pullman; these are *not* engagement songs.

2 My mother's Indian name, Hoptonix (X̱apt'íniks) Sawyalilx̱, was her legal Indian name. Her Christian name was Ellen Wanto (Wántux̱); later, the BIA changed it to Ellen Saluskin. Names are very complicated; they show how the federal government issued different names to people. Ellen's grandfather, Sawyalilx̱, took her home after her father, Oscar Wanto, died and changed her name to Hoptonix Sawyalilx̱. The government gave Sawyalilx̱ an English name, Yakima George, then the rest of his family became Georges. That is why my nieces and nephews are Georges.

3 Red willow bark and alder bark were also used by women to make dye used for designs in weaving and basketry.

CHAPTER 4
Experiences and Reflections

Pina'ititámat Wak̲'íshwit

When I was growing up, my curiosity revealed many things: plants, animal and wildlife. I found out there were rivers and lakes, fish and birds. I began to study how they existed where we lived. Later, after puberty, I was taught about being human, and began to notice that some of my relatives spoke different languages, and I learned to recognize the different basic expressions.

My first experience, as a child, about how the wild creatures reproduce came from my big brother, Oscar. He showed me the nests of the feathered ones, birds, ducks, and geese, that flourished in the environment where we lived. He identified the larger birds, the eagle, hawk, crane that built their nests up higher; the magpie and crows lower. Their habitats were trees, brush, marsh, and for dryland birds, he named them all. He told me to respect their nests: "Do not touch the nest when it is occupied. Do not touch the eggs, because you contaminate them and the mother will abandon them. The eggs would not hatch because their mother was not there to help the babies come out of the eggs, and they would die."

He said it was alright to observe them from a distance, but not to frighten the mother. Sometimes she had to leave them to go look for food, and the babies were left alone in the nest: "Do not touch them."

The same rule applied to other animals: newborn puppies and kittens are not touched until they begin to suck. The mother might let you touch them, but when you play with them too soon, they get distressed and die.

I had the benefit of a traditional education. The Storyteller was my educator about the value of Native culture, and how to respect other people and all of Creation. The Whipman disciplined the children and so taught the children to love and respect each other and our parents and Elders. These lessons were all in the Native language spoken in our village, including the dialects spoken by our visitors who were Plateau People. I am now sharing these lessons. I include a selection of my observations and teachings, some about sacred things, such as medicine power, and some about everyday life, such as farming. Some practices I tell about are no longer used, or have changed over time. I discuss only what I observed and was taught.

PÁPAWILAALAKWT

Ínknash px̱wípx̱winx̱a túnx̱it awkú patk'íx̱ta íx̱wi niimíma myánashma shúkwat, anakú íkuuk anakúsh shyapuwítki pásapsikw'asha skúulitpa, ku íchi íkuuk tiin anakúsh itḵ'íx̱sha sápsikw'at myánash piimínk tiináwit.

Íkw'ak aw Tayx̱łáma ku Nix̱yawiłáma ku maykwáanik íkwa Níimipuma aw papx̱wípx̱wya ku myánashma aw íchi íkuuk ásɨnwisha piimínk sɨ́nwit tł'ápx̱it kutskútsk, anakú tł'aax̱w aw tun itx̱ánasha anakw'ɨ́nk pawaníkx̱a pápa'iisht.

Íchi íkuuk anakúsh íchi iwá táakwɨn páax̱amit íchi íkuuk k'upípit tł'aax̱w tun anakúsh páwilaalakwtsim. Aw íkuuk cháwk'a tiin i'ayáyasha pinmiláyk'aysim ayáyataysim, aw iwá páwilaaylakwsimk'a awkú tł'aax̱w tun. Kuna aw íkush tx̱ánasha íchi sɨ́nwitki Ichishkíin.

COMPETITIONS

I worry about what it is that this younger generation will want to know because now they are learning the white people's ways at school, and the Native people want to teach the children their own Native culture.

And the people from Tygh Valley and Nixyawi [Umatilla] and farther over there, the Niimipu Nez Perce people, are concerned, as now their children are going back to speaking their own language [although not perfectly fluently], and they say this is turning into what they call a contest. [This is what I have heard from Elders.]

Just like now, our war dance and circle dance and everything is becoming only a contest. Now a person is not dancing for his own enjoyment, now everything is only a contest, and that is what is happening to our language too.

Awna pápawilalaakwsha shin ishúkwasha ɨlɨ́x̱tx̱aw sɨ́nwit Ichishkíin, chi myánashma aw íchi kuuk papawiláalakwsha íkushkink. Kútyaash áwna nch'ínch'imaan íkush: "Pimásapsikw'ashax̱a awkú íchishkiin sɨ́nwit, ku maykwáanik pawyá'ishax̱isha. Awkú pimásapsikw'ata mayk ɨláx̱ sɨ́nwit chishkín."

Now we are competing to find out who knows more vocabulary in the Native language. These children are competing with each other in this manner. I told the Elders, "They are improving their spoken language." [They are trying very hard to learn more and more words and sentences. It is helping and inspiring them to learn.]

Ku míimiish áḵ'inunx̱ana áyatma nch'ínch'ima papawiláalakwsha walptáyktki íchi tł'ípat wáashat, wilalík wáashat, íchi walptáykt ku papawiláalakwt íchi iksíkski kiwkíwlaski pawalptáykinx̱ana. Íkw'ak papawiláalakwɨnx̱ana.

A long time ago I used to see the older women having a singing contest using modern social dance songs, and the rabbit dance. When they sang these songs they were holding small drums [round hand drums]. That is how they competed. [When you are drumming this way, my mother told me you should rock, rock forward. In this way, you keep the rhythm even and all the drummers are in unison. She was a good drummer. If her partners had to join a different team, she pulled me in to drum with her team. The male judges picked the winners.]

Figure 4.1 shows the Owl Dance at Tulalip for a canoe regatta, and 4.2 shows an older Owl Dance at the Celilo Salmon Feast. The Owl Dance could be part of a contest, but more often people just danced for pleasure. The women chose their dance partners. The men are drumming and singing. Notice that the girls each have one feather inserted on the beaded headband; this is because they are single. Married women have two feathers.

FIGURE 4.1. Mimanú Wáashat (Owl Dance) at Tulalip for the canoe regatta, circa 1960. Harriet Shelton dancing with Alex Saluskin, center, Jobe Charley, right. Courtesy of Virginia Beavert family photo collection.

FIGURE 4.2. Mimanú Wáashat (Owl Dance) at the Celilo Falls Salmon Feast, circa 1942. This photo shows an older form of the celebration than figure 4.1. Courtesy of Yakama Valley Libraries.

Ayáyat itx̱ánana íkush íkw'ak míimi anakúsh palaláay tíyatiyat. Chaw shin isx̱ɨ́x̱ɨnx̱ana, paysh chawsh shiin ák'inunax̱ana ínch'a, anakú papúutinx̱ana ku pasx̱ɨ́x̱inx̱ana áwtya awkuníik pimáyanwax̱ana.

Long ago there was a lot of enjoyment and laughter. No one was angry because they lost, and I never saw anyone get angry, when they lost they just took it for granted.

Ku kúshx̱iish áḵ'inunx̱ana papawiláalakwtyaw ts'xwiilí pátuktki. Laxs áyat ipátuksha nax̱sh ts'xwiilí. Tɬ'aax̱w tun, awák nɨ́mnɨwit íchi wíi'uyt, waláts'x̱wikt, shapátutit, cháwiinknikt, shapátpnit, pɨ́tḵ'ɨpt, wáawḵukt tɬ'aax̱w íkw'ak anakúsh haay panáwnak'ix̱ana.

I have seen a teepee contest where one woman sets up one teepee. It includes everything, especially the most important part at the beginning, tying the poles together at the tip, then setting it upright, wrapping the canvas around the poles, spreading the canvas out, lacing the front together, and then staking it all down. [As my mother used to do it, the poles in the back are a little longer than those in the front, so that when you set it up, the two in the back brace the two in the front. Then the rest of the poles are added onto those four most important bracing poles. Some people have three instead of four. I helped with the spreading and staking; my job was to climb up the front to lace the canvas when we made our camp. The women made a ladder out of cotton rope zigzagged on the poles to climb up in order to lace.]

Anakw'ɨ́nk awkú lɨkkɨ́ptx̱aw ináwnaḵ'i pɨ́nx̱ush íkw'ak awkú i'íishɨnx̱ana. Awkú patíyasha patíyasha áyatma. Íkw'ak iwachá úytnash íkush áḵ'inuna.

The one who finished first, won. And the women would laugh and laugh. That was the first time I saw that done.

Íkw'akna aw íchi íkuuk páax̱amitki, kupípitki papawiláalakwsha. Palaláay pátuksh táala kwnak itx̱ánana ku aw ikks íchi ttáwax̱t iwyáninx̱a nax̱shk'anáx̱shk'ayaw páax̱amityaw iwínasha. Ku paysh awkú iwá nɨ́mnɨwit shix̱ paax̱amiɫá anakúsh shíx̱tx̱aw pina'isíkw'anx̱a. Íkw'ak awkú iwiláalakwilaalakwsha ku anísha palaláay táala. Pch'i itúx̱sha.

Now we are having contests with war dancing, circle dancing, and other dances. And we have high stakes set up for contests and our young people travel long distances, going from one powwow to another powwow to compete. The most talented war dancer, who will make the best showing of himself, will win. That's to show that the one who wins the most will make a lot of money, and come home rich.

Kush ák̲'inuna aw íchi kpaylk ɫmamatúmak'a awkú papawiláalakwsha k'upípitki ku awkú tɨɫ'ápx̱i chaw pashúkwasha shuyaputɨ́mit kútya awkú pawáshasha buspa túpan airplanepa ku pawáynasha wiyátyaw tiichámyaw pawiláalakwatasha k'upípitki. Ku tiin anakúsh wíyatyaw iwínax̱a ishapáwayx̱tisha kaa ku káakɨm kwnak pawáshasha. Pawínasha pawilaalakw'át'asha mɨnán k'upípitki túkin páax̱amitki. Áyatma ka'áw papáax̱amisha papawiláalakwsha. Pt'ilíma papáax̱amisha.

And I have observed the women Elders are now participating in the contest, the circle dance, and although they do not speak English they will get on the bus or airplane and they will go long distances to participate in the circle dance. Now the people are going far away, packed in the car. They are going in order to compete, to where they circle dance and war dance. And now the women are war dancing in the contest. Girls are war dancing.

Ku aw íchi íkuuk iwyátunx̲sha kúshx̲i wát'at íchi kiwkíwlasnan. Míimi tiin iwát'ax̲ana łwáayki ku aw íchi wáawk'a lɨkkɨ́p pawát'asha kɨ́tu ku tiin miskilíiki ishapáwyiit'atwɨyiit'atsha wɨx̲á.

And now there is another thing that is changing, how they hit the drum [the rhythm]. A long time ago they used to hit the drum slowly and now they hit it too fast, and you can barely move your feet [stepping sideways as in circle dance] to keep up. [There is a special, graceful way to move your feet and body sideways, and my mother would be very strict about the proper way to dance when she was judging].

Chaw míshkin ayáyataysim wíilst'at kwnak páax̲amitpa, anakúsh míimi iwachá ayáyataysimnam wyápnisha kunam wáashasha, chaw mish páwilaalakwtpa túpan. Íkush aw íchi íkuuk itx̲ánasha íkw'ak aw iwá pashtɨnwítki íkush tx̲ánat anakú íkush áwa piimínk px̲wit áwa; táaminwa ipx̲wísha "áwilaalakwtaash íkwɨnkink inmíki wapsúx̲witki." Kuna aw íchi íkuuk íkush namách'ak'a tx̲ánasha tíinma.

Now it is impossible to run out and join in the contest for pleasure, like it was a long time ago, when you would go out there and dance for enjoyment, not to compete in the contest. This is what is happening now. That is the White way. That is the way they think now, competitively, "I'm going to win with my cleverness." And this is happening with some of our Indian youth. [There is a related problem that a few Indian children have in school. These children have respect and values and do not want to brag about themselves and show off. It is hard for teachers to understand children who do not want to compete. I was competitive and always tried to beat the boys in races, so perhaps I learned to be competitive in school.]

Chaw míshkinna awkú myánashmaman áwɨnta, "x̱áwx̱shɨnk." Paysh laak íkushkinksim awkú pa'anísha táala pimanaknúwitay ttúushma.

It is difficult to tell the children to "stop." This might be the only way for some of them to earn a living.

BONE GAME / PALYÚUT

My first recollections and observation of "Indian gaming" (a term now used to refer to casinos) was when I was a child, around 1930. I watched my mother play the women's hand game the Native people call *palyúut,* "bone game," or "stick game." When a person began to play, she had to place a matching bet with someone on the other side. *Lamtús* is the word for opponent. When you hold up an article to bet with someone on the opposite side and that *lamtús* matches it, this is called a *pa'alyúut* or a "bet against each other." This will be described further below.[1]

The bone game was a social activity played among the local women for recreation. During hop harvest time they played against visiting tribal people.[2] This is when the Native people were active in fruit- and hop-picking activities

FIGURE 4.3. Bone game being played at Moxee Hop Ranch, circa 1938. Courtesy of Virginia Beavert family photo collection.

around the Yakima Valley. Indian people came from Canada, the coast, and the surrounding Northwestern states. Each tribe played bone game during the weekends when they were given two days off from work.

I remember walking around among the army tents at a Moxee Hop Ranch, looking at the different tribal people cooking outside their tents. They looked different from our people and they spoke a language I did not understand. They were friendly people. My mother would go to the Moxee Hop Ranch to play on Friday nights, and she played all night. When a team lost one game, they immediately began bargaining bets for the next game. The activity lasted all day Saturday until late midnight and then it was shut down because the players had to get ready to work on Monday.

Áwayayanx̱anaash anakú áyatma papa’alyúux̱ana. Íkwna waayk itútisha áyat, ku cháwiiłtx̱sha isíkw’ashamsh anatún áwa alyúush. Chɨ́nik íshatknik paysh náx̱shin áyatiin páshix̱ani alyúush, ku pa’isíkw’a túkin kwɨ́łx̱i páshwiniki pats’áanisha.

I used to admire the way the women played. There on the far side a woman stands, and she is raising her hand to show what she has to bet. And on this side, one woman might raise her bet, and show it to the woman across from her, to see if she thinks it is of equal value to what she is holding. [*Ts’áanisha* means to match the value of the item shown.]

Paysh papúuchnik “ii” pakú, níiptik patamákyuu, ku pawx̱íya pachúpa. Chaw míimi kuuk, pa’alyúux̱ana táala, awkłáw ayatmamí patún: ɨstíyaas, tɨnú uu ɨwíix̱ lisháal, sapk’úkt wawx̱paanmí uu páwayki k’pɨtłimá.

And if they agree on both sides, they say *ii* [“yes”] and lay the items together. There was no money bet at that time, only women’s things: bracelets, shawls, and woven corn-husk or beaded bags.

Áyatma pimáwapawax̱ana shíx̱simki patúkin: káatnam wíwapshani, chátł’umx̱i tsɨ́mti chátł’umx̱shki, wímshyaki luxlúx wɨx̱inshmí, ɨwáywiyi ɨmtsa’ímtsa, luxlúx ɨstíyaasyi.

The women would always wear their best clothing: their hair in long braids, a brand new bandana on the head, and pretty earrings of shiny abalone shell, wampam bone necklaces, and shiny silver bracelets around their wrists.

THE GAME

The women sat in a straight line opposite one another. There were usually ten or fifteen players on each side. The "guesser" or "captain" of each side sat in the middle and she took care of most of the guessing activity. She also took care of the sticks that were given up when she missed a guess. A person on the opposite side was holding a pair of bones and the captain was supposed to guess which hand the white bone was held in. She missed if she did not choose correctly.

Eleven sticks and two pairs of bones are used in the game. Each pair of bones has one white bone and one with a black band around it. The women's playing bones were small enough to fit their hands. The object of the game is to guess which hand is holding the white bone. When the guesser points instead to the hand that has the black band, she must give up one stick. There are ten sticks in the game and one in the middle. The one in the middle is an extra stick that might help recover a losing game.

The game starts when the guessers "match" each other. They each hold a pair of bones and try to outguess one another. Sometimes they might both continue missing by pointing to the hand that is holding the black band several times. When one player finally misses and the other does not, she must give up the bones and the middle stick. The other ten sticks are distributed equally, five sticks for each side.

FIGURE 4.4. *Palyúut* (bones used to play bone game), 2016. Courtesy of Brittany Parham.

A song is started by the winning guesser and she distributes a pair of bones to each of the players sitting on the left and right side of her. They hide the bones and decide how to hold them; then they must bring both hands out in plain view. They swing their hands, keeping time with the song. The guesser on the opposite side will then try to guess in which hand the other player holds the white bone. Each player has one hand closer to the center of the line of women, and one hand closer to the outside of the line. Figure 4.4 shows the possibilities for which bones will be held in the inside hands and so also the possibilities for the guesses that the opposing captain could make. For example, the top two white (unbanded) bones represent the scenario in which both players hold white bones in their inside hands.

If the guesser points with her index finger down to the ground, she is guessing that both the white bones are held to the center, in other words, that the player seated to the opposing captain's left is holding the white bone in her right hand, and the one sitting on the right of the captain is holding the white bone in her left hand. This is shown in Figures 4.5a and 4.5b.

If the guesser is right, then both players give up the bones. But if the black bones are held in that position, the guesser has missed and she gives up two sticks.

If the guesser believes the white bones are in the outer hands of both players, she will raise her right hand with the palm facing towards her body and the first, second, and third fingers curled under; the thumb points backward (like hitching a ride) and the forefinger points straight across to the left. Figures 4.6a and 4.6b show this way of pointing.

If the guesser believes that one white bone is to the center and one is to the outside (in other words, that both opposing players have the white bone in their right hand or that both opposing players have the white bone in their left hand), she will point to the left or the right, palm towards the body, in the direction of the outside white bone.

When one person is holding the bones, the guesser's hand is pointing to either the right or left.

A bone game can last all night and is won only when all sticks are taken by one side.

FIGURE 4.5A. *Tɬ'ut pachúpa* (guessing both white bones are to the center). Courtesy of Jaeci Hall.

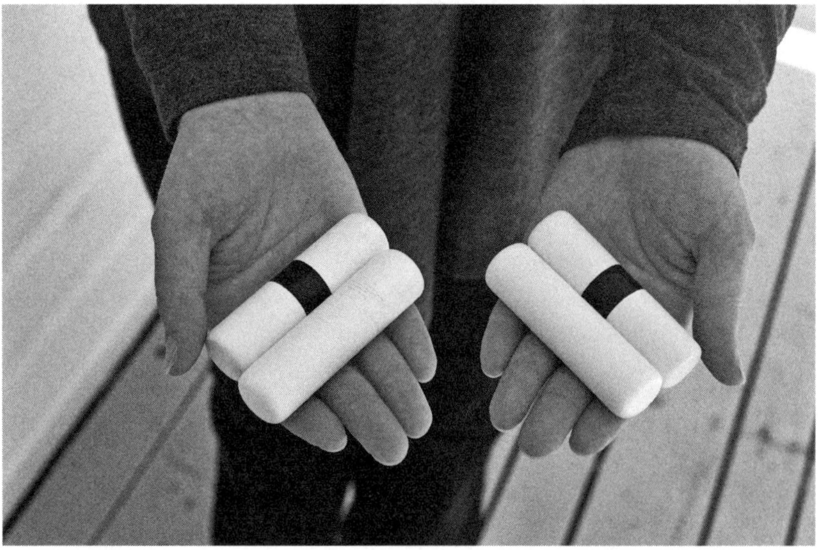

FIGURE 4.5B. *Tɬ'ut pachúpa* (white bones are to the center), 2016. Courtesy of Brittany Parham.

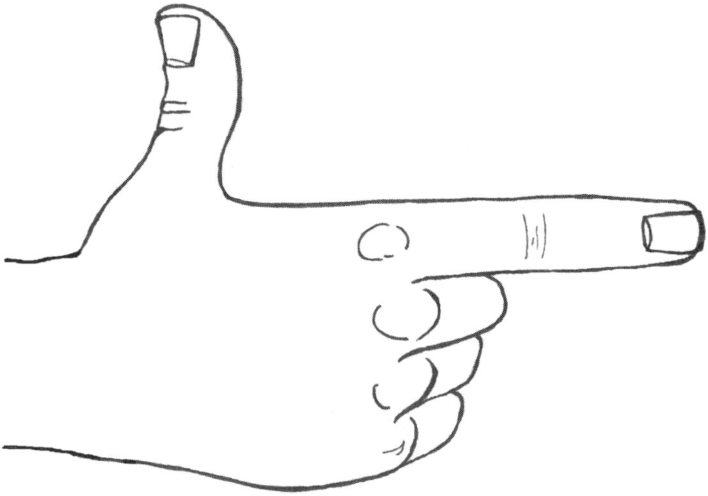

FIGURE 4.6A. *Papúchan* (guessing both white bones are to the outside). Courtesy of Jaeci Hall.

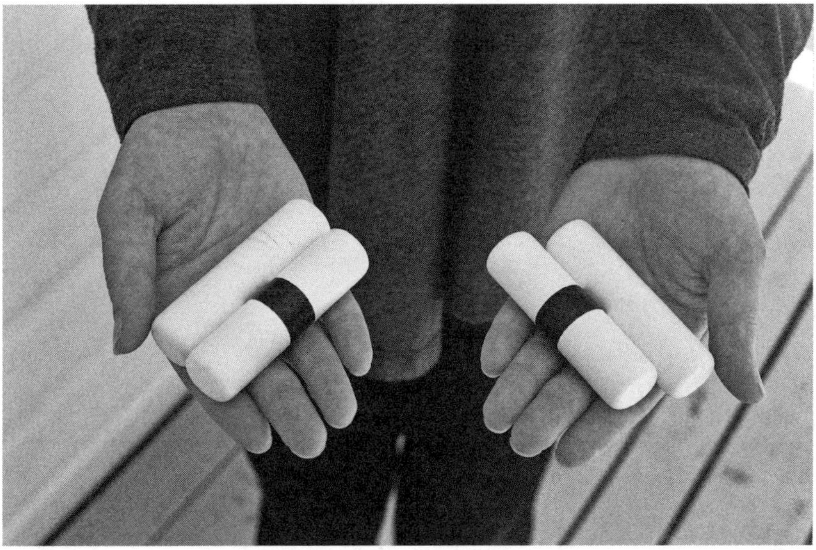

FIGURE 4.6B. *Papúchan* (white bones are to the outside), 2016. Courtesy of Brittany Parham.

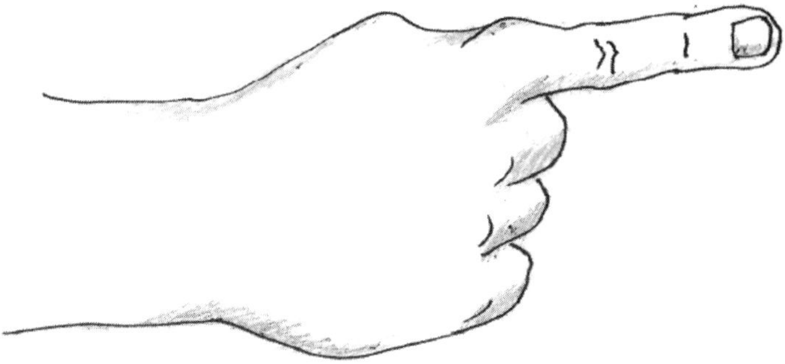

FIGURE 4.7A. *Tł'ut nax̱sh wikayklánan* (guessing a single bone holder). Courtesy of Judith Fernandes.

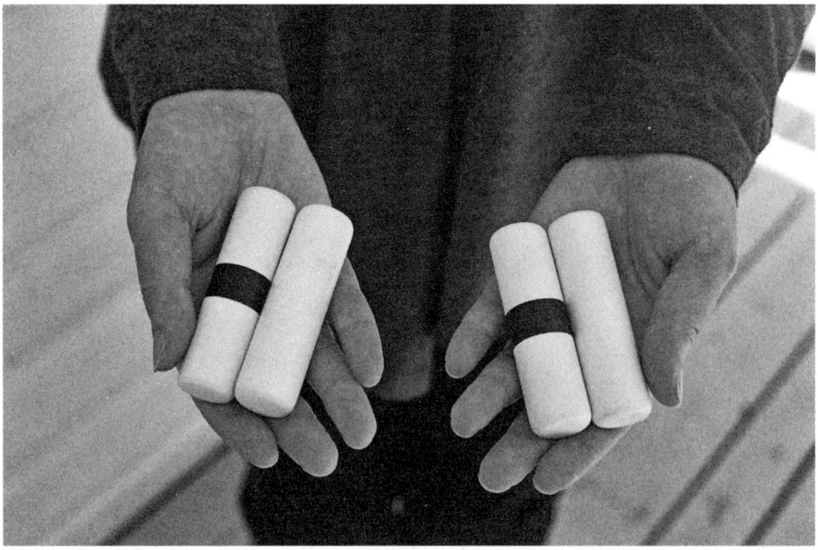

FIGURE 4.7B. White bone to the outside, 2016. Courtesy of Brittany Parham.

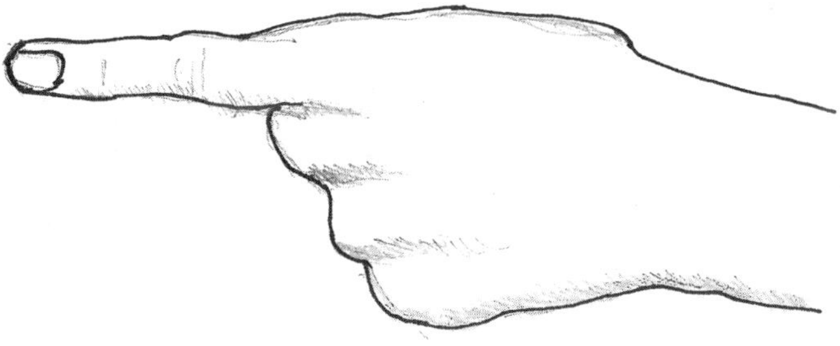

FIGURE 4.8A. *Tł'ut naxsh wikayklánan* (guessing a single bone holder). Courtesy of Judith Fernandes.

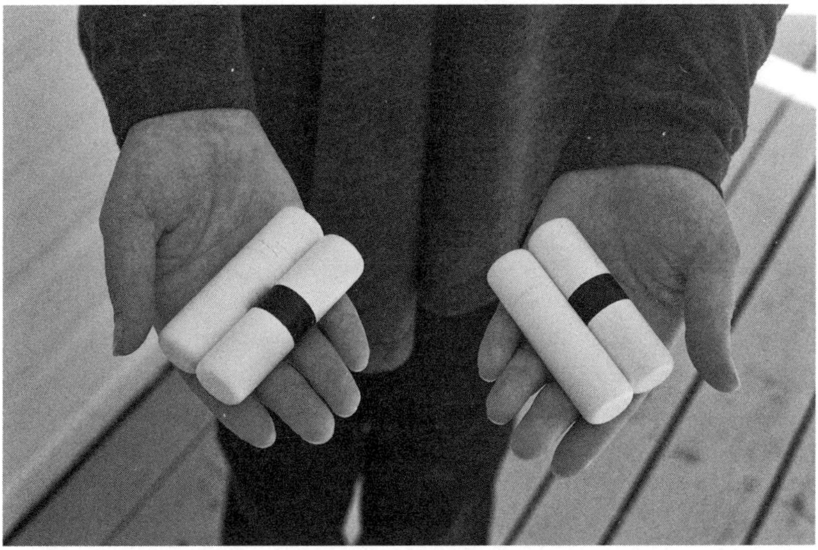

FIGURE 4.8B. White bone to the inside, 2016. Courtesy of Brittany Parham.

Áwacha ayatmamísim wán-
paash palyuutpamá. Ku k̲'shɨshní
pawíitkwapaniix̲ana niiptík ɨpáp,
kwáysim kwáysim, wánpaashyaw.
Kuuk míimi chaw pawalptáykx̲ana
kiwkíwlaaski. Awínshma
pawát'ax̲ana twánan wat'atpamáki.
KinChúuchma íkw'ak panáchika
kiwkíwlaaski walptákt palyúutpa.

The women had their own songs. [There are special songs the women sing that are softer than and not as harsh as the songs the men sing.] They hold their hands in fists and swing them back and forth evenly, keeping their hands together, in time to the music. [This is not like the men, whose hands are not held together.] And long ago they did not play with drums. The men had a pole in front of them and they would keep time on it with a stick. The Canadians brought that drumming while playing bone game.

KinChúuch means British Columbia; *KinChúuchma* means Canadian Indians. It should be mentioned that when the Canadian Indians came is when the manner of wagering changed. It was the first time the women began betting money. Indians from other areas would come to pick hops, and they were bone game players. They bet the money they had earned working in the hop fields. It was the only valued item the British Columbia and Coast Indians would accept since they did not wear the Sahaptin Plateau type of jewelry or clothing, or carry the beaded handbags.

FARMING AND FISHING / TAMANÍKT KU NP'ÍWIT

Íkush awkú iwachá tunx̲túnx̲
kútkut, ttúushma piimilksá kw'ɨnk
nisháyktpa pashapáttawax̲ɨnx̲ana
awkú tamaníksh, anakú awkú
páwisapsikw'ana shapáttawax̲t
tamaníksh tíinmaman. Kush awkú
máytsk̲i patáx̲shishana kú awkú
tamaníkshnan paták̲w'tkatax̲ana
áyatma.

There were different kinds of work, and everyone would grow a garden or farm at their home, because the Indians had been shown [by the government] how to grow vegetables. [This went beyond victory gardens—Indians were encouraged to farm on their own allotments, raising food and animal feed.] So early in the morning they would get up and the women would go outside to weed the garden.

Ku kúshx̱i awínshma awkú pakútkutshana patúpan áytalupa, uu pasháx̱tɬ'x̱shana tun íchi alfalfa, kw'ɨnk pawaníkinx̱a waskú uu mísh pashapawananúushana. Ttúushma k'úsiki paḵḵanáywix̱ana ku túkin músmustsɨnki anatúntya áwacha ḵaaw ḵaaw kútkut, íkw'ak íkush anakúsh máytsḵi máykutkut.

And it was the same for the men, they were out there working in the wheat, or cutting alfalfa, what they call *waskú*, or maybe irrigating it. Some of the men were busy with horses or with cattle, whatever they had for separate jobs in the morning.

Awínshma awkú uyt pmáx̱ush wát'uy pax̱wyákɨnx̱ana, anakú awkú pawyatsímaksha tun k'úsi tun músmustsɨn awkú pax̱wyáksha ku pa'áshx̱ama awkú kw'áx̱i tkwátatya, ku kw'áx̱i kpaylk ánach'ax̱i awkú pakútkutɨnx̱ana úyknik. Íkush awkú áwacha wyáx̱ayx̱t.

The men would be the first to go sweat, after they had fed the horses or cattle. After the sweat, they would come in and eat their breakfast, then go back out and continue to work. That is the way they lived.

Íchi íkuuk chawtún áwa kútkut awinshmamí ku awkú ttúshma patkw'anínkw'aninx̱a táawnpa. Ttúshma awkú pachíisha k'aaw mɨnán pak'úsha chaw tun kútkut tawnáapak'a. Ku tɨ́knik'a túnx̱mana awkú pawyánawyuusha kuna pakútkutnanisha anakw'ínk míimi tíinma panáktkwaninx̱ana, anakúsh pakútkutɨnx̱ana haps tmaanítpa, tɬ'aax̱w íkw'ak anatún áwacha kútkut pashtɨnmamí ku awkú pa'íwshɨnx̱ana tíinmaman kútkut kw'ɨnk pashapákutkutɨnx̱ana. Íchi íkuuk awkú áwa tunx̱mamí.

Today the men have no work and some of them are just walking around town. Some of them are drinking and gather together in groups—no work, supposedly. And instead, different kinds of people [migrant workers] come to do the work on the Indian Reservation. The Indian people used to work in the hops and pick the fruit. Now all of the manual labor work and compensation that was provided by the farmers to local Indian men are no longer available. They used to pay the Indian people for the work that they had them do. Now it is someone else's job.

Íkushna awkú íchi tx̱ánasha ku cháwna átḵ'ix̱sha íkushna wáta awkú niimí myánash, ku míshkinna awkú niimíki sápsikw'atki pashíx̱wita, túnna awkú ásapsikw'ata anakú aw iwyátunx̱sh íchi tiichám.

This is what is happening to us now, and we do not want this to happen to our children, and how will our children benefit from our teaching, what should we teach them, since this world is changing?

Ku túnx̱k'ana awkú tkwátat wa ttuush, cháwk'a awkú nɨ́mnɨwíit anakúsh tkwátat tiichámknik. Anakúsh ttuush iwá shapáttawax̱ni asht ɨníitpa, uu túpan shapáḵ'iki mɨnán túpan tkwasáypa ku ittáwax̱sha kwnak cháwk'a tiichámpa.

And some of our food is changing, the food is no longer from the land. Some is grown in a house, or hanging somewhere, in a bucket, and they are no longer grown on the earth. [This is referring to food grown in greenhouses, or hydroponically.]

Anakúshx̱i awkú niimí tiichám iwyátunx̱isha. Awkɫáwna áytalu ttush áytalu íkw'ak awkú pɨ́nch'ax̱i iláamsha anakú tiichám iwyátunx̱sha awkú cháwk'a tun áwa x̱túwit tiichamnmí shapáttawax̱tay aytalúnan kwɨnkínkna awkú átawtnukix̱a. Anakúshna ásaypnanix̱a chilwít tawtnúk ku kunkínk awkú íttawax̱sha ánch'ax̱i úyknik. Anakúshna awkú áwichaychaysha tiichámnan.

And our land is changing. We have only the grains, and some of the grains are also disappearing, because the land is changing. Now the land has no strength [nutrients] to grow and that is why we fertilize it. Thus we are feeding it bad things with that fertilizer in order to make the grain grow. It seems like we are spoiling the earth.

Kúna chiish aw ists'úupsha cháwk'a iwánasha anakúsh iwánanx̱ana míimi uu cháwk'a ipúuyix̱a anakúsh ipúuyix̱ana. Palaláaaay ipúuyix̱ana íchna tiichámpa, anakúsh kkɨmkkɨ́m wá'aaw ɨníitiniitnan ttuush.

Now our water is drying up, the river is no longer filled with water like it used to be a long time ago, and it does not snow like it used to snow. There used to be lots of snow here on this land, it would pile up as high as some houses.

Kunkínk iwachá palaláay chiish íchna tiichámpa, anakúsh wána iyákkɨmkx̱ana, kúshx̱i míimi anakúsh itúux̱ix̱ana wána wiyátyaw anakúsh itúux̱ix̱ana, ku kwnak awkú tiin iwátḵukx̱ana kuunák, ku iwats'úlaksha.

In that way there was a lot of water in this land, because the water used to flow and filled up [the river]. And the river used to freeze, it would freeze way down deep, and there the people bore holes in it and they went ice fishing.

Nayáyasintash wats'úlakɨnx̱ana, Taptíil wánapa ɨsɨ́mayaw. Nayáyas iwaníkshana Oscar. Iskáwix̱ana x̱yáaw ílkwaas ku ílkwx̱ana iksíks ilkwsh inmíyay láts'muytay. X̱wíimichnik túux̱pa, kush álwaachix̱ana.

My brother and I used to fish in the Yakima River for white fish. My brother's name was Oscar. He would gather dry twigs and build a fire for me to keep warm on top of the ice, and I'd watch the fire.

Itúkx̱ana ḵ'íya ku wátḵukipa túux̱pa ishapáwalux̱ana chíishyaw.

He would bait a hook and line and in the hole in the ice, drop the line down in the water.

Áwnash awkú iwyáalakwx̱ana kwnak tɬ'anx̱ itasɨ́x̱ɨnx̱ana túnin ku yɨpáx̱shkan. Pamúnnash iwináchikuux̱ana, itamáatx̱ana tkwalá, ku ánach'ax̱i itúkx̱ana. Kw'áx̱i itasɨ́x̱ɨnx̱ana, ayáyat ḵ'ínupa iwíisklikwiiisklikx̱ana nɨwítkan ku waḵátsalkan.

I stayed and watched the hook while he skated up and down the river. Once in a while he'd come back to pull the fish out and bait the line. Then he would continue skating, twirling back and forth. [Like ice skaters in the Olympics.]

Shix̱ iwá tkwátat ɨsɨ́may tkwalá. Chaw áwa ataa'ɨláx̱ yápaash, anakúsh áwa atachiishpamaanmí.

White fish is good food. It does not have a lot of oil, not like those that come from the ocean.

Íkush iwachá míimi íchi tiichám. Tł'áax̱wnan tuun patkwátax̱ana, ɨsɨ́may, kúshx̱i áwacha átaw tkwátat íchi íkuuk, anakw'ɨ́nk awkú pawyá'anakwsha íkuuk, aw íchi x̱wɨn, x̱wɨn anakú áwa pala-láay pipsh ku cháwpat awkú shix̱ tkwátat apx̱winúux̱a x̱wɨ́nnan. Ku tíinma panátx̱anax̱ana íkw'ak awkú x̱wɨnmí áwa palaláaytx̱aw anakúsh tawtnúk pɨnmipáynk wáwnakw-shashpa anakú áwa palaláaytx̱aw. Inak̲núwisha pɨnmipáynk wáwnak-shashpa tawtnúk anakwɨnkínk x̱tu i'aníx̱a pípshpipshnan, anakw'ɨ́nk íchi íkuuk páshtɨnma pawaníkx̱a calcium, íkw'ak awkú íkwtɨnk áwa x̱wɨnmí pinmipáynk wáwnakw-shashpa, kuna tɨ́knika awkú áchaay-sha anakú áwa palaláay pípshpipsh wáwnakwshashpa kuna awkú áwanakwsha íchi íkuuk. Fertilizerna awkú áwanisha uu míshna áta-maynaksha túpan tk̲únipa, ák'aatsha.

That is the way this land was a long time ago. They used to eat every-thing, like the white fish, and they had a valued food that nowadays is thrown away, the suckerfish. The suckerfish has many bones, that is the reason people will not eat it. The suckerfish has a lot of medici-nal value in its body. The bones provide the minerals to strengthen bones with the nutrient people call calcium. The suckerfish provides calcium and protein in our diet. People should take advantage of this resource instead of throwing it away. [In Sahaptin winter legend-telling season, between December and January, my grandmother would boil the head and take it apart, one bone at a time and tell us the legend each bone represents, the important lessons children should know. That is the reason the Indian people say "The Suckerfish is wise."]

Kúshx̱i íchi asúm, asúm iwachá páyu átaw míimi tkwátat shápshpa x̱yaaw nák'anint anakúsh chíwat tkwátat, kúshx̱i ínat'yi itx̱ánax̱ana ílkwshpa, ku tł'aax̱w awkú áwananx̱ana pɨnmínk yápaash ku awkú k̲'ɨsk̲'ɨs tkwátat shix̱ anakúsh chákw'ɨlktpa. K̲'ɨ́sk̲'ɨs Ichishkíin tamáshwiktpa anamkú áchakw'ɨlkta k̲'ɨs tkwátatnan anakúsh iwíinashax̱a potato chips.

And there is eel, the eel used to be a very valuable food, to take dried in your lunch, it was filling food, and you could also crisp it over the fire, and all of its grease will drip out of it, and it will become crispy. *K̲'ɨ́sk̲'ɨs* in the Indian language translates to the sound when you bite into crispy food like potato chips.

Nch'iwánapaatash kwnák wáwtukx̱ana np'íwitpa Wɨshx̱amípa, kush áḵ'inuna (nɨmmawíit palaláay) ásum payáwtaanx̱a. Ayáyat ḵ'ínupa pawáach'aksha pshwápa palálp'asha Áanki, anakúsh ḵ'ínupa sx̱áwkaas.

At the Columbia River where we camped during fishing season among the Wishx̱am people, I saw many, many eels floating in the water, attached to flat rocks in the river reflecting in the sun, looking like shiny black flintstone.

Ínx̱tway Estherintash áwihananuykx̱ana Piil Slúskɨnan (Bill Saluskin, my step brother) anakú inp'íwitax̱ana chimáawaknik anakwnák iskúulishana.

My relative Esther and I would pester Bill Saluskin when he came to fish there from Chemawa, Oregon, where he was going to school.

Átash áwku wáawk'a ihananúynx̱ana kutásh ishápwawch'akx̱ana asúmki tpɨshpa kutash wíitux̱ɨnx̱ana wiyánax̱tisha.

When he could not stand us any longer, he'd stick eels on our faces and we'd run back to camp crying.

Íkush iwachá íchi míimi tkwátat miimá, ku cháwk'ana mun íkush átkwatax̱a anakú iláamshax̱i kw'ɨnk awkú íchi ásum anakúsh iḵátx̱anasha tawtnúki ku ttuush awkú iwá chaw ts'aa tkwátatay. Iwánax̱a awkú ttuush tun cháychay chíishyaw ku kw'ɨnk awkú patkwátasha pmách'ax̱i kuunák ku áwashsha kw'ɨnk cháychay tun pɨnmipáynk wáwnakwshashpa.

This is how food was a long time ago. We no longer eat like that, eel is disappearing, and it is also now becoming contaminated; some is not fit to eat. The poison flows into the water and then they eat it too, that poison gets into their body.

REMEMBERING MY GRANDMOTHER, X̱AX̱ÍSH / P'ƗX̱T NAKÁŁASAAN, X̱AX̱ÍSH

Kush awkú wachá wáawka iksíks ashkú nakáłas iwachá nch'ík'a awkú ttáwax̱t, ku tƚ'aax̱wnan tuun ishúkwaashana pɨnk. Áwnash íkuuk anakúsh px̱wínx̱a, mɨnánx̱it awkú íkw'ak ikwɨ ishúkwaana tuun wíkut.

I was still young yet when my grandmother was already very aged, and she knew many things. Now when I think about it, I wonder where did she learn everything she knew, how to do everything?

Tƚ'áax̱wnan shiin isápsikw'ashana niimípa nisháyktpa. Ku na'íłasnɨmnash awkú anakúsh ishax̱áshana, inák ashkú wáawk'a wachá iksíks, kush chaw awkú ámshtk'ukɨnx̱ana nakáłasaan, tƚ'ápx̱iish awkú kwnáx̱i wachá táaminwa. Kush átk'inx̱ana mish imísha, kush chaw kw'ɨnk anakúsh isápsikwashana sɨ́nwitki, "Íkushnayk'aynash íchi íkush kúsha," mish chaw, áwtya ináktkwaninx̱ana kush íkwɨn átk'inx̱ana.

She used to teach many people these things at our home. Later my mother added onto my teachings, because I was too small [when my grandmother was living], and I did not pay much attention to what was going on, although I was there all of the time. And I would watch what she was doing but she did not say or explain to me, "I am doing this for this reason"; she continued to work and I watched her.

Tƚ'áax̱wnatash mish wíimix̱ana. K'úsikitash atmaanísha kkúushnan tuun naníknan, kutash awkú nánasha anakwnák iwá wawtkáwaas ku ílkwsha ku ipshaanákwsha awkú lápuulpuulpa, ku kw'áx̱i awkú iwáshukɨnax̱ana kuunák uu mish aw iníchx̱ana, ku i'íłax̱yaawisha. Tƚ'áax̱wnash íkw'ak átk'inx̱ana íkushx̱i kútyaw. Kush áwapiitasha ttuush, kush awkú iksíks íx̱wi wachá myánash.

We did everything. We picked filberts and pine nuts from horseback and then we would take them to our camp and she would bake them in the ashes. [*Pshaanákwsha* means push a group of things into the hot coals or ashes.] Then she would winnow it or store it, or dry it. I saw all this as she worked. And I used to help her, even though I was still a little child.

Táaminwaash anakúsh isháapax̱ana ánachnik. Lisháalkiish iwaláḵw'ɨp'ɨnx̱ana kúshx̱i iwáyuumix̱ana ánachnik pɨnmipáynk. Kwɨnkínknash awkú chaw x̱átamkanwix̱ana k'úsiknik. Wíyattash wínax̱ana kúsh awkú wyápnunx̱ana, íkushnatash wyáninx̱ana nakáłasin míimi k'úsiki.

She would always bundle me up with a shawl. She would tie me snug against her, and pull me up tight behind her. That is how I was kept from falling off the horse. When we traveled far, I would fall asleep as we went, that is how my grandmother and I traveled around by horseback a long time ago.

Ku ɨníitpa anamún awkú itáx̱shix̱ana kush awkú ínch'ax̱i táx̱shix̱ana kúukx̱i, anakú isɨ́nwix̱ana ku iwalptáyksha máytsḵi, ku isɨ́nwisha tł'áax̱wki túkin itɨmnanáx̱ɨnx̱ana máytsḵi, kúshx̱i iwalptáykɨnx̱ana ku ipúux̱ana kwnak íkw'ak ɨwínsh anakw'ɨ́nk itáx̱shiya niimípa tiichámpa.

And at home when she woke up, and I woke up at the same time, then she would start talking and singing in the morning, she would tell stories about all kinds of things, and she would sing and repeat the songs that that Prophet brought back when he awoke in this land.

Íkushkinknash isápsikw'ankx̱ana nakáłasnɨm máytsḵipa. Kúuknash wachá íx̱wi iksíks niimípa nisháyktpa. Palaláaynatash pawyák'ukuux̱ana tíinma, kútya pmák ámchnik papnúnx̱ana. Nayáyas Oscarx̱it awkú ipnutwíix̱ana kuumanák, anakú awínshmasim pawachá, ttúushma pawachá ínpimx̱ma.

This was her way of teaching me, in the morning. At this time I was the only very young child in the household. We also had lots of people who would stay with us, but they slept outside the house as they traveled through. My brother Oscar must have slept with these people, who were mostly men, some our uncles.

Palaláay anakúsh áwacha walptáytk ku sápsikw'at sɨ́nwit, íchi niimíki waḵ'íshwitki, mɨshkwyáamkt íkw'ak íkwɨnkink maysx̱máysx̱ isɨ́nwix̱ana anakú uyt itáx̱shix̱ana, iwalptáykɨnx̱ana, inatx̱ánax̱ana "Áwshtaymashaash chɨ́mtinan łkw'ínan."

There were a lot of songs and teachings about our religion, our belief, this is what she spoke about everyday when she would wake up. She used to sing and she would say, "I am meeting the new day."

Íkush áwacha tx̱ánat nakałasaanmí, ku itł’yáwya kush, íx̱wi wachá paysh pax̱at’umáat uu mish túskas anwíkt íx̱wi.

Thus was the life of my grandmother, and when she died, I was still only perhaps seven or eight years old.

Kush chaw awkú tuun anakúsh áshukwaana nɨ́mnɨwit, anakúshnash áḵ’inuna náktkwanint tł’yáwitnan, kúshx̱iish áḵ’inuuna anakúsh pɨnmikínk shúkwatki, íchi wáashatki ishapá’ata chilwít-wapsúx̱nan wáwnakwshaashknik nax̱sh ɨwinshmɨ́knik.

I never learned much beyond what she taught, although I saw the preparation for burial, and I also experienced her knowledge when I watched her use her religion to exorcise the devil from the body of a man.

Kush áḵ’inuna itkw’á’ata shwát’ash, uu lawiishḵ’íshish ɨwínsh itkw’á’anakwa wáwnakwshashnan. Ku i’áta ámchan anakúsh awkú ik’áatna nakáłas, “Átɨnk, áwyaalakwɨnk, wínak, atk ámchan, wínak, anamɨ́niknam wyánawisha!” Ik’áatna kuunák chilwítnan, chilwít wapsúx̱nan. Itútya ɨwínsh lawiishḵ’íshish itk’wanátya, itk’wá’ata ámchan, ash aḵ’inúshana kuunák ink inmíki áchaashki.

I saw a shadow walk out, like a cloud, or a shadow from the man. It left his body and went outside when my grandmother evicted the bad spirit, saying “Get out, leave, go, go outside, back to wherever you came from!” She evicted that bad thing, the devil and the shadow from the man stood up, and walked across the floor and walked outside, and I saw that with my own eyes.

Ku kw’ɨnk ɨwínsh anakuunák pá’ashshana kwiiník, awkú ix̱áx̱anayka ku ipnúna, anakú mun itáx̱shya ku awkú iwachá shix̱, kw’áx̱i ishíx̱iya awkú kw’ɨnk ɨwínsh ku icháynachya ku ishapáttawax̱na pɨnmínk myánashma, chaw awkú túwin ánch’ax̱i úyknik páshapyáwya, anakú lawiishḵ’íshishin awkú pawyálaakwa.

And the man that this thing had possessed, he fell back and he slept. When he woke he was better, he got married and raised his children, and nothing further bothered him ever again.

Kush chaw ashúkwaashana mish kw'ɨnk iwachá ɨwínsh anamísh pának'ninx̱ana kwiiník chilwítin, awkłáwnash áḵ'inuna anakúpat ánasha niimíyaw ɨníityaw. Anakúsh tun i'át'ɨlpx̱a k'usík'usi kunam awkú iwátkwnanuuta. Kúshx̱inam itkwatatát'ata anakúsh áwatta áchaash, ɨtɨ́t íkw'ɨtta kunam ichanpát'ata. Íkw'ak íkush awkú iwachá kw'ɨnk ɨwínsh apatkú ánasha ɨníityaw niimíyaw kupat áwalaḵ'ika aykáwaasyaw, awkú pináwapyaasha, nápu awínshiinpat miskilíiki áchaḵuksha.

And I never knew who this man was or how this bad thing affected him, I just saw him when they brought him into our house. It was like when a dog goes mad, and it will attack you, and it wants to eat you, and its eyes will grow hard, it will show its teeth and it wants to bite you. That is how that man was when they brought him into our house and tied him to a chair, and he was struggling and two men were barely holding him down.

Nakáłas awkú iwɨ́npa kw'alálkw'alal itamáata pɨnmiknínk łp'áanaḵknik, iwínanuuna kuunák ɨwínshnan, ku ichátika wát'uychnik, ku í'ína, "Áwmash shúkwaasha, shínnam wa. Wáshnam áymɨl." Awkú páwatkwnanuux̱ana, kupat miskilíiki áchaḵukɨnx̱ana. Awkú ichatikúuna ku anakú mun ichatikúux̱ana, ixɨ́ppɨnx̱ana kw'ɨnk ɨwínsh, wáwnakwshash awkú tł'aax̱w áx̱ɨppɨnx̱ana, ku awkú iwátkwnanuux̱ana nakáłasaan.

My grandmother took her bell from her sally bag [this is the bag where she kept all of her important things], and went up to that man and rang it in front of him, and said, "I know you who you are. You are evil!" He attacked her, and they had difficulty holding him back. Then she rang the bell towards him, and when she rang the bell towards him, now that man shivered, his whole body would shake, and he would try to attack my grandmother.

Awkú iwyánknika, ichátika, iwalptáyka awkú ku iwyánknika aw, awkú kw'ɨnk ɨwínsh anakúsh mish pináwapyana anakúsh íchi núsux̱ pináwapyata anamkú átamawinatta chíishknik. Kúshx̱i awkú kw'ɨnk itx̱ánana ɨwínsh, pináwapyana, húuypat awkú áchaḵuka, awkú áwḵanɨna, kwnak táakwɨnpa aykáwaaspa kútya iwachá kwaat káshtki.

She went around and around him, ringing the bell, and singing [the specific song for this purpose]. Then that man struggled, like a salmon struggles when you throw him out of the water. That is what happened to this man, he struggled, they barely could hold him down, he twisted around there on that chair, but he was bound securely.

Awkú iwyanknikwyanknikúuna awkú wát'uychnik itútya, ku ɨ́na, "Áwnam átta, áwnam átta íkuuk, áwapawx̱ink, shákwinan, áwnam áwyaalakwta, áwnam túx̱ta anamɨ́nik íchi wyánawya, kunam aw wíyat wínata, atk, wínak!" Awkú x̱túwiki awkú kush iníya sɨ́nwit x̱tu ichátika ku awkú áchaash áwiinatma awkú ɨwinshmí.

Then she went around him, round and round him, and she stood in front of him, and she said to him, "Go out, leave now, I want you to release this man, you must go back to wherever you came from. You go far away, get!" She kept trying to drive him out with words, and ringing her bell, and the man's eyes popped out at her.

Kush ínch'a awkú tútishana łamáay, íkush ashkú pak'áatna pa'ɨ́nx̱anaash, "Ámchan wínak, wíyat íkuuni ámchan." Kúshx̱iish awkú wachá ḵw'shɨm, awkúsh ḵw'shɨ́mna kush awkwnák awkú piná'iłamayka, kush átk'ina kúunak ɨwínshnan, mish itx̱ánashana. Kush chawmún túkin anakúsh ínch'a wyáych'unx̱ana ashmáal wachá kwnak káła, kush px̱wínx̱ana nakałasánɨmnash inaknúwita, táaminwaash íkush px̱wínx̱ana, kushkínknash chaw wiyáych'una.

I was standing there hidden, although they told me, "Go out, far away [to a safe place]." But I got stubborn and so I disobeyed and I hid myself there, and I saw what happened to that man. And I was never afraid as long as my grandmother was there, and I thought my grandmother would look after me, I always thought that, for that reason I was not afraid.

Awkú x̱túwiki, x̱túwiki awkú isámx̱nana kuunák chilwítnan. Awkú i'átɨma kw'ɨnk awkú anakúsh lawiishḵ'íshish chmuk, ku íkuuni awkú wíyat itútya nakáłas, ku átkika awkú itkw'á'atkika, kush ts'áapa itkw'áwaawna kwnɨmk, ku átkika awkú pchɨ́shpa.

Then with great strength, my grandmother then spoke hard to that evil one. Then it came out like a black cloud, and my grandmother stepped aside and it went out, passing close by me, and it walked out the door.

THE POWER OF MEDICINE MEN AND WOMEN / X̱TÚWIT TWATIMAMÍ

Íkushnash áḵ'inuna inknínk anakúsh inmíki áchaashki íkw'ak tx̱ánat, kush palaláay íkush tuun áwiḵ'inuna ashkú wachá anakúsh íx̱wi iksíks ttáwax̱t. Twátima pakútkutsha túpan payúwitnan, ku tuun iwítx̱anax̱ana íkwɨnnash aw tƚ'aax̱w áwiḵ'inunx̱ana íkush inmíki áchaashki. Kush kunkínk áshukwaasha mɨƚ áwacha x̱túwit, anakwmák pawachá shúkwaani.

That is how I saw that happen with my own eyes, and I witnessed a lot of things like that as a child when I was still growing up. The medicine people worked on a patient and some unusual things would happen, that is what I used to witness. And that is how I know how much strength they had, those who were given the power to be medicine people. [*Shúkwaani* means knowledgeable; here it means knowledgeable about the spirit world].

Pashúkwaashana tun átaw, pánya x̱túwit, hawláakin túwin. Kush kuunák ínch'ax̱i awkú áḵ'inuna, kush chaw áshukwaasha ink, cháwnash inách'a túnɨm isámx̱nana, íkush íkw'ak, anakúsh x̱túwit iníya túnɨm. Cháwnash wa tun x̱túwit túpan, anakúsh íchi pawachá twátima. Chaw. Áwtyaash wa ínch'a íchi walím tiin, awkƚáwnash ḵ'ínutkisim tuun áshukwaasha, kúshx̱iish áwapiitax̱ana, anakúsh twátimaman kuts'k tun wapíitat. Íchi ƚmamatúma ashkú pa'atƚ'áwix̱ana, "Wapíitataam," anakúshx̱iish áḵ'inunx̱ana kútkutyaw.

They knew valuable things, and they were given special power by a spirit. And I witnessed these things but I myself do not do the medicine work, nothing ever gave me that power. I do not have that power like the medicine people. I am just an ordinary person and I only know by witnessing, although I used to help a little bit. [For example, they needed supplies and water, and I could bring these things. I could also see what they were going to need shortly, and would bring that. I did not understand what it all meant. I just followed the directions instinctively.] These Elder women used to ask me, "Come help me," then I would see things as I helped.

Ashkú áwaashiinix̱ana iksíksknik ttáwax̱tknik twátimaman, anakú pawánpx̱ana kush áwaashiinix̱ana, kush anakúsh patamkáshax̱ana. Chawsh áshukwaasha mish awkú kw'ɨnk íkw'ak iwá patamkáshat. Kush patamkáshax̱ana k'úpkw'ppa kush panákwaashax̱ana pak'úpkw'pki, inmíki k'úpkw'pki piimipáynk k'úpkw'ppa, kush chaw mun shínɨm anakúsh i'ɨ́na íkush íkw'ak iwá íkushnayk'ay.

When I was a little girl I used to dance for the Medicine Men. When they had their winter dance, I would dance for them, and they would put me on their back. I do not understand the meaning of that, putting me on their back. And they would put me on their back, and they would carry and dance with me back to back. [The men would bend forward and dance and stomp with a child on their back. They would call a child out and carry the child like this. The word *tamkáshasha* refers to this.]

Kúshkinnash chaw áshukwaasha túyay awkú íkw'aknash íkush pakúx̱ana míshnash awkú ink kwɨnkínk tx̱ánax̱ana, awkɫáwnash aw px̱wínx̱ana paysh laak pimáwapiitasha pmáktya, cháwnash awkú ínch'a px̱wínx̱ana, inách'ax̱iish pawapíitasha uu mish chaw, cháwnash mish px̱wínx̱ana kunkínk.

And I did not know why they did that to me, and what was supposed to happen to me, except I wondered if they were helping themselves. I never thought they were helping me, but I did not worry about it.

Áwnash mɨ́łman íkush x̱wɨsaatúma panákwaashana anakúsh k'úpkw'ppa, awkłáwnash awkú áshukwaasha náx̱shnɨmnash iníya wánpaash, kush ɨ́na "Anamkú tun átaw átḵ'ix̱sha kut, kunam íchi áp'ɨx̱ta íkuunak wánpaashnan. Cháwnam aw mish áwanpta, áwtyaam áp'ɨx̱ta." Ash ku mun wáshax̱ana átaw papawilawíix̱tpa, kush áp'ɨx̱ɨnx̱ana kuunák íkw'ak ku awkú inátx̱anax̱ana, "Inaknúwitaam chɨ́nɨm wánpaashnɨm." Kush awkú ápx̱winx̱ana kush px̱wínx̱ana, "Shíx̱nash inaknúwita, cháwnash wyáwḵta." Íkushnash íkw'ak px̱wínx̱ana. Ashkú íkush ɨ́na, áshkú wachá mayknch'ík'a awkú ttáwax̱t, paysh mɨł pútimt ku niipt, mɨł pútimt ku mɨ́taat anwíkt.

There were some old men who danced with me on their back, and there was one I remember who gave me a song, and he told me, "Whenever you do something important, or if you want to do something, remember this song. You do not have to sing it, just remember it." And when I used to ride in an important race, I would remember it. He would tell me, "This song will take care of you." And I used to remember, "It will take care of me, I won't have an accident." That is what I used to think. When he told me this, I was a little older, perhaps twelve or thirteen years old.

Áwacha waníkt Tímiti Tsúuts. Kutásh wachá náx̱sh wayx̱titpamá k'úsi iwaníkshana Sir Timothy, kush áwanpanix̱ana Tímitinan wánpaash ashkú áwashax̱ana pawilawíix̱tpa wánpaash ashkú áwashax̱ana pawilawíix̱tpa Sir Timothynan, kutásh cháawiyat táamiinwa wát'uynx̱a, awíishɨnx̱ana.

He was named Timothy George. We had a racehorse named Sir Timothy, and I sang Timothy's song when I rode him. Sir Timothy ran, and we won almost every race.

Íkw'ak awkú íkush pawachá twátima míimi, kush chaw ínch'a wa tun twáti, kush chaw míshkin awkúmatash ɨ́ntax̱nay, "Íkush íchi iwá twáti tx̱ánat." Chaw, kush ashkú chaw áshukwaasha. Awkɫáw twátisim ishúkwaasha tun áwa piimínk x̱túwit, míshkin kw'ɨnk iwɨ́npa x̱túwit, uu túpan áwa kw'ɨnk níyi x̱túwit túyay. Chaw mun twáti iwá x̱túwit níyi tɫ'áax̱wyaw túyaw, awkɫáw láxsyaw payúwityaw.

That is how the Medicine People were a long time ago, but I am not a medicine woman so I cannot tell you, "This is how it is to be a medicine person." I do not know that. Only the Medicine Doctor knows what his own power is, or how he will call it forth, or how his given power is to be used. The Medicine People—healers—are not given power to heal everything, only one sickness. [The Medicine Men never were questioned. When someone did challenge them, it was time to get out of the way because they would be angry and show their power.]

Íkw'ak íkushnash pa'ɨ́nx̱a ttúushma nch'ínch'ima ttáwax̱tma anakwmák pashúkwaasha. Íkw'aknash awkú ikwɫ áshukwaasha íkwɨnkink. Kush áykɨnx̱a íchi kpaylk wanpɫáma anakwmák panáwanpsha, panúu "Wáshnash twáti, awsh wánpsha," ku mɨnán awkú íkw'ak pa'ɨyáx̱na wanpt uu mish aw papúusha túuman? Íkw'akx̱iim awkú paníta wánpaash, kunam pa'ɨ́nta, "Íchimash wa wanpsh." Cháwnash mun shínnɨm íkush ínach'a ikúya.

That is what I have been told by the Elders who know these things. That is all I know about that. And I listen to those who are singing, they say, "I am a medicine person, because I am singing," and I wonder where they found [or were given] this song, or are they appropriating it? They [Medicine People] could give you a song at a Medicine Dance, and they would say to you, "Here is your song." Nobody did this to me.

Kútya awkú pamún íkush, íkushx̱inam awkú twátinɨm iníta wánpaash, kunam awkú áwanpanita kuunák. Ku paysh laak íkush íkw'ak áwa, anakú pawá iksíks íx̱wi ttáwax̱t. Íchi cháwk'a shin íkush ikúx̱a, anakúsh wínat pɨ́t'x̱ánukkan waḵítt íkushnanak, kush cháwx̱i áḵ'inusha mun wáḵ'ish pa'anísha túuman.

But they also say, when a medicine man gives you a song, then you can sing it for them. And perhaps that is how they obtained it, because they are very young, these singers. Nobody goes to the mountains anymore to look for their power, and I have not yet seen these people heal anyone.

Cháwx̱iish ayksh íkw'ak, anakú twátima íkushnayk'ay pawá, anakúsh wáḵ'ish anít payúwitmaman, cháwtya aw iwá wánptpasim. Íkw'ak wanpt iwá anakú anakúsh pimá'ishax̱anix̱a, anakú niimí wáwnakwshash waḵ'íshwit nax̱sh anwíkt anakúshna tɬ'aaaax̱w niimí x̱túwit awkú iláamnx̱a, ku chɨ́mtipa anwíktpa kwnak kw'áx̱i ishíx̱ix̱a, anakúsh piná'ishix̱ix̱a kw'áx̱i anakúsh íchi anakúsh íchi iwá shyapuwítki battery. Awna ku battery táakwɨnix̱a láamɨnx̱a x̱túwit, kuna chɨ́mtiki kw'áx̱i batteryki x̱tu tx̱ánax̱a íchi flashlight tun íkushna wa wáwnakwshash niimí.

And I have not heard [or seen] that yet, healing through singing alone, because medicine people are medicine people for the purpose of healing the sick, not just for singing. [Singing can renew or heal the power, but it is not the main power.] That song is for strengthening oneself, because our bodies and our spirit all throughout the year lose strength. [The winter dance is for renewing ourselves. Medicine men and women regain their power through this dance.] During the new year it gets better, like healing itself, just like in English we say a battery recharges. And our battery loses power, and with a new battery we become strong, like a flashlight, that is the way our body is.

FIRST FOODS CEREMONY / KÁ'UYT

Kushkínkna tx̱ánax̱a íchi ká'uyt, anakúshna íniix̱ix̱a kwnɨmk ká'uytnɨm ánach'ax̱i wyá'uyt chɨ́mti, anakúshna íshix̱anix̱ana wáwnakwshash anakúsh mish chɨ́mti kw'áx̱i tx̱ánax̱a. Kuna awkú náx̱shyaw anwíktyaw awkú wayksh x̱túwit, kwnak niimípa wáwnakwshashpa, waḵ'íshwitpa, ku tɨmnápa.

In that way we have our First Foods ceremony, the food repairs us and then we start anew, so it heals our body and we become new again. And then for the next year we start over with strength in our bodies, spirits, and hearts.

Íkush awkú íchi áwa mɨshkwiyámkt tiinmamí, tł'áaaax̱wpa túpan iwá ḵaawḵáaw, íkush, chawna awkú wa tł'áaax̱wpa túpan wapsúx̱, chaw, íkush iwachá míimi anakúsh tiinwít; ku awkú íchi shyapuwítki awkú patx̱ánax̱a, pawíwanikanix̱a tímash pashtɨnmí tímat. Anakú laxs itx̱ánata, tiin níyi x̱túwit íkushpaynk, awkú patímax̱a anakúsh tł'áax̱wmaman awkú pawáyuumisha kwnáx̱i tíinmaman, kuna chaw mun wachá tł'aax̱w kúsksim.

And this is how the Indian religion is, in everything it is thus separate, we are not each one knowledgeable about everything. This is the way it was a long time ago; now the white people's ways have us reading about this [Indian religion] in books. An incident only happens once, when one Indian person is given strength for this purpose, then the author writes it down and they include everyone, all the Indians, but we are not all alike.

This refers to when the teachings of a particular area or the words and actions of a particular prophet or medicine person are applied to all tribes and people, when Indian religion and ways are generalized across all Indians. However, the strength of medicine people is individual, specific to each person. Tribes and bands, even among the Sahaptin people, each believe a bit differently and have different Holy Men and Women. Individuals have different spirit guides that hold different healing powers. People have different beliefs in God, and Nature and Christianity. Not everyone has a spirit guide; some people, like me, have no spirit guide.

TRAVELING ON EEL TRAIL / WƗSHÍNWƗSHINT ASÚM ƗSHCHÍTPA

Anamɨnánnam wyáninta níimipa tiichámpa, kwnák iwá átaw tɨmnanáx̱t uu tun watít. Tł'ápx̱iim íkuuk wyanínshata táwnpa kunam áshta tkwatatpamáyaw, kwnáknam áp'ɨx̱ta, "Ah, íchnatash sháakwɨnin lɨsx̱aam papachɨttwíishana, kutash mɨsámsashana patúkin." Íkush iwá páp'ɨx̱t kúshx̱i p'ɨx̱t tuun átaw tɨmnanáx̱tnan.

Wherever you travel on our land, there are valuable stories and legends. Even now when you travel to town and you go into the restaurant, there you will remember, "Oh, I remember, here is where my friend and I shared lunch together and we joked around about something." This is how we recall an incident, or an important story.

Míimi anakú chaw iwachá ɨshchɨ́t, anakúsh iwá íkuuk. Tíinma pawɨshínwɨshinx̱ana k'úsiki uu wɨx̱akílk pawyanínx̱ana. Kumánk iwachá ɨshchɨ́t waníki "Asúm Ɨshchɨ́t."

Long ago there were no roads, as there are now. People moved around by horse or by foot. Since then, there has been a path named Eel Trail.

Napíshish iwaníkshana Saptix̱awáy. Áwacha na'iłasaanmí pishísh. Áwacha pshɨ́t, áwanikshana Oscar Wantux̱, pɨnmínk áwacha pat, Saptix̱awáy. Pawachá Palouseknik ttáwax̱t. Oscar Wantux̱ iwachá pɨ́tł'ani; kushkínk chaw áwacha napusaasnmí tiin waníkt.

My great-aunt's name was Saptix̱awáy [Margaret Wanto]. She was my mother's paternal aunt. Her father was Oscar Wanto, and Saptix̱awáy was his older sister. Their heritage was from Palouse country [on the Snake River]. Oscar Wanto was baptized; for that reason my paternal grandfather did not have an Indian name.

Saptix̱awáyintash k'úsiki panátix̱ana Asúm Ɨshchɨ́tpa atashkú mánax̱ana uu tmaanítax̱ana wíwnu Psawaaswáakułkan. Chaw itḵ'íx̱ɨnx̱ana tux̱t Asúm Ɨshchɨ́tpa, kutash túx̱ɨnx̱ama túnx̱pa ɨshchɨ́tpa. Anakú wáawk'a ix̱át'ult'ulta tkwátat, awkú íchaayta.

Saptix̱awáy and I climbed the Eel Trail on horseback when we went root digging or to pick huckleberries at Twin Buttes [in the Gifford Pinchot Forest]. She did not want to come down the Eel Trail coming home, so we took a different route. The food on the pack horse would bounce it around [going down the trail] and it would spoil while traveling.

Palaláay tíinma pawínaxana pɨ́t'xanukkan íkwnak ɨshchɨ́tpa; kwɨ́nik Winátshaknik, Wanaɫáma, ku Kw'sɨ́sknik, pamɨ́nik.

Many Indian people used Eel Trail en route to the Cascade Mountains; some came from Wenatchee, Priest Rapids, and Snake River, and others.

PÁTUXNAT WÁXSHAMPA

EEL TRAIL AND THE INDIAN WAR

Asúm Ɨshchɨ́t waníkt iwachá átaw tɨmnanaxtpamá. Palaláay átaw txánat kwnamánk iwá. Kwnák ikwíitana Asúm Ɨschɨ́tpa nch'i tamanwitpamá superintendent Bolin, tawnáapak'a ítɫxatktnak'it tiinmamíknik. Kwnákpat áwaptaymana xáyin Mɨshíil, anakú páshtɨnmapat tɫ'áaxw náxsh nisháykt Mɨshíilnan áwitɫ'yawyanya.

Eel Trail has a famous name and history. Many revered things took place there. There the government supervisor Bolin came riding up the trail after he had talked peace with the Indian people. There Mɨshíil and his kinsman killed Bolin. Mɨshíil was getting even for when the white people massacred his entire family. This was the incident that started the Indian war against the United States Army.

Íchitya iwachá chcháanwyi pátamun tiinmamípasim. Awkú shuyápu Nch'i Wɨ́xaniináwtunxna tímashpa uu páyshtya iwachá chcháanwyi tiin tɨmnanáxt.

This, however, was a thing known to Indian people only. The white person Big Foot changed it on the paper or perhaps the Indian version was kept secret.

Íchix̱it áwacha chcháanwyii wánikt Mɨshiilmí ku pɨnmínk x̱ɨ́twayma tíinmamí.
Nch'i Wɨx̱aníipat (Big Foot) tíinma áwanika Lucullas McWhorternan, anakú x̱ɨ́tway aníya tíinmaman. Iwapíitama anakú áwacha shapyáwit tíichamki tamanítpa pápanasht, míimi 1900pa. Kúshx̱i tamashwikłá chaw iwachá chnamánk, chaw tuun ishúkwaashana anakú iwachá tunx̱ tiin.

This would have been done to protect Mɨshíil and his family. Big Foot is one of the names given by the Indians to Lucullus McWhorter, who befriended and supported Yakama Indian people against settlement and the government in the early 1900s. Or perhaps the translator was not from here and he did not know, because he was from a different tribe.

Wáx̱shamki pashtɨnmí tímani tɨmnanáx̱t iwá chaw tkw'íikw. Wáa'awpat tíinma ákuya páshtɨn súltsasmaman kwnák Wáx̱shampa. Tł'áax̱wpat tun átyanɨpa: limíil, tkwátat, k'úsi, winánpsh, ku nch'i twínpaash. Kupat áwapawx̱ina cháwpat áwitł'yawya. Íx̱wi iwá íłamayki kw'ɨ́nk nch'i twínpaash. Chaw mun pa'íyax̱na íchɨn łkw'íyaw.

McWhorter's written account [of the battle field called Wax̱sham, above Eel Trail] was not correct. The Indians won the battle with the white soldiers at Wax̱sham. They took everything from the soldiers: mules, food, horses, arms, and big rifles. They drove the soldiers into a ravine and released them. They did not kill them. [This is important to note because it shows how the Prophet's teaching concerning killing influenced their conscience.] One aforementioned big rifle [a howitzer gun] is still hidden. It has never been found to this day.

Íkushnash awkú áwyap'ɨx̱nanishana nakáłasaan sɨ́nwit anakútash tł'áax̱wmaman máytsḵi itíitax̱shix̱ana. Ip'ɨ́x̱nanishana sɨ́nwit nch'ínch'imaman.

This is how I remember my grandmother's words when she would awaken us with her reminiscence in the morning. She was remembering the Elders' version of history. [And, I remembered this story while traveling on the Eel Trail with my aunt Saptix̱awáy.]

WATÍT'AAS ÁYAT	LEGEND WOMAN
Íkushnash awkú wɨshánatpa áwyap'ɨx̱nanix̱ana nakáɫasaan sɨ́nwityaw. Atashkú wyák̲w'iyamka Asúm Ɨshchɨ́tpa, kwnáktash ák̲'inunx̱ana Watít'aas Áyatnan. Íkw'ak Áyat iwá áwtni. Cháwnam awawtk'íwita.	Thus I remember my maternal grandmother talking while traveling around. When we reached the upper rim of Eel Trail, there we saw Legend Woman. That woman is sacred. Do not make a fool of her. [Legend Woman is a sacred woman who will grant your wishes. At this place by Eel Trail, she is near the top of a mountain, lying on her back with her arms outstretched and is said to be embracing you lovingly. You are supposed to approach her with respect and love.]
Páyshnam átk̲'ix̱ta túyaw atɬ'áwit, átawnam tun ánita, kú nam ɨshnawáyta. Páyshnam awawtk'íwita kunam tun lapaalakwá ɨluyɬimá ánita, kunam íkw'ak ímktya pinásapilɨmta. Cháwnam tun ts'i'íix̱ áwyax̱ta.	If you want to ask for something, give her something you value, and humble yourself. Then she will pity you and grant your wish. If you make fun of her, and you give her something grimy, you will ridicule your own self. You will not successfully accomplish anything.
Táaminwanam átmaakta Watít'aas Áyatnan. Íkush inátx̱anax̱ana nakáɫas X̱ax̱ísh.	Always respect Legend Woman. This is what my grandmother X̱ax̱ísh said.

LEGEND: RATTLESNAKE AND EEL / WATÍT: WAX̱PUSHYÁY KU ASUMYÁY

I include the following legend as an example of the sort of story we children might hear in the mountains. This is a legend my father, Henry Beavert, told. This too took place at Asúm Ɨshchɨ́t (Eel Trail). Wíshx̱am Village was at Dallesport, located on the north side of the Columbia River across from The Dalles, Oregon. The cliff north of Wíshx̱am is the place Eel and Rattlesnake, the animals in the legend, used as their diving board when they dove into the Columbia River. There were lots of rattlesnakes there. They had a huge den covered by a flat smooth stone the size of an average-size slide. It was a wonderful place to play, because every time you slid down, the rattlesnakes made a lot of noise.

During fishing season people who were related by blood or through marriage gathered there to fish for salmon and to dry eels. The flat table rock in the Nch’iwána (Columbia River) provided an ideal place for eels to stick on the smooth stone to stabilize themselves. You could look down into the river and see sheets of eels waving back and forth fastened on the rocks. There was also a large rock with a face. It was called the Widow Rock. Families told the children not to play at these two places. They were warned about getting bitten by rattlesnakes, and the Widow Rock was taboo.

The glossary presents some of the vocabulary used in this legend.

Míimi tɬ’aáx̱w tun íchna tiichámpa isɨ́nwix̱ana anakúsh namákna íkuuk sɨ́nwix̱a. Íchi watít anakú Wax̱púuya ku Asumyáyin pawachá tiin. Pasɨ́nwix̱ana ku patkw’ánatix̱ana anakúsh imk ku ink. Nay!

Long ago on this earth everything talked as we do now. This legend takes place when Rattlesnake and Eel were people. They spoke and walked around as you and I do. *Nay!*

Iwachá nch’iiii tánawit áanknik pátupa ku kwnak iwɨsháynaka Wax̱púuya.

There was a huge cave on the south side of Mount Adams and Rattlesnake made his home there.

Aw ik’pɨ́sishana ku Wax̱púuya piná’iḵ’piḵ’pshana, pinawshúwashana anwíktay.

The weather was becoming cold and Rattlesnake was weatherizing his home, getting ready for winter.

Pɨ́nch’a Asumyáy iwisalílshana áx̱mi Nch’iwánaknik, ku itk’ína Pátunan; “Ah, áwnash wíiwinasha íkuuni, la’áknash áwyach’aakta nax̱sh yukaasínsnan.”

At the same time old Eel was hunting away from the Columbia River, and he looked toward Mount Adams [and said to himself]: “I think I’ll go in that direction a ways, perhaps I’ll see a buck.”

Awkú iwínana iksíks wánapa ku páwyapaatpa túnx̱kan iwínana.

He walked beside a small river and came to a fork where he turned the wrong way.

Wíiiyat iwínana ku iwyáłamayka. “Míinnash awkú wínata?”

He went far and lost his direction. “I wonder where I should go now?”

Awkú ts’áak’a Pátuyaw kwnak iwyách’aaka Wax̱púuyanan. “Ay x̱ay, míshnam íchi mísha íchna?” pá’ɨna Asúmnan.

And then when he was nearing Mount Adams he met Rattlesnake. Rattlesnake greeted him. “Greetings friend, what are you doing here?”

Ku iwíinpa, “Ay x̱ay, áwnash paysh wyáłamayksha kush aw k’asáwisha kush anáwisha.”

Eel answered: “Greetings friend, I believe I’m lost and I’m cold and hungry.”

“Aw, áwnam wínamta inmíyaw ɨníityaw kumash sáypta.” pá’ɨna Asúmnan.

Rattlesnake said to Eel: “You must come to my home and I will feed you.”

Awkú Asúm itkwátana ku iláts’muyna. Ámchnik awkú ipúuya ku k’pɨs itx̱ánana.

Eel ate and warmed himself. Outside it began to snow and it became cold.

Pá’ɨna Wax̱púuyayin; “Cháwnam awkú míshkin túx̱ta. Áwnam anwíkta íchna. Áwnash awkú lalíwanx̱a ilksá.”

Rattlesnake told him: “You cannot go home now. You must spend the winter here. I get lonesome here all by myself.”

Awkú anwíka Asumyáy Wax̱puuyaanmípa.

And then Eel spent the winter at Rattlesnake’s place.

Íkw’ak pápax̱witát’ashana wáwnakwshash ku waḵ’íshwit Asúmnan Wax̱púuyayin.

Rattlesnake actually wanted to steal Eel’s name and body.

Aw iwúux̱mya ku Asúm itux̱át’ana.

When spring approached Eel wanted to go home.

FIGURE 4.9. Drying lamprey eels at the camp of Billy Barnhart. Photo by Lee Moorhouse. Special Collections and University Archives, University of Oregon Libraries, Eugene, PH36, photo ID# 5609; and the Confederated Tribes of the Umatilla Indian Reservation.

Pá'ɨna Wax̲púuyayin, "Áwna pawilawíix̲ta. Páyshmash ink wiláalakwta kush ink awkú tx̲ánata Asúm, kunam paysh imk tx̲ánata Wax̲púsh."

Rattlesnake told him, "Let us have a race. If I beat you then I will become the Eel, and you will become the Rattlesnake."

"Ii," ikúya Asúm Wáx̲pushnan, anakú páyu itux̲át'ashana.

Eel agreed with Rattlesnake because he really wanted to go home.

Awkú pá'isikw'ana tawnáapak'a k'aywátx̲aw ɨshchɨ́t wánakan Wáx̲pushin, íkw'ak pásaptayakshana yanwáy Asúmnan.

Rattlesnake showed him what was supposedly the shortest route to the river, that was how he cheated poor Eel.

Awkú papawilawíix̲na.

So they raced.

Ának iwachá Asúm anakú chilwít ɨshchɨ́t pá'isikw'ana Wax̱púuyayin.

Eel was way behind because Rattlesnake had showed him the wrong route.

Anakú ts'áak'a pawyánawya Nch'iwánayaw Wɨshx̱aamípa, Asumyáy inúkshya chíishnan ku ix̱túna ku iwayáwawna Wax̱púuyanan ku ix̱átamaliikika wánayaw pɨ́nx̱ush.

As they approached the Columbia River at Wishx̱am, Eel smelled the water, gathered all his strength, and slipped right past Rattlesnake and plunged into the river first.

Íkush iwiláalakwa Asumyáy Wax̱púuyanan saptayakát'atyaw.

This is how the Eel won the race when Rattlesnake was cheating him.

Íkush iwá pátiix̱wat, "Cháwnam ásaptayakta shiin. Shíx̱nam wáta tiin."

The moral of the story is: "Do not cheat anyone, be a good person."

HORSES / K'ÚSIMA

MÁYTSḴI TÁX̱SHIT PAWILAWÍIX̱TPA

EARLY RISING AND HORSE RACING

Míimi tíinma patkwátax̱ana awkɫáw wɨsháanakwi, uu mísh, pá'ilayi saplɨ́l. Chaw tun yápaash anakúsh mɨ́laa yápaash ku aw íchi íkuuk ílachx̱i yápaashsim saplɨ́l patkwátasha, anakúsh ílachx̱i yápaashpa. Kunkínk awkú ttush tíin ichx̱íisha.

Long ago people used to eat only bread baked in the ashes, or else bannock bread. [My mother made good bannock bread but gave up on me ever learning.] There was no oil, or only a very little bit, but now we eat fried bread soaked in oil. That is how some people gain weight.

Míimi tiin iwachá k̲'áyu anakúshx̲it awkú paysh laak anakú it'úk pakútkutɨnx̲ana, kúshx̲i pakútkutsha łíikw'i. Máytsk̲i patáx̲shisha ku pakútkutsha. Áykɨnx̲anash míimi "Cháwnam t'áwk'umta, táx̲shitaam máytsk̲i." Kutash aw íchi íkuuk namách'ak'a táwk'umnx̲a táaminwa, ínch'ax̲iish awkú táwk'umx̲a, miskilíikiish táx̲shix̲a máytsk̲i. Kush míimi táx̲shix̲ana cháwx̲i íx̲wi ik̲'áyx̲shamash kush míimi táx̲shisha, kush wachá palaláay kútkut kush awkú nɨwít awkú kútkutɨnx̲ana, íchi wáa'aw atashkú wyáninx̲ana k'úsiki pawilawíix̲ɨnx̲ana.

A long time ago, Indian people were lean, and it was probably because they worked hard, they worked all day. In the morning they woke up and they worked. I used to hear them say a long time ago, "Do not oversleep, get up in the morning." And now some of us always sleep in, I too sleep in, I barely get up some mornings. And a long time ago I used to wake up real early, when it was still dawn, I would already be up. And I had a lot of work to do and I worked right away in the morning, especially when we were going around horse racing.

Táx̲shix̲anatash íx̲wi sts'aat, kush míimi áshapawiliilawisha k'úsimaman, wíinkniksha nax̲shk'anáx̲shk'aash, awkú áshapawiliilawix̲ana anakwmák awkú pawáyksh wáyx̲titay.

We would wake up when it was still dark, grooming and exercising the horses. I rode them around the track one after the other, I would be exercising those that were going to race that day.

Lɨsx̲aamnash áshapawiinknix̲ana náx̲sh mayl łwáayki, áshapalax̲uyx̲ɨnx̲ana, anakú nɨwít pawayx̲titát'ax̲ana. Náakni ánach'ax̲i, kush náx̲shpa kwátapa Áliksaanɨm ɨnx̲ana, "Áshapax̲twik!" Kush áwapawx̲inana áshapawayx̲tix̲ana tł'áax̲wki x̲túwitki náx̲sh kwátayaw.

I'd go around one mile really slow, to warm them up, but they wanted to run. At the quarter mile pole, Alex would tell me "Blow him out!" and we would gallop full speed a quarter mile.

Na'íɫas iwachá sapak'paasɫá k'úsimaman. Inaktkw'anínx̱ana isapák'paasitx̱ana, ku ának awkú ikúukix̱ana kutásh ishapátkwatx̱ana tɫ'áax̱wmaman. Ishx̱ɨ́mtɫ'ɨnx̱a, "Ɨ́knash ɨɫáx̱tx̱aw kútkutɨnx̱a."

My mother's job was to walk them out afterwards, and after she was done she had to cook breakfast for the whole crew [always toast, oatmeal, coffee, juice]. She used to complain, "I have the hardest job."

Palaláay natásh wachá kútkut. Wacháatash náx̱sh shapawashatpamá, ku náx̱sh tamantatyí ptáx̱ninsh k'usimamíyay shapáwashatay. Inmí pimx̱ iwachá páyu t'ɨnú. Páysh amíis-kutkutɫáma pak̲w'shɨ́x̱ix̱ana x̱aayx̱ pnunáɫ, awkú maykɨláx̱ ishapákutkutɨnx̱ana.

We had a lot of work to do. We used to carry quite a lot of horses—we had a great big truck and trailer with stalls inside that could carry six horses and supplies. Alex [my stepfather] was very strict. Those who had sneaked out to a party and had not slept the night before had to exercise twice as much.

Ɨ́kw'ak íkushnatash kútkutɨnx̱ana tɫ'áax̱wma tɫ'áax̱wmatash kwmak wyánɨnx̱anaatash wachá kushkúsh kútkut kutash awkú táx̱shisha máytsk̲i kutash awkú kútkutsha.

That is the way we used to work together, those that went around racing with us. We had separate tasks. Each one had a job to do and we would get up early and work.

Ku muun awkú ik̲áyx̱ɨnx̱ana ku anátshamsh Aan, ku kpaylk awkú páshtɨnma pawíyu'utyu'utsha ku pakútkutsha pawíi'uysha kutash míimi awkú namách'a tíinma náwnak̲'ix̱ana kútkut. Kutásh chawmún pashúkwiinix̱ana, míshnatash wachá k'úsima, ku pamɨ́shtɫ'ɨnkɨnx̱ana "Túyay awkú íchi pmách'a panáchiksha íkwtɨnk íchi walím k'úsima?" íkuushtash pa'ɨ́nx̱ana.

And when it got light and the sun rose, and white people began to move around and begin work, we Indian people would have already finished our work. They never knew what we had, what quality horses we had, and they would complain, "Why are they bringing those Indian ponies here?" [They were referring to our thoroughbreds.] That is what they used to say to us.

Kuutash awkú áwilalaakwilalaakwɨnx̲ana k'úsima niimíki ku kpáylknatash awkú patmáakna. Áwnatash uyt anakúsh chaw patk̲'íx̲na tíinmaman, wáa'aw ashkú wáshax̲ana, ku awínsh-masim íkush pawachá washałá, kush awkú inách'a ínpɨmx̲nɨm ishapáwashax̲ana pawilawíix̲tpa. Ishapáwach'akanix̲ana waníkt kush awkú wáshax̲ana. Aw nɨmnɨwíit pasx̲íx̲inx̲ana íkw'ak páshtɨnma washałáma awínshma, chaw patk̲'íx̲shana ku áyat iwáta washałá pawilawíix̲tpa.

Then we kept winning and winning, beating them with our horses, then they finally began to respect us. At first they didn't like the Indian people especially when I used to ride, since at that time only men were jockeys. My stepfather used to have me ride in the race. He used to sign me up, then I would ride. Then they would get very angry, those white men jockeys, they did not want a woman to be a rider in the horse race.

Ashkú uyt wɨ́npa tímash pawilawiix̲tpamá wáshat k'úsinan, iwachá ashkú wachá pútɨmpt ku páx̲aat anwíkt 1936pa anwíktpa Kánatapa.

When I first obtained my jockey's license I was fifteen years old, in 1936, in Canada.

Cháwnatash wachá washałámaatash ku nákwɨshachikika wayx̲titpamá k'úsima. Ix̲wí paskúulishana ku mún skúulit áx̲awshx̲tax̲nay kutash kuuk pa'áwtkw'ɨmtax̲nay.

We didn't have male jockeys with us, they were still in school, and when school was over, they would have caught up with us.

Kwɨnkínknash inák pashapáwinpa tímash. Kush haay awisíkw'ana myáwax̲maman áshukwaashaash íkush wáshat.

That was the reason I had to apply for the jockey license. First, I had to show the officials I was an experi-enced rider.

Kuuk cháwx̲i mɨł pawachá áyatma washałá tímashyi. Kuush awínshma pawałána washátwiit. Awkú pastríkya awínshma washałáma.

There weren't many women who were licensed jockeys, and the men refused to ride in the race with me [in it]. The men jockeys went on strike.

Myáwaxmapat áwna: "Kuumísh, aw pɨlksá ipawilawíixta ku iwáta iishłá." Awkú chɨmk'usiyíima pa'atłáway, pimátiiyawka; "Áwtash wáyxtita niimí k'úsima." Ku miskilíiki washałáma áwku papawilawíixna.	The officials told the jockeys: "All right, she will race all by herself and she will be the winner." The horse owners begged to keep their horses in the race, and the jockeys were finally convinced to ride the race.

All of us spoke Ichishkíin while traveling the racing circuit.

THE AMERICAN INDIAN HORSE

To the Plains and Northwest Natives in the United States, a horse was useful for their survival. A horse was part of the family and was treated with affection and trust. During my childhood where I grew up in Sih', my family had many horses. Most of the horses were gentle. I would catch one and crawl on it, and ride away. All the children in my family rode bareback; they didn't need a saddle to ride on.

The earliest use of horses was mainly for travel. There were no roads, only trails. The *ts'íkts'ik* (wagons) could go just so far into the forest before they had to stop; wagons were stored at these end points. Then travelers packed their supplies on the *shapaashappamá k'úsima* (pack horses) and continued on *k'úsiki* (horseback) on their journey to wherever they were going.

My father had *kutkutpamá* (work horses), Percherons, to take care of because he was a *tamanikłá* (farmer). He plowed eighty acres of land where we lived and he raised hay and grain for feed or trade. He crossbred packhorses with draft horses such as Percherons or Clydesdales, which were used for farming. They were trained to drag farm equipment. This was difficult for the horses that were not familiar with a harness.

Every year in the springtime, my uncles *tkwaynpt* (rounded up) wild horses in the hills and drove them into a corral and branded them. The best horses were picked and tamed for riding. The women picked out the gaited horses because they were comfortable to ride on long-distance journeys. The Indian women preferred them when they went to the mountains to dig roots and pick berries. Some people call these horses *wilátksht* (gaited) for the way they travel.

I was too young at that time to witness the *pawilawíixt* (horse races) the Indians competed in at the different racetracks that historians have written about. It must have been a sight to see. I heard about it later as I grew older when they talked about different tribes who came to compete against the Yakama Indians. It was later, when I became a licensed jockey to ride thoroughbred horses, that my experience with horse racing began.

The storytellers talked about the war horses that were just as *shatawí* (brave) as the warriors when they were at war with the enemy. It was told that *natílas* (my great-great-grandfather on my mother's side), X̱aniwáshya, had a Medicine Hat horse. It was a white horse and it had one black ear and a black circle around one eye. The horse was his *pátash* (fetish) that had something to do with his Spirit Guide protection. Medicine Hat horses are a rare type; a white pinto with color only on the ears, around the eye, on the same side, and over the chest. Only the warriors who had proved themselves in battle were allowed to ride them. The Indians believed a warrior who rode a Medicine Hat into battle was invincible. The Plateau People journeyed to Shaḵúulkt Sioux (Plains Indian) country periodically to obtain buffalo meat and many Indians were killed when they trespassed into the prairie to hunt the buffalo.

Now horses are used for pleasure riding and competition. In parades on horseback, Indian cowgirls and cowboys show off their regalia. In the rodeo the horse is used for the bucking bronco, and ridden in events such as racing and roping. The wild horses are no longer rounded up, tamed, and utilized for farming and transportation as they were in the "old days." They are inbreeding in the hills and mountains.

MY HORSE TRAINING AND RACING DAYS / NÁKTKWANINT PAWILAWIIX̱TPAMÁ K'ÚSIMA PAWILAWÍIX̱TPA

My experience with horses during my horse racing days began when I purchased my own thoroughbred horse. After World War II, I began saving money to help my favorite niece with her education. Right after she graduated from high school, she eloped. I was very upset. Instead of giving the money to her, I decided to buy a horse. I went to the Washington State Fair at Puyallup, and began to observe horses.

One day I watched horses getting saddled in the paddock. There was one rank horse a trainer could not saddle. He constantly kicked the horse in the belly, and the horse reared. Other people got involved and finally put a saddle on him. He was led around the paddock and every time he came by me he would look me straight in the eye and whinny. He would pull away from the trainer and want to come to me. Of course, he was jerked away. Finally he got my attention. I began looking him over. He looked sound and well balanced. He looked like he was about fifteen hands high, and had a good coat. I went to the racing office and consulted my friend, the racing secretary, and he was appalled! "Why do you want that awful horse?"

I offered the money that was usual for a horse in this class, the eight thousand dollar claiming race. There are different classifications of horse races on

FIGURE 4.10. Watch these women ride: the author is in the center. Courtesy of Ellensburg Public Library, RDO-155.

the daily racing program. The highest is the stake race. Horses that make it to this class are the winners of several races; they are classified on their race earnings.

The claiming race lists horses that are eligible to run for the purse. The dollar amount (the purse) is written down under the horses' name on the program. They are the lower-class horses; some of which may never have won a race before. Anyone who wants to claim a horse in a race can offer the amount listed to take the horse. An eligible claimer is a person who is actively racing his own horse in the race meet. I was not eligible to claim the horse because I was not racing any horses at this meet, but I wanted to claim this particular horse that was giving everybody difficulty in the paddock. My friend said I could get him cheaper after the race. We watched him go to the gate. What a disaster! He refused to cooperate, reared in the gate, and was left behind by the other horses.

The race distance was one and one-sixteenth mile. He started two lengths behind the last horse, and he finished fourth. I wanted that horse. After the race, we asked how much the owner would sell him for. The horse was contracted by the trainer, who wanted to get rid of him. I paid eight hundred dollars for him! I noticed his halter had a metal plate on the cheek strap with his name on it. This meant he came from a prosperous stable.

The horse came to me and we walked down the shed row. I turned him over to a gentle trainer who was Indian. We put him up in his own stall and began to treat him with respect. He did not act up; he just relaxed. I began training him early in the morning in the way my parents trained their thoroughbred horses. A retired jockey at the shed knew my new horse and he made friends with him. The jockey was from California and knew about the horse because he was California-bred. His sire was Hilo Sun, from Hawai'i. His name was Siskiyu's Sun. We worked with Siskiyu for one week and I entered him in the governor's handicap, the biggest race of the season and the most expensive purse.

Everyone I knew advised me against it but I had my confidence in the horse and so did my jockey. We won that race easily. He behaved like a gentleman, as long as I was in sight and talked to him. He made enough money in that race for his care during winter and into spring. Siskiyu earned three good mares for me; one mare in particular who won a feature race for me in Victoria, British Columbia. Common sense and kindness can bring an amazing response from a horse. They have their own way of responding that is beneficial to both parties.

I would like to tell you about two more horses. Indian TomTom was a small sorrel thoroughbred horse, spoiled so bad his owner could not handle him, so they turned him over to my boss who trained a large stable of horses, and I was hired as a groom. I was between jobs and had time on my hands and could not think of a better way to use my time.

Indian TomTom bit and kicked anyone who came near him. One day I was given the responsibility of his care. I worked with him for a week and won his confidence. We gradually became friends. My boss was training some horses at Santa Anita, California for two weeks. When he returned to Yakima Meadows, I surprised him by showing him how well TomTom was doing. He let me braid his tail and clean his hooves without him acting up. We took him out on the track and he clocked fast enough to enter a race, and he won. Before this he had been lazy and made no effort to run. TomTom went ahead and won three more races, then the owners took him back. I lost any future commissions, after all my work.

Another horse in our stable could barely walk. Again my boss gave him to me to take care of. I discovered his problem was an infection around his hooves and it was very inflamed. I do not know why the other grooms never detected this problem. I guess they were afraid of him because he kicked and charged at anyone who came near him. I used an old Indian remedy and cured his problem. This horse went out and won several races, and then my boss took him to California. He won a few races there and died on the track of a heart attack. I wondered if he missed me.

The skills I learned for training were passed onto me by my parents who raced thoroughbreds for many years. When I was a teenager, I exercised their horses and did chores around the stable. My trick-riding friend showed me four tricks to do on a running horse. Another friend taught me to relay on a horse. I would jump from the ground onto a running horse, ride around the racetrack, jump off and jump on the next horse. This takes a lot of training. One has to be physically fit and strong. Riding on a jockey saddle takes a lot of skill too, and a rider has to learn a few tricks about safety when competing against the male jockeys. They did not want women riders on the racetrack. Fortunately, I rode horses that took care of me.

Horses have feelings of pain as well as feelings of security and joy. It all depends on how they are handled. A trainer working on a recognized racetrack has skills to detect horse problems. The trainer can make or break a good horse. A groom must also have a lot of horse sense and veterinarian skills. Grooms at a race are professionals too. When the trainer or owner tells you what he wants from his horse, it is up to the handler to do his best to provide it. When I owned my own horses, I tried my best to be close to them.

YɨKɨ́T K'ÚSIMA

Nax̱sh páshtɨn áyat itímana nch'i tímash k'usimamíki. Iwaníksha Judith Dutson. Awkɬáwakut láxs k'úsi shúki iwá kwyaam yɨkɨt k'úsi. Ttuush iwá winaninɬá nisháykt-knik. Ttuush iwá wapáwx̱ini anakú naknuwiɬáyin chawk'á míshkin pánaknuwita. Awkú yanwáyma payɨkɨ́tix̱a.

WILD AND FERAL HORSES

A white woman wrote a book about horses. Her name is Judith Dutson. She says there's only one true wild horse. Some of them [the ones we call wild but not those she refers to as wild] traveled from home. Some are released when a caretaker will no longer take care of them. Then the poor creatures are undomesticated and become feral.

Íchi yɨkɨ́t k'úsi iwá wáayk atáchiishknik anakwnínk pawá Chálmilma tíinma. Nax̱sh ttáwax̱t tiichámknik Russia, Mongolia ku Kazahkstan. Chɨ́ma kwnik pawá ttáwax̱t Chálmil, pasɨ́nwix̱a máyktunx̱, anakúsh wa namák íchna tunx̱túnx̱ tíinma Shíwanish, Nix̱yáawiknik, Shɨmnáashuknik, ku Wanałáma. Íkush pawá kwnak waayk atáchiishknik. Kwnak kw'ɨnk k'úsi laxsímk'a yɨkɨ́t k'úsi ittáwax̱na waníki Sha-palski (she-val-ski). Namákna áwanikx̱a Taḵawáakuł. Áwa chmuk t'shɨsh ku twin ku iwá twáp'skii chmúkki pnɨ́x̱knik twínyaw.

This first truly wild horse comes from across the ocean, from the Asian people. One line comes from Russia, Mongolia, and Kazakhstan. These are Asian people, but they spoke differently [from the main population], just like we have different people here such as Nez Perce, Umatilla, Simnasho, and the River Tribes. So they're from across the ocean. That is where that only wild horse, called the *Prezewalski*, comes from. Our name for it is *taḵawáakuł*. It has a black mane and tail, black feet, and a black stripe along its spine clear down to its tail.

Náx̱sh ánach'ax̱i iwá k'úsi íchna niimípa pɨ́t'x̱anukpa kúshx̱i ku iwaníksha ḵaashḵáash. Chaw áwa twáp'ski k'úpkw'p. Náx̱shk'a átaw k'úsi niimí tiinmamí iwá wilátksh. Kúshx̱i íchi páshtɨn áyat tímashpa tɨmnanáx̱t ishapáwach'aksha wilátksh k'usimamíki. Nakałasaanmí X̱ax̱íshmi áwanikshana Píli Puts; iwachá luch'á k'úsi ku iwachá wilátkshkt.

There is one other similar horse in our hills called *ḵaashḵáash*. It does not have a stripe on its back. Another important horse to our people is the gaited horse. Judith Dutson also wrote about the *wilátkish* [single footer]. My grandmother X̱ax̱ísh named hers Billy Boots; he was a brown gaited horse.

The only one true wild horse on earth today, the *Prezewalski*, also known as the Asiatic wild horse, vanished from Asia and Russia in 1969. As of January 2004, the most recent count showed there were 154 *Prezewalski* in North America (Dutson 2005). In the wild, only offspring produced within a species can perpetuate the species. Cross-breeding never happened in the wild because of the geography and the roaming habits of wild horses.

Mustangs are not wild horses. They are descendants from escaped domestic horses who are living in a wild undomesticated environment. In cases where cross species are in captivity, the resultant offspring, known as hybrids, will often be infertile.

Wild horses are considered a nuisance because they roam in large numbers and deprive cattle of their grazing area. However, horses take care of the grass they eat. They roam under the supervision of the stallion. Stallions do not stay in one place and eat up all of the grass; they preserve it by taking the herd from place to place. They do not trample the mountain water supply. They take turns drinking at a spring and leave it clean and intact. Cattle are not careful. They trample the springs until they dry out; gradually they deplete the watering holes that have been there for many years. Figure 4.11 shows some Yakama Nation horses being rounded up.

The other day while riding in a car discussing different computer screens and screen savers, I mentioned to my friend that my computer screen had a scene from our Indian Reservation showing a large herd of wild horses. I told her the history behind how it became so special. My friend, from the University of Washington, wished to learn about how to dig a special root that the local Natives were digging for food at that spring season. We went from the lower valley to a higher elevation and were looking for roots when we saw a herd of wild horses. Figure 4.12 shows one of these herds.

Her husband grabbed his camera and sneaked up on them. It was interesting how soon the stallion sensed the man. He immediately began dividing his herd into three groups. There were several colts and mares in one group to the left. On the right were a bunch of older-looking horses, and in the center, where the stallion stationed himself, were two three-year-old colts.

When the man snuck up closer to take his picture, the stallion signaled the herd by whirling himself to the left. The group of mares and colts took off. Next the photographer stuck his head up from where he was hiding, and the stallion again signaled and the remaining groups fled. He was able to capture the stallion in the center, with another to the left and a few fleeing mares and colts. I treasure the psychology that stallion showed to protect the mares and colts. They were able to flee as the remaining herd distracted the perceived predator.

Survival is the watchword for all living species on this earth. Sometimes we ignore the benefit of staying on good terms with nature.

Wild horses are wise and people desired them for traveling in the wild country. They were trained for mountain travel. Figure 4.13 shows a packhorse, although this one is more decorated than most for traveling. The high saddle was for safety when traveling in high country. You could also hang packs around it. The baby on its board would also travel this way. A *twinpamá* (back strap tied under the tail and attached to the saddle) kept the saddle from slipping while going downhill. A neck strap stabilized the saddle in the other direction, going uphill.

FIGURE 4.11. A roundup of Yakama Nation *yikít k'úsima* (wild horses). Courtesy of Yakama Nation Wildlife, Range, and Vegetation Resources Management Program.

WɨSHÍNWɨSHINT PÍT'X̲ANUKPA

Chaw kuukitpamá inánax̲ana anakú níchi áwacha shapálkw'ishpa Pátupa. Kúshx̲i áwacha x̲yaaw tkwátat níchi kwnak. Łstiinmí áwacha ilachx̲tpamá, ku nch'i kuukitpamá tkwsay shapálkw'iki. Awkłáwtash nánax̲ana pnútay awshníks, shátay, ku síilhaws, anatún iwá maysx̲máysx̲ wyax̲ayx̲tpamá patún.

Atáwtx̲aw awachá aytalú, saplíl, shúuka, suul, ku yápaash kúukitay.

CAMPING AT MOUNT ADAMS

X̲ax̲ísh never packed cooking supplies because she had these items buried at Mount Adams. She also cached dry food there. She had an iron skillet, and a large iron cooking pot stored there. We only took along our bedding, blanket, and tent, and other domestic necessities we needed everyday.

The most important were the grain, bread, sugar, salt, and tallow for cooking.

FIGURE 4.12. *Yikít k'úsi* (a wild horse). Courtesy of Yakama Nation Wildlife, Range, and Vegetation Resources Management Program.

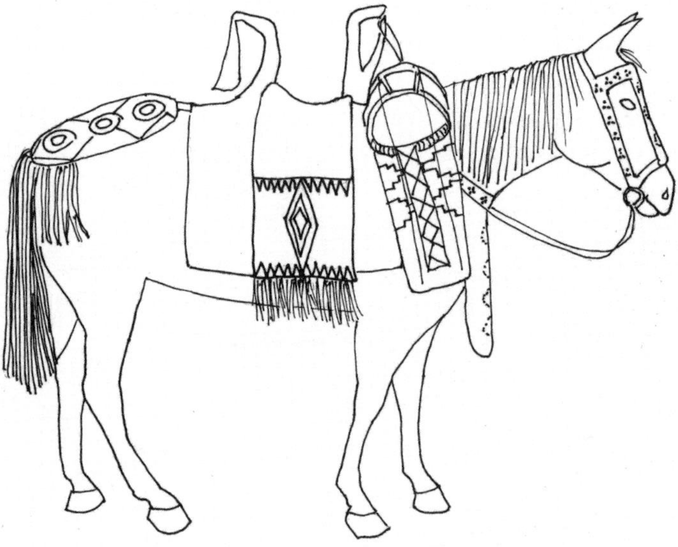

FIGURE 4.13. *Shapaashaptpamá k'úsi* (a pack horse). Courtesy of Judith Fernandes.

Awínshma nɨwítpa wisalílx̱ana, kutash nɨkwɨ́t tkwátax̱ana. Íkw'aktash wachá átaw wyanínt k'úsiki íkush. Anakú tkwátat íx̱wi iwachá miimáwit. Tɬ'aax̱w tun átaw tkwátat iwachá pɨ́t'x̱anukpa—tawtnúk, táwax̱, tmaanít. Iwachá ɨt'úk íkwɨn wɨ́npatat, ku awkɬáw k'úsiki iwachá íkwɨn wínat.

The men hunted right away for meat and we would eat. The journey traveling on horseback was important to people because it was the only way to obtain food. Most of the food was in the mountains—the medicine, tobacco, nuts, and fruit. It was difficult to reach food-gathering places except on horseback.

Yɨkɨ́t k'úsi ishúkwaashana wyanínt iyíyapa tiichámpa kwɨnkínk pa'atáwishana íkushmamank k'úsimaman. Pa'ítɬx̱atkx̱ana ku awkú patɨmnánx̱ana wyaníntpa pɨ́t'x̱anukpa.

Wild horses are wise traveling in the wild country, people desired horses like that. They tamed them and depended on them for mountain travel.

Iwachá nch'ii pawilawiix̱tpamá támiwnat Pátupa kwnak tíinma pawyák'ukx̱ana ku panáchikx̱ana k'úsi. Ch'ikwásh iwaníksha, kwnak íx̱wi iwá pawilawiix̱tpamá.

There was a racetrack on the other side of Mount Adams where Indians gathered and brought their horses to race. Ch'ikwásh is the name of the place, and the racetrack is still there.

Kúshx̱i, Táp'ashnaḵ'itpa lak'ítit, iwá nisháyaas, ku kwnáx̱i iwá íkwtɨnk, náx̱shk'a iwachá Tx̱ápnishpa. Ts'aa MúlMulyaw, anakwnák iwá káatnam íkuuk.

At the ridge of Simcoe Mountain is a village site and there is also a racetrack, Edge of the Timber, at Cleveland, Washington. Near the White Swan Longhouse is another racetrack.

BILLY BOOTS / PÍLI PUUTS

My great-grandmother had a *ḵaashḵáash* horse she called Píli Puuts, Billy Boots. He was gaited, and he walked single footed (a four-beat gait where the horse moves one foot on the ground at a time), which is valued by Indian women for long-distance travel, especially to the mountains. This is his story.

Nakałasaanmí atáw k'úsi awaníkshana Billy Boots. Íx̱wiish wachá, paysh, pútɨmt anwíkt kúuknash ilksá pashapáwashana wɨshánatpa k'úsiki pɨ́t'x̱anukyaw.

My great-grandmother's beloved horse was named Billy Boots. When I was still about ten, they let me ride alone when we were moving by horseback to the mountains.

Iwachá iyíya wyánint pɨ́t'x̱anukpa, wáa'aw ts'aa Pátuyaw anakwnák iwíihaykshamsh plash puuymí chiish.

Traveling in the mountains on horseback was dangerous, especially when you got near Mount Adams where the white snow river came rushing down.

Billy Boots iwachá míima anwíkt k'úsi. Cháwnash áshukwaasha mumán iwachá. Kúshx̱iish chaw áshukwaasha mɨnán iwɨ́npa nakáłas. Paysh iwachá chwiksh Billy Boots; anakú Sawyalílx̱ iwachá nch'ii twáti ku palaláay áwacha patún íkushpamank. Sawyalílx̱ áwacha ám Nakałasnmí.

Billy Boots was an old horse. I do not know how old he was, and I didn't know where my grandmother acquired him. Perhaps he was payment to her medicine man husband, Sawyalilx̱, because they had many things given to them for that, healing people.

Úytnash panákwɨshanax̱ana waláḵ'iki wasat'áwaaspa ashkú chaw áshukwaashana cháwiitk'uk k'úsinan. Kush Billy Bootsnɨm shix̱ ináktkwaninx̱ana.

At first [when I was too young], they used to tie me on the horse because I didn't know how to guide the horse with the reins. But Billy Boots took care of me.

Íkush awkú pawá k'úsima. Páyshnam shix̱ anáktkwaninta ku imanách'ax̱iim panáktwaninta.

That is how horses are. When you take care of them, they also take care of you.

Atashkú nknínx̱ana Pátupa, yáx̱waykx̱anaatash k'úsiki. Kw'ɨnk wána iwachá páyu tł'ínaaw ku chiish iwánashana x̱túwiki. Páyu shaax̱! Kuush wyáych'unx̱ana.

When we went to Mount Adams, we went across [the Cispus River] by horseback. The river was very wide and the water was swift. Very scary! And I was frightened.

Nakáłasnɨmnash i’ɨ́nx̱ana, “Cháwnam wyáych’uta, Píli Pútsnɨmnam ináktkwaninta.”

My grandmother told me, “Do not be afraid. Billy Boots will take care of you.”

Áwnash awkú lɨmḵ’ínx̱ana anakú iwyalachalíix̱ana wánayaw. Kush amts’íx̱wanx̱ana íkwɨlkin shaax̱ inúu chiish.

Then I would close my eyes when he stepped into the river. I would listen to the sound of the violent river.

Awachá kwak kumánk ɨshchɨ́t aníyi kwnak wánapa anakúshx̱it tun watikáwaas waayk wánanan aníyi pshwapshwanmí. Ku tł’aax̱w niimí k’úsima pashúkwaashana mɨnán pawyáwatika. Kunkínknatash watwáa wyáwaykx̱ana.

This must have been an old [horse] trail made at the river; it was like a stairway made of stone, clear across the river. And all of our horses knew where to step. That is how we crossed safely.

Ka’áwtya awkú pamún shapáashapi k’úsi itx̱nímłamáykɨnx̱ana ku ix̱atamalíix̱ana ku iyawáynax̱ana.

Sometimes a pack horse misstepped and it would fall in and drown.

X̱ax̱ísh, nakáłas, iwachá wapsúx̱. Sápḵitwani ishapáshapx̱ana k’úsipa. Chaw tł’aax̱w tun náx̱shpa. Kwɨnkínk chaw áyawiiłamaykx̱ana kwaas patún anakú shapáshapsh áyawaynax̱ana.

My great-grandmother, X̱ax̱ish, was wise. She knew how to pack supplies securely on the horse. She separated them equally. That was why it was not a total loss when one pack of supplies floated away.

NOTES

1 In restructuring the noun *palyúut*, bone game, *alyúu-* is the verb and *pa-* is the plural person prefix. When we place the prefix before the verb we add the glottal stop, separating the two *a*’s. The *–t* is added to the end to make the verb into a noun. We then have the word *pa’alyúut* meaning “betting against one another.”

2 “Hop harvest time” means the time for picking hops. Hops are an industrial crop used in the making of beer. People used to pick them off the vine by hand. Now hops are picked with machines.

Conclusion

Wánaḵ’it

Íkwaalnash aw tɨmnáx̱nɨmsh inmíki, ash tun inách’a inmíma nch’ínch’ima pasápsikw’ana átaw shúkwaat. Ttuush íkuuk myánash ɨshnawáy ittáwax̱sha chaw shíyin pasápsikw’asha pɨnmínk tiináwit ku ichishkínk sɨ́nwit. Átaw iwá Ichishkíin sɨ́nwit tɬ’aax̱w shimín. Íkw’akmash awkú wa imínk waḵ’íshkwit.

I have shared this far about how my Elders taught me the important things they knew about. There are children growing up today who do not have anyone to teach them Indian culture and Ichishkíin language. Language is important for everyone. That is part of your spirit of life.

Íkuukna tímasha íchishkink sɨ́nwit anakú cháwk’a niimí plus p’íx̱ɨnx̱a wyát’ish anakú wáawk’a tɬ’áax̱wnam túnɨm inákpalayksha. Ku paysh íx̱wi chɨ́ma myánashma pawíwanikta íchi tímash ku kuts’k tun pashúkwaata ku pasɨ́nwita Ichishkíin. Kwɨnkínk pasápsikw’ata piimínk myánashma.

Now [in these modern times] our brains cannot remember words because there are too many interruptions in the environment. We write things down. Perhaps these children will read this writing some day and go to school to learn their language. Then they can teach their own children to learn the language.

Niipt pamápa wa íkuuk tx̲ánatpa (pashtɨ́nwit ku tíinwit) pimápax̲aapsha íchi namák tíinma. Kuna chaw míshkin áwyawaawta kuunák. Kushkínk haay myánash pɨ́nch'ax̲i iwáta kúɬx̲i sapáskuu-lyi ku kpaylk iwáta tmáakni pashtɨnmí. Íkuuk iwá íkw'ak kútkut shuyaputɨ́mtkisim. Ku paysh myánashma paskúulita niiptík, Ichishkíin ku shuyaputɨ́mptki, kwɨnkínk awku pimanaknúwita.

We Indian people are wedged in between two cultures, and there is no way for us to avoid it. Nowadays the Indian children must have equal education as the white people before they are shown any respect. Now those skills are taught in English, and perhaps when the child learns both Ichishkíin and English, they will be able to survive [in the modern world].

IN CLOSING

Tɬ'áax̲wna aw tun wyátunx̲isha kpaylk íchi, uu palaláay anakúsh tiin cháwtya aw íchi tiin nɨ́mnɨwit áwtya tɬ'aax̲w páshtɨnma túman, anatúman aw pawá tiin anakúsh íchi tx̲ánat. Ku papx̲wípx̲wishax̲i awkú pmách'a pak̲'inkúshax̲i aw tɬ'áax̲wna aw tun wyátunx̲isha pawápnamanx̲ana anakúshx̲i namákna aw wápnaman-sha, px̲wípx̲wisha túkinna anakúsh íshix̲itax̲nay ánach'ax̲i, íshix̲itax̲nay kuts'k wapíitat tun niimí.

And now everybody is changing lately, everybody including the Native people and the white people, anyone who is human, and they are worrying, because they see the changes that are going on, they see we are changing. Others too are groping for solutions just as we are groping. We are wondering how can we make things better again, how can our help make it a little better?[

Láakna myánashmaman átiis-kawkta íchɨnki ku pmách'a awkú tun anakúsh wapíitat pa'aníta íx̲wi, laak pápawapiitata awkú tɬ'ápx̲i pawáta tunx̲túnx̲.

Maybe if we call attention to the young generation they might also help make things better, maybe they will all help each other even though they are of different races.

Ku átaw iwá Ichishkíin sɨ́nwit. Aw ttuush tiinmamí Ichishkíin sɨ́nwit álaamna míimi, awkɬáw mɨ́laama anakúsh panápayunsha piimínk Ichishkíin sɨ́nwit, ku panaknúwisha piimipáynk nisháyktpa, piimipáynk tɨmnápa, kunkínk k̲waat anakúsh papíksha tiináwit.

And our Indian language is important. Some people's Indian languages disappeared a long time ago, and only a few are still defending their Indian language, and they have kept it in their home and in their heart, for that is how they have held onto their heritage.

Kunkínknash ínch'a k̲k̲anáywisha íkushkink kútkutki.

That is the reason I pursue this work.

Appendix

Guidance for Academic Researchers

I am often asked in academic settings about how non-Native researchers should conduct themselves in tribal communities. What does a researcher, particularly a non-Native researcher (or someone from another Native culture) need to know before beginning to work with a Native community, beyond technical and intellectual knowledge such as how to operate recording equipment and how to deal with areas without electricity? Here are several important factors.

KNOWLEDGE OF CULTURE AND HISTORY

How much do you know about the people you plan to work with? Some of the background information you should gather does not have to do with your particular field. Some of this information will be available to you at a public library, tribal library, or tribal museum. Some will only be available once you establish relationships with individuals in the tribe you plan to work with, since some of what you need to learn is typically unwritten. Be aware that you may find inaccurate information in published sources.

Before you proceed or early in your conversations with tribal people, gather information about:

- The current population of enrolled members
- The languages and dialects of the community—even those you are not working with
- Tribal history, mores, and traditions
- The tribe's experience with treaties. Was there a treaty? When was it signed? By whom? When? What were the circumstances of the treaty,

its signing, and ratification? How many bands and tribes were included in the treaty? Read the treaty, and pay attention to any reserved rights.

- Geographical statistics about the reservation lands. What are the traditional lands, and how do these compare to the current reservation? Are there closed areas of the reservation?

TRIBAL RELATIONS

Find a member of that community who wants to work with you. This person should be well known and respected, able to take you to social ceremonies and introduce you to people. Then talk to that person, and ask him or her to go with you to discuss your project with the people on the tribal level that he or she recommends you speak to first. In the Yakama Nation, we have a culture committee. Go to this group and state your purpose. Tell them how your work is going to benefit them as well as yourself. The work must benefit the tribe.

If your work will include language materials, the tribal and/or culture committees will want to know if these will be translated, and if so, by whom? Will they be written down? Using what writing system? Will tribal members be able to read them in the system you plan to use?[1]

Finally, the tribal council will have questions about access. In the past, some ethnographers put barricades around the research material they collected on Indian reservations, making it unavailable to the tribal members who had provided the material and to their families. Who will have access to your recordings? Who decides this? Who will be responsible for the stored material after you complete your work? Will the research be safely kept? If there are recordings, will they be available on the Internet? (In my experience, many tribes will say "No!") Come to some consensus regarding copyright, as this is a difficult issue.

There are places on reservations where outsiders are not allowed and you will need special permission to go there. For example, on the Yakama Reservation we have closed areas that are protected by guards and gates. Only the tribal council can give permission to enter. If anybody approaches you, they will ask to see your paper signed by the tribal council or culture committee before letting you through.

If the tribal council agrees to your proposal, you have permission to go on the reservation and do your study. They are not going to tell you how to do your research but they will want to know that the person whom you have selected as your helper will be with you at all times, to pave the way for you. In certain homes especially, where you may need to get information, you will need to be accompanied.

The resource person you are working with will know other tribal members who can help you. You need to consider how much you can pay per interview. Your budget needs to be adequate for your project. Some individuals will accept only goods, not money, and this can be expensive. A Pendleton blanket can be two hundred to three hundred dollars, and a beaded bag three times this. Others will be glad for the opportunity to work for money. Some people will refuse compensation, depending on their individual values and possibly on the topic you are asking about. Your resource person can help you to know what is appropriate.

ETHICS AND RESPECT

Culture is an essential part of language. One without the other cannot function. The researcher must respect the language and culture of the people he or she works with. Tribal communities are liable to welcome a person who is comfortable around tribal people. However, there is a limit. Native people may have rules about, for example, female and male contact. Maintain an awareness of protocol and ask your resource person to keep you informed and educated about how to behave.

You must know how to conduct yourself properly at ceremonials and social activities. For example, longhouse ceremonials are strict about how to enter the longhouse. Men and women do not sit together; they must separate at the entrance. The man will go to the right side and the woman to the left side of the room. Children must be kept still, and may not play on the floor of the longhouse. If your children cannot behave this way, leave them home. You too should be aware of when you can converse, because conversation may interrupt an important occasion. One time faculty members from a university were invited to the longhouse. They stood around in groups holding discussions when they were supposed to be sitting down quietly in their proper places. In the meantime, the leader of the longhouse was waiting for them to quiet down.

Getting involved in social and ceremonial activities paves the way for acceptance. When I was a student at Central Washington University I taught high school teachers a course on American Indian culture. This was part of their retaining State of Washington teaching certification. An opportunity came up for the whole class to attend a memorial service for someone who had passed. The teachers arrived before I did, and were at first mistaken for distant family members of the deceased person. To be on the safe side, sincerely state your intention to help and your purpose in being at a memorial to the family. When I got there I found my male students working diligently putting the building into order and setting up tables and chairs. The female students were in the kitchen helping to prepare traditional foods, and one was actually making frybread. Several teachers made lifelong friends at that ceremony.

Research, archiving documented material, and handling ownership involve important responsibilities. I first encountered some of these in my work with Margaret Kendall.

MARGARET (KIT) KENDALL

My early experience with Margaret (Kit) Kendall began when Melville Jacobs, professor of anthropology at the University of Washington, Kit's advisor, sent her to the Yakama people's land to study culture. This experience taught me about the importance of archiving documented materials. Kit asked for permission to make movies and record the fishermen at the rapids at Celilo Falls. In order to reach the fishermen, we had to ride across the Columbia River on a tiny box suspended from a wire cable, one that was used for sending sacks of fish to shore. So we rode in that little box over the tumbling water. It was frightening as we precariously dangled, swinging back and forth over the river. There were several little islands separated by gorges and we crossed to each island separately. It was worth the effort.

We documented men fishing at Celilo Falls talking about their heritage as fishermen; the Chief of Celilo Falls discussing fish conservation; the telling of legends; and narratives of women cutting and drying salmon and baking filet fish in the open fire. We photographed the rapids and salmon jumping out of the water, as well as pictures of social dances in the Longhouse.

Kit was reliant on people who contributed their cultural knowledge, performing tasks like skinning a deer and processing the hide into tanned buckskin, doing beadwork, weaving cornhusks, making baskets, and telling stories and legends about geographical sites brought into existence by Coyote. With help from Yakama people, we collected specimens of medicinal and food plants in the mountains, and we preserved plant specimens in wooden panels, labeling each with information identifying the location and soil type where each plant was found. Kit filmed an entire Indian wedding ceremony and a Wedding Trade between the Yakama and Umatilla Tribes. The bride was a Umatilla from the Shoeship family, and the groom was Yakama from the Alexander Saluskin family.

When Kit Kendall died, the data stored in her house was lost. There is no written information available as to where the collection was sent. The Jacobs

FIGURE A.1. The Samish canoe races at Tulalip, circa 1938. From left, Kay Northover, Kit Kendall, the author, Vera Yallup, a Sohappy girl, and an unknown girl. Courtesy of Virginia Beavert family photo collection.

Foundation, at the University of Washington in Seattle, has no record of it, nor was it mentioned in her will. Unfortunately, I was somewhere else when she died so I was unable to make an inquiry about the collection. Kit's collection should have been archived and made available to the Yakama Indian Nation, which granted permission for her research on the reservation.

This is one reason why tribes are reluctant to give research permits when they are approached by linguists and anthropologists, unlike when they hire researchers as witnesses in court cases and have control of all information. The loss of this material also presented a personal problem for me because I was appointed to work with Kit by the Yakama Tribal Council and therefore was responsible for the contacts made with the Yakama people who gave of their knowledge. In this way, Kit's research also fell on my shoulders. This made my involvement precarious, and jeopardized future involvement with researchers who desired to work on the Yakama reservation.

Researchers must be prepared to answer the following questions when approaching the tribe: What will happen to the data after it is documented by the researcher? Will the tribe have access to it? Who owns it? Who owns the copyright—the funding agency, the university, or the researcher? Who is responsible for any misuse of research collected? Who has the authority to decide these issues?

Áwnash tł’iks tɨmnanáxta naxsh ayatmíki. Iwaníkshana Margaret Kendall, kútya itḵ’íx̱shana iwáta waníki “Kit.” Iskúulishana Sityátł’ɨnpa. Pɨnmínk sapsikw’ałáyin páshapawinana Yakmułmamíyaw tiichámyaw, pashapátwakstɨmishana tiináwit kwnamánk tiichampamá. Kúshx̱i anakwmák pasɨ́nwix̱a kúsksim ku ipapáykɨnx̱a.

Now I will tell a story about one woman. Her name was Margaret Kendall, but she wanted to be called “Kit.” She was attending school at Seattle. Her instructor [Dr. Melville Jacobs] sent her to the Yakama people’s land, she was sent to study culture about the land, to those Sahaptin people who spoke one language and could understand each other [regardless of dialectal differences].

Uyt iwinanúuna Pak’ułámaman ku i’atł’áwya tímashyaw wiyanín-tay kútkuttay tímanipa tiichámpa. Áshix̱nanyapat náwtmiyush, kupat ániya tímash. Kúuknash ínch’a áwapiitashana Joe Meninaknan wiyatímat Nch’i pák’upa.

First, she went to the Tribal Council people to ask for a permit to allow her work on the reservation. They liked her presentation and they gave her a written permit. That was when I was helping Joe Menineck record the minutes for the General Council meeting.

Kush pak’ułáma paníya kútkut twíntwint Kítnan, ku tamáshwikt anakú ikw’imátax̱nay tíinmaman. Áwnatash wyanína áwatł’awya tíinmaman tɨmnanáx̱tyaw. Áwpat palaláay tíinma áshix̱nanya kútkut kupat á’iłux̱nuuna. Ishapáwach’akaanya sɨ́nwit hawláak ɨstí sɨnwitpamáyaw, kúshx̱i iwípikchashya ḵḵanáywityaw:

The Tribal Councilmen assigned me to accompany Kit, and to translate when she talked to the Indian people. We went around the Reservation asking the men and women for interviews. Many Indians liked her work and they were willing to record their voices on wire recorders, and she also took pictures of people working. [In the photographs:]

Awínshma patknísha np’iwitpamá. Pa’anísha pipshmí x̱apiłmí. Awisíkw’ashanapat miimawít twapwiinaynaktpamá ḵ’aláx̱.

The men are making dipnets. Some are making bone knives. They were showing her the ancient zigzag log corrals for horses.

Áwnatash áwatł'awya áyatma-man isíkw'atyaw, tun áwa átaw shapáwach'aktay. Náx̱shnɨmtash áyatnɨm isíkw'ana shúwat yáamash-nan, ku ilámx̱shkt lɨmíslɨmɨsnan. Áyatin pashapátutya ts'xwíili, ku paḵá'ilkwsha asht ílkw'shpaspa.

We asked the women to show whatever was important to them for recording. One woman showed us how to skin a deer, and process it into buckskin. Two women put up a teepee and built a fire inside.

Tł'aax̱w awkú tun pawínakpayshka: páwaykt, wáp'at, chchípnat, ts'apx̱mí wápaas ánit.

They shared all kinds of crafts: beadwork, yarn weaving, tule mat making, and cedar basket making.

Átaw aníya shapátk'it papshx̱wíit, Nixyawiłáma ku Yakmułáma pawachá píwnashma.

She made a movie of an Indian Wedding Trade, between the Umatillas on the woman's side and the Yakamas on the man's side.

Íkushnatash awkú kútkutna. Ttúushma watít pashapáwach'aka sɨnwitpamáyaw, ttuush aw walímtɨmnanax̱t. Íkw'ak áwacha átaw piimiláyk'ay myanashmamíyay. Anakú íkuuk piimínk myánashma amts'íx̱watax̱nay. Pɨ́t'x̱anukpaatash wyanína ápikchashya patúun kákya-maman, ku píniipt wɨx̱ánimaman.

That is how we worked. There were some legends told on the wire recorder, and some were unrecorded. They thought that would be important for their children, for the time that their children could have had access to it now. We went to the mountains to take pictures of wildlife, animals, and birds.

X̱nítnantash áx̱niya ku itamaníka pɨnmipáynk nisháyktpa. Áwx̱i awkú áttawax̱na, chaw ttuush.

We took some wild root plants and transplanted them. Some of them grew, others did not.

Kkúushnantash atmaaníya ts'ák'a Pátuyaw. Áwilax̱yawyaatash, ku chaw átashix̱ ílax̱yawya.

We picked filbert nuts near Mount Adams. We dried them but they did not dry very well.

Húuytash áwaḵitna kw'ɨ́nchnan. Náxshnɨmtash áyatnɨm isapsikw'áyat'ashana támakt kw'ɨnch.

We could not find black moss food. One woman wanted to teach us how to bake black moss.

Kúshx̱itash chaw shínɨm isápsikw'ana támakt wáḵ'amunan. Anakú míimi ilátamawna.

Nobody was able to show us how to process *waḵ'amu* (camas) because it had already dried up.

Sawítkx̱i míimi ilátaashka chaw túyay tkwátatay.

The Indian carrot plant had already disappeared, or it was unfit to eat.

Íkwłtash ḵḵanáywya Yákimupa tiichámpa, kutash wiyíit'ana Nch'i Wánakan. Kwnáktash shix̱ pax̱ɨ́twayna tíinma, ashkú inák tíinma pashúkshana shínnash wa.

This is how much time we spent recording on the Yakama Reservation, and we moved on to the Columbia River, at Celilo, Oregon. The Indians there were very hospitable, because they all knew me. [They liked Kit too, after they became acquainted. She was not shy about participating in social activities.]

Átway Lawátnɨmtash inámunx̱ana. Ku pániya ts'wáywit kw'ímat np'iwiłámaman ɨmáawipa anakwnák panp'íwishana awínshma.

Átway (deceased) Tommy Thompson, called us his granddaughters [just a term used by Elders]. He gave Kit the right of way to the fishing site on the islands and permission to interview the fishermen.

NOTES

1. The Yakama Nation approved the orthography I use in this book. See pg. 164.

Ichishkíin–English Glossary

INAWAWÍKSH KU TMAYÍKSH / WEDDING DOWRIES

Inawawíksh / Male Dowry

ɨwínat deer meat
k'úsi horse
lɨmɨslɨmɨsmí wapáwat táatpas tanned hide outfit
músmustsin cattle
sháptakay hide suitcase
twinúushush eagle feather headdress
útpaas buffalo robe
x̱yaaw núsux̱ dry salmon

Tmayíksh / Female Dowry

ɨwáywish necklaces
k'pɨt beads, shells, dentalium
shimx̱ buckskin dress
wápaas root and berry basket
x̱laam ts'apx̱ɨnmí cedar basket
x̱yaaw x̱nit dry roots

TŁ'YAWITPAMÁ PATÚN / FUNERAL PREPARATION MATERIALS

Ɨwínsh / For Men

ɨḵ'am (chaw wíyayti) moccasins (undecorated)
ḵ'ɨx̱lí tule mat
max̱áx̱ white clay
nch'i ílamx̱shki útpaas lɨmɨslɨmɨsmí big smoke-tanned buckskin blanket
pátash medicine bundle (if shaman)
pipshmí ɨwáywish ku táwk'ɨsh bone breastplate and choker
plash lɨmɨsmí kapú white tanned buckskin coat
sapak'ílks hider
shápɨnchaash, luts'á Indian paint (red)
shátay/ útpaas blanket (Hudson Bay or Pendleton)
táatpas shirt
tawáx̱pas tobacco pouch
walách'wiksh belt
wásɨmtatasay buckskin or buffalo robe
wilyakí white buckskin pants
x̱wayamanmí wáptas golden eagle feather (to hold in right hand)

Áyat / For Women

chátł'umx̱sh bandana
chímti lisháal new shawl (Pendleton)
ɨmtsa'ímtsa ɨwáywish bone or shell necklace

ḵ'ɨx̱lí tule mats

kw'alálkw'alal brass bell

ḵw'laapsh shɨmx̱ plain buckskin dress

łḵ'am, chaw wíyayti moccasins (undecorated)

max̱áx̱ white clay

nyach plain leggings

pátash medicine bundle (if shaman)

patł'aapá basket hat

plash lɨmɨsmí white tanned buckskin

plash táatpas white buckskin dress

sápk'ukt beaded or cornhusk bag

shápɨnchaash Indian paint (yellow)

t'alptmí ɨwáywish ku tawḵ'x̱sh wámpam beads and choker

walách'wiksh belt

x̱wayamanmí wáptas golden eagle feather (to hold in right hand)

TŁ'YAWITPAMÁ SÍNWIT / FUNERAL VOCABULARY

átna- to die

átnat dead person, deceased person

átway late, dead, deceased person(reference term)

áwx̱sha- to miss, feel loss of, mourn

áwx̱sha mourning ceremony

cháawi- die (gentler term than tł'yáwi-)

Cháawk'a iwá. S/he is gone.

hawláak tiichám spirit world, heaven (empty land)

iix̱- wash, clean (clean body)

íkkɨmi- fill, cover

laḵayx̱it'áwaas candle light (often associated with the Shaker church. Some people want a candle lit all night at the wake.)

náḵ'itx̱aw tkwátat last meal

nákwat'uy- lead, officiate, preside over

nakwat'uyłá leader, especially in longhouse

náx̱ti- cry, weep, grieve

ni- give

ních- bury, put away, store, save, keep

páwinit, wínit giveaway ceremony

puuks casket, box, locker

talapúshak- pray (associated with the Shaker Church)

tamáynak- bury, lock up, deposit, incarcerate, place in ground

tanamútɨm- pray (usually associated with Christian praying)

tł'yáwi- die

tł'yáwit death, corpse, wake

tł'yáwiyi the spirit of the deceased

wáash longhouse floor, dirt floor in middle of longhouse

walptáyk- sing (people singing or insect noise)

waníkt tl'aax̱wsimk'a say the dead one's name for the last time

yáwatash grave, graveyard, cemetery

XWYACHITPAMÁ SÍNWIT / SWEATHOUSE VOCABULARY

aláala devil's club (nettle)

álayt edge of waterway

apíłapł leaf

awnámk naked

áwshniksh floor

ayún, ayút bear root

chiish water

ílkwaas wood

ilkwsh fire

k'asáwi- be cold (person)

ḵ'ix̱lí tule mat
láxuyx̱t hot
láx̱wayx̱t hot (air)
małáa clean
nák'uk- gather
nank cedar
papsh white fir
patísh branch
pchɨsh door
płɨx̱ love medicine
płx̱u fresh/green (of plant)
pshwápshwa rocks
pshx̱u sagebrush
psúni alder
sápx̱wnati- crawl
shapáshukwaa- talk, introduce to
shátay blanket
shchápa rose hips
sutł'wanpáwas dipper
tamḵ'ikskúla soap vine
tamsháashu rose, rosewood
tanamútɨmt prayer
tax̱sh willow
tiin person, Indian
tkni twine
tḵúni hole, pit
tkwsáy bucket
tsawktsáwk red hot
tunís matches
twána- follow, go with
wapsíki cotton rope
waypx̱t upstream
wíi'uyt first/to begin
wiḵ'áat lukewarm (liquid)
xwyach sweathouse
xwyák- sweat (as in bathe)

WATITPAMÁ SÍNWIT / LEGEND (RATTLESNAKE AND EEL) VOCABULARY

aan sun
ámchnik outside
anáwi- be hungry
anwíkt year
asúm eel
Asumyáy Legendary Eel
áx̱mi away from water
chiish water
chilwít bad
iksíks little
ɨníit house
ɨshchɨ́t path, road
isíkw'a- show
k'asáwi- be cold (person)
k'aywá short
k'pɨs cold
kwnak there
lalíwa- miss, be lonely for
láts'muy- warm up, warm oneself
łkw'i day
míimi long ago
myánashma children
Nch'iwána Columbia River
núkwshi- smell something
Pátu Mount Adams
pawilawíix̱- race, compete
paysh maybe
páyu very much
puuy snow
px̱wí- think
saptayák- cheat
sáypta- feed
shix̱ good
sɨ́nwi- speak

tánawit cave
tawnáapak'a supposedly
tiichám earth, land, country
tíix̱wa- inform, notify
tk'i- look at, stare at
tkw'ánati- walk around
tkwáta- eat
ts'aa near, nearby
ts'muuy warm
túnx̱kan wrong way
túx̱- return home
tx̱ána- become, happen
wána river
watít legend
wáx̱push rattlesnake
Wax̱pushyáy, Wax̱púuya Legendary Rattlesnake
wiláalakw- race to win
wɨsalíl- hunt
wɨsháynak- stay, camp, move in with
wɨshúwa- get ready
wúux̱ɨm springtime
wyáłamayk- get lost
x̱átamalii- fall into water
x̱ay friend (male to male)
x̱tú- try hard
yanwáy pitiful, poor

TTUNX̱ SHÁPINCHAASH K'USIMAMÍ / HORSE COLORS

chmaakw dark gray
chmuk black
k̲aashk̲áash buckskin with black
kawxkáwx palomino
k̲uyx̱ white
liláwlilaw bay with white belly
luch'á brown/red bay
máamɨn appaloosa (spots only on rump)
pa'áx̱ buckskin with white
pátatkw'ikwi buckskin with dark stripe down back; or uniformly orange
patł'úmx̱i boldface
shiwíwshiwiw chestnut sorrel
shkw'íishkw'i liver-color sorrel/brown
shukawáakuł like sugar (bluish-white, white mane and white eyes)
tak̲awáakuł golden with black stripe down back and spider web stockings
támtl'aki paint
túk̲tuk̲ útpaas leopard Appaloosa (spots all over)

PAMÍSHPAMISH TX̱ÁNAT K'USIMAMÍ / HORSE ACTIONS

cháwayna- pull/drag
piná'awk̲anin- roll over
pináwx̱i- lay down
tkw'anáti- walk
tłúpwayuna- jump over
wákmuyk- buck
wáyx̱ti- run
wíik̲iit- trot
wilátkshk- walk single footed
wilátkshkt gaited horse
x̱wnáti- canter

References

Beavert, Virginia, and Sharon Hargus. 2009. *Ichishkíin Sínwit: Yakama/Yakima Sahaptin Dictionary*. Seattle: University of Washington Press.

Beavert, Virginia, and Joana Jansen. 2011. "Yakima Sahaptin Bipartite Verb Stems 1." *International Journal of American Linguistics* 77, no. 1: 121–49.

_______. 2013. "Agent Case Marking in Sahaptian." In "In honor of Scott DeLancey." Special issue, *Functional-Historical Approaches to Explanation*, edited by Tim Thornes, Gwendolyn Hyslop, Joana Jansen and Erik Andvik, 131–54. Amsterdam: John Benjamins.

Beavert, Virginia, and Bruce Rigsby. 1975. *Yakima Language Practical Dictionary*. Toppenish, WA: Consortium of Johnson O'Malley Committees, Region 4.

Beavert, Virginia, and Deward E. Walker. 1974. *The Way It Was: Anakú Iwachá: Yakima Legends*. Yakima, WA: Franklin Press, Consortium of Johnson O'Malley Committees, Region 4.

DeLancey, Scott, and Victor Golla. 1997. "The Penutian Hypothesis: Retrospect and Prospect." *International Journal of American Linguistics* 63, no. 1: 171–202.

Dutson, Judith. 2005. *Storey's Illustrated Guide to Ninety-Six Horse Breeds of North America*. North Adams, MA: Storey Publishing.

Hargus, Sharon. 2001. "Quality Sensitive Stress Reconsidered." *University of Washington Working Papers in Linguistics* 20: 25–56.

Hargus, Sharon, and Virginia Beavert. 2001. "Initial Clusters and Minimality in Yakima Sahaptin." *University of Washington Working Papers in Linguistics* 20: 1–24.

_______. 2002a. "Yakima Sahaptin Clusters and Epenthetic [ɨ]." *Anthropological Linguistics* 44: 231–77.

_______. 2002b. "Predictable versus Underlying Vocalism in Yakima Sahaptin." *International Journal of American Linguistics* 68: 316–40.

_______. 2005. "A Note on the Phonetic Correlates of Stress in Yakima Sahaptin." *University of Washington Working Papers in Linguistics* 24: 64–95.

_______. 2006a. "Word-Initial Clusters and Minimality in Yakima Sahaptin." *Phonology* 23, no. 1: 21–58.

_______. 2006b. "High-Ranking Affix Faithfulness in Yakima Sahaptin." In *Proceedings of the Twenty-Fifth West Coast Conference on Formal Linguistics*, edited by Don Baumer, David Montero, and Michael Scanlon, 177–85. Somerville, MA: Cascadilla.

_______. 2012. "First Position Clitics in Northwest Sahaptin." Presented at meeting of the

Society for the Study of the Indigenous Languages of the Americas, January 5, 2012, Portland.

_______. 2014. "Northwest Sahaptin." *Journal of the International Phonetic Association* 44, no. 3: 319–42.

Hunn, Eugene S. 1990. *Nch'i-Wana, "The Big River": Mid-Columbia Indians and Their Land.* Seattle: University of Washington Press.

Jacobs, Melville. 1929. "Northwest Sahaptin Texts." *University of Washington Publications in Anthropology* 2, no. 6: 175–244. Seattle: University of Washington Press.

_______. 1931. "A Sketch of Northern Sahaptin Grammar." *University of Washington Publications in Anthropology* 4, no. 6: 85–291. Seattle: University of Washington Press.

_______. 1934. "Northwest Sahaptin Texts" [English translations]. *Columbia University Contributions to Anthropology* 19, pt. 1. New York: Columbia University Press.

_______. 1937. "Northwest Sahaptin Texts" [Indian text]. *Columbia University Contributions to Anthropology* 19, pt. 2. New York: Columbia University Press.

Jansen, Joana Worth. 2010. "A Grammar of Yakima Ichishkíin/Sahaptin." PhD diss., University of Oregon.

Jansen, Joana, and Virginia Beavert. 2010. "Combining the Goals of Language Documentation and Language Teaching: A Yakima Sahaptin Case Study." In *Building Communities and Making Connections* 62, no. 80, 62–80. Cambridge Scholars Publishing in association with GSE Research.

McWhorter, Lucullus V. 1952. *Hear Me, My Chiefs! Nez Perce Legend and History.* Caldwell, ID: Caxton Press.

Pandosy, Mie Cles. 1862. *Grammar and Dictionary of the Yakama Language.* Vol. 6. Trübner.

Rigsby, Bruce Joseph. 1964–71. Sahaptin field notebooks, 10–18. Unpublished ms.

_______. 1965. "Linguistic Relations in the Southern Plateau." PhD diss., University of Michigan, Ann Arbor.

Rigsby, Bruce, and Noel Rude. 1996. "Sketch of Sahaptin, a Sahaptian Language." *Handbook of North American Indians* 17: 666–92.

Ruby, Robert H., and John A. Brown. 1986. *A Guide to the Indian Tribes of the Pacific Northwest.* Norman: University of Oklahoma Press.

Swanton, John Reed. 1952. *The Indian Tribes of North America.* No. 145. Baltimore: Genealogical Publishing.

Index

adultery, 60
After Burial Ceremony, 69. *See also* death and mourning
alder bark, 90, 101
Alderdale, 21
American Indian Language Development Institute (AILDI), 13
ashxyatúu, 57*fig.*
Awátam, 6, 23. *See also* Parker

Baby Board Island, 26
Beacon Rock, 39
Beavert, Harris (Henry) (Aylux) Wataslayma (father), 22, 138; Aylux (childhood name), 58
Beavert, Oscar Wantux, Latp'áama (older brother), 60, 103, 121, 125; Wa̲xwín (childhood name), 60
Beavert, Virginia, Tu̲xámshish: academic research, 11–13; birth, 15; getting lost, 15; horse racing, 147–50; military service, 8; occupations, 7–9; relationship with great-grandmother, 17, 24, 124–25; teaching, 9–11; Water Woman, 96
Bickleton, 22, 59
bitterroot (*pyáx̱i*), 29, 47
bluebird, 19
Blue Mountains, 15
bone game, 79, 110–18, 110*fig.*, 112*fig.*, 114*fig.*, 115*fig.*, 116*fig.*, 117*fig.*, 157. *See also* stick game
braiding of the bride's hair (*wápshat ámtanatnan*), 54, 54*fig.*
bridal shower, 55, 55*fig.*, 57
British Columbia (Canadian Indians), 118, 149
Brooks, James, 9

camas, 28*fig.*, 29, 170
camp of Billy Barnhart, 141*fig.*
Camp Chaparral, 99
Cashmere, x*map*, 23
cedar baskets, 51, 53, 57, 59
Celilo Falls, 25*fig.*, 25–28, 78, 105–106, 166, 170
Celilo Falls Salmon Feast, 106*fig.*
Central Washington University, 9–11, 165
Charlie, Mussie (maternal aunt), 15, 23–24
Chief Shawaway (Umatilla Chief and father's paternal great-grandfather), 60
childbirth, 32–33; birth hut, 33; circumcision, 33; diapering, 36, 57; newborn, 33; umbilical cord. *See also* diapering ceremony
Chinook Jargon, 18
Chipmunk and Witch Woman (legend), 38
ch'lay, 20, 26
chokecherry, 19, 86, 100
children: early childhood training, 37; newborn, 33
circle dance, 108–109
Columbia Plateau, 5
Columbia River, 5, 22
Coming-Out Ceremony, 41–42
Coming Together Dance Ceremony, 43, 58. *See also* engagement
cottonwood, 19
Cowiche Stream, 6
Coyote, 38, 168
Coyote, Ruth, 35*fig.*

cradleboard, 33–34, 35*fig.*
Creator, 31, 38, 60, 81, 89, 97–98
currant, 19

Dalles, The, 25, 138
Dawes Act of 1887, 16
death and mourning, 61–63, 65–66, 74; death song, 29, 64; dressing ceremony, 64; funeral bundle, 63–64; funeral songs, 63, 66
deer, whitetail, 19, 20
Dempsey, Espirita M., 12
dentalium shells, 51, 60
devil's club, 90
diapering ceremony, 36, 57
divorce and separation, 23, 42, 60. *See also* adultery
dowry, 34, 45, 52, 60; female 22, 50–51, 59, 97; male 22, 50–51, 53, 53*fig.*, 59, 97
dried beaver testicle, 90
drying lamprey eels, 141*fig.*
duck, wild, 19

earth lodges, 6
eels, lamprey, 19, 123, 139
Eel Trail, 135–38
Eisenhower High School, 11
Elders: assistance with childbirth and childrearing; 33–34, 36–38, 103; guidance of, 29, 31, 39–42, 58, 62, 64, 66–67, 80, 88, 97; marriage selection, 22, 42, 45, 50, 92; medicine and, 91–92, 132; and preservation of language, legends, and culture, 5–6, 8–12, 44, 103–105, 137, 159; storytelling, 74; suicide, views of, 80, 82–83; widow-making ceremony, 76–78. *See also names of individual ceremonies*
Ellensburg, 85
engagement, 45, 48–49; engagement dance 21–22, 42, 47; meeting of two people dance ceremony 45. *See also* winter dance

Fall Bridge, x*map*, 5
farming, 118–23
filberts, 169
First Christian Mission, 26
First Christian Mission Boarding Residence, 24
First Food Communion Ceremony, 28. *See also* Root Feast
First Foods ceremony, 134
First Menses Initiation Ceremony, 22
fishing, x*map*, 5, 118, 139; Wɨshx̱am fishing site, x*m*, 26
food, traditional: 55, 86, 118–23, 134, 166; taboos, 67, 72, 79. *See also specific foods*
Fort Simcoe, 26

gathering and preparing food, x*map*, xvi, 5, 17, 19–21, 26, 28*fig.*, 29, 52, 135, 139, 141*fig.*, 152–53, 155
General Allotment Act. 16. *See also* Dawes Act of 1887
George, Andy (maternal cousin), 25
George, Jesse, Tsasat (maternal great-uncle), 25
George, Johnny, X̱ayawat (maternal great-uncle), 18, 25
George, Johnson (maternal cousin), 25
George, Ned (maternal cousin), 25
George, Thomas (maternal cousin), 25
George, Timothy (maternal cousin), 37, 131
George, William (maternal cousin), 25
Gifford Pinchot National Forest, 15, 135
Goldendale Ridge, 6, 59
goose, 19
Grandmother Water, 98–99

Hanford (Hanford Nuclear Reservation), 5
Hanford Reach, x*map*, 5, 20–21
Hargus, Sharon, 11
Heritage University, 12–13. *See also* Fort Wright College; Heritage College
Hess, Thomas, 12
Hilbert, Vi, 12
Holy Men/Women, 40, 134
hops, 118–19, 157
Horn Rapids Dam, x*map*
Horse Heaven Hills, 6, 22

horses, 18, 19, 142–52; American Indian horse, 146; Billy Boots, 151, 156–57; and burials; 64; gaited horse, 151; Indian TomTom, 149; Medicine Hat horse, 147; pack horse, 154*fig.*; racing, 147–150, 148*fig.*; Siskiyu's Sun, 148–49; *ta<u>k</u>awáakuł*, 147, 151; training, 147; war horse, 147; wild and feral horses, 150–52, 153*fig.*, 155
huckleberry, 19
hummingbird, 19
hunting, x*map*, 5, 15, 18, 21, 40, 51, 93, 101
hunting, fishing, and food-gathering map, x*map*

Ichishkíin, xi, xii, xiii, xvi, 3–4, 6–7, 9, 11, 13–14, 83, 104–105, 146, 159, 161
Ichishkíin (Yakima) Practical Alphabet, 7, 13
Icicle River, x*map*, 23
Indian gaming, 110. *See also* bone game or stick game
Indian Trade Marriage, 22, 29
Indian Wedding Trade, 45, 51–52, 60

Jacob, Roger, 13–14
Jacobs Foundation, 10
Jacobs, Melville, 8, 10, 166, 168
Jansen, Joana, 13–14
Jim, Maggie, 15–16
John, Mary, 29
John Day, 5

Kendall, Margaret (Kit), 8–9, 166, 167*fig.*, 168
Kiksht, 26
Kittitas-Ellensburg, 5, 85
Kittitas Valley, x*map*
Klikatat (<u>X</u>wáł<u>x</u>waypam) 5, 7–8, 22–23, 58
Klickitat River, x*map*
Klug, Linda, 9

languages and dialects: Ichishkíin, 5; Klikatat, 7–8; Nez Perce, 5, 104; Umatilla, 104
legends. *See* specific legends
Legend Woman, 138
Lewis River Klikatat Band, 5
Lincoln Public School, 24
Li<u>x</u>ups (maternal great-grandmother's sister), 28
longhouse, 6, 21, 63, 172; dances and, 45–46; 48–49; 58; funerals and, 65–66, 69–70, 73–74, 79, 81; longhouse religion, 19, 62, 97–99; religious Prophet 19, 60; religious songs, 29, 51, 98–99; ways, 24, 28–29, 165. *See also specific longhouses*
Lower Snake River Palouse, 23
Lushootseed, 12

magpie, 19
marriage, 5, 21–23, 34, 51, 54, 58–59, 61, 76; bridal shower, 55; bridal veil, 51, 52*fig.*; engagement, 42–45; traditional ceremony 52, 57, 60, 77. *See also* dowry, Indian Trade Marriage
McCoy, Esther (maternal cousin), 26
McCoy, Johnny (maternal cousin), 25
McCoy, Margaret (maternal cousin), 26
McWhorter, L. V., 6, 137
Medicine Men/Women, 18, 37, 49, 59, 65, 98, 129–30, 132–34
Medicine Valley, 6
Meeting of Two People dance ceremony, 45
Mellon Foundation, 12–13
Menineck, Isabel, 29–30
menses hut, 41–42
Mid-Columbia River Bands, 5
military service, 8
Moses, Clifford, 12
moss, black, 169
Moxee Hop Ranch, 110*fig.*, 111

naming (ceremony), 36–37
National Science Foundation Fellow, 13
Nespelem, 6, 14
Nez Perce, 5, 7, 23, 99, 104, 151

Northwest Indian Language Institute (NILI), 13–14

Old Wantux (mother's paternal great-grandfather), 16, 23, 101, 135
Oregon (tribes; Sahaptin people), x*map*, 4–5, 13, 15, 22–23, 25, 58, 123, 138, 170
orphans, 32, 39, 41, 76
Owl Dance, 106*fig.*

pack horse, 154*fig.*
Packwood, 23
Palmer, Elit, Latp'áama (father's maternal great-grandfather), 60
Palouse, 78, 135
Pandosy, Father Charles Marie, 7
Parker, 23
pemmican, 20
Pendleton, 5, 15
Pendleton blankets, 62, 171, 183
peppermint, 20
Pine Creek, 5
Pinkham, Joe "Jay," 100
plants, traditional, 19–20. *See also specific plants*
Plateau Penutian, 5
Porter, Larry, 9
powwow, 108
prayer, 97–99
pregnancy, 32–33, 42; new parent observations, 32
Priest Rapids, 5, 136
primrose, 19
Prosser, x*map*, 20
prune tree, 20
Pshwánapam Bands, 5, 23, 25
puberty, 40. *See also* menses hut

Randle, 23
Rattlesnake and Eel, 138–42
Rau, Violet, 12
Redhorn, Eileen, Walulmay, née George (maternal cousin), 25
Redhorn, Jesse, 25
Richland, 20
Rigsby, Bruce, 5, 7–9, 14
Root Feast (First Foods Ceremony), 7, 28, 134
rose hips, 90
rosewood, 90
Rude, Noel, 9

Saddle Mountain, 5
sage, 90
schools: Lincoln Public School, 24; Toppenish High School, 101; White Swan Public School, 25. *See also* First Christian Mission boarding residence
Sahaptian, 5
Sahaptin, xi, xvi, 4–6, 13, 20–23, 43, 45, 48, 58, 61, 79, 122, 134
salmon: Chinook, 20; dog, 21; spawning/gathering grounds, 21. *See also* Hanford Reach
Saluskin, Alexander (Hawaaya) (step-father), 7–9, 23, 26, 100
Saluskin, David (step-uncle), 23
Saluskin, Ellen, X̱apt'íniks (Hoptonix), née Sawyalilx̱ (mother): birth, 22; children of, 16, 16*fig.*; death and funeral, 73–74; digging roots, 28*fig.*; divorce, 17; getting her power, 18–19; marriage, 58–60; name, 37, 101; remarriage to Alex Saluskin, 23
Saluskin, George (paternal step-grandfather), 23
Saluskin, Rudolph Valentino (younger half-brother), 26, 29, 100
Satus Stream, 6
sawíkt (Indian carrot), 170
Sawyalilx̱, Emma, Timinsh (maternal grandmother), 7, 23
Sawyalilx̱, Yakima George (maternal great-grandfather), 18, 22–23, 25, 101, 156; Medicine Man 18
Schuster, Helen, 9
Selah, x*map*, 6
Selam (family), 27
Serenade Ritual, 22, 61, 101
serviceberry (juneberry), 19

Shaker Church (religion), 7, 17, 98; prophet, 19, 28–29, 36, 54, 60, 68, 74, 78–79, 83, 97–98, 125, 134, 137; prophet songs, 66, 98, 125
shaman, 7, 37, 62
Shíshaash (Porcupine) (paternal great-grandfather), 22, 59
Siłá (*Sih'* Village), 17, 19, 22, 29, 85–86, 87, 91, 146
Silama, 66
sikáywa, 29
Smithsonian, 10
Snake River, x*map*, 5, 135–36
Soap Lake, x*map*, 5
soap vine, 90–91, 173
songs: death, 29, 64; food, 28; funeral, 63, 66; social, 21, 48, 51, 105
Spokane, x*map*, 6, 12
steelhead, 20
stick game, 110. *See also* bone game
Storyteller, 38–39, 74, 103
suckerfish, 122
suicide, 80–83
Sunnyside Dam, 6
Sutterlict, Greg, 14
swallow, 19
Swanton, John R., 6
sweathouse, 83–84, 87–96, 98–10; earth, 89; conduct at, 93; participating, 92; prayer, 97; preparing, 89; stones, 89; wood, 89; Wood Chopper, 89; women's practices, 96. *See also specific plants*
Sweowat, Louie, Shuyawt (maternal cousin), 28–29

taboos, 40, 42, 139; family planning, 32; pregnancy 32; pork, 18; puberty, 40; widowhood; 74, 78–79
talking circle, 100
talking stick, 99
Taytnapam, 5
Tayx, 5, 104
teepee, 6, 107, 169
Tenino, 5
Tieton Stream, 5
time ball, 43
Time Ball Keeper, 43
Timentwa, Louise, Chashtkw'l (paternal step-grandmother), 23
Tkwasayat (maternal great-grandmother's sister), 25
Toppenish, 7, 12, 18
Toppenish Longhouse, 28
Toppenish Stream, 6
Toppenish Wildcats, 101
Trout Lake, 18
Tulalip, 15, 24
Tux̱ámshish (mother's paternal great-grandmother), 37
Twin Buttes, 15, 135
Tygh Valley, 104

Underriner, Janne, 13
Union Gap, 6
University of Arizona, 13
University of Mexico, 10
University of Oregon, xv, xvi, 7–8, 13–14, 35, 55, 141
University of Washington, 12
Umatilla, x*map*, 5, 7, 14–15, 22–23, 45, 58, 60, 166
Umatilla-Cayuse, 23
Umatilla Indian Agency, 15
Umatilla River, 151
Umtuch Olney, Hazel, 12
Upper Cowlitz, 5
Upper Nisqually River (Mɨshiil), 5
U.S. Air Force, 99
U.S. Bureau of Indian Affairs, 10

veterans, 13, 99
violet, 20

Walla Walla, x*map*, 5, 22
Walker Jr., Deward, 9
Wanity Park, 11
Wanto, Margaret, Saptix̱awáy (maternal great-aunt), 135
Wanto (Wantux), Oscar (maternal grandfather), 15–16
Wapato High School, 11, 101

Warm Springs, 5, 13–14, 23
Warren, Dave, 10
water, importance of, 6, 47
Wawyúuk Sahaptins, 5, 20
Wayam, 5
Webb Hodge, Frederick, 6
wedding: ceremony, 54–57; feast, 56*fig.*; modern, 56*fig.*; veil (*pátł'umx̱sh*), 52*fig.* *See also* dowry; engagement; marriage; Indian Wedding Trade
Wenas, 6
Wenatchee, x*map*, 44, 136
Wenatchee Range, 6
Whipman, 37–38, 61, 84, 103
whipping ritual, 37–38
White Bluffs, 20
Whitefoot, Ambrose, 27
White Salmon River, 5
White Swan, x*map*, 26, 30
White Swan Longhouse, 30, 155
White Swan Public School, 25
widowhood: substitute spouse, 77; taboos regarding, 74, 79; widow-making ceremony, 74–78
Widow Rock, 139
wild apple tree, 20
wild rose, 20
Willie, Mary, 13
willow bark/tree, 34, 37, 90, 91, 97, 101
winter dance,15, 37, 130, 133
Wishx̱am, 123, 142
Witch Woman, 38. *See also* Chipmunk and Witch Woman (legend)
Women's Auxiliary Corps, 8
Woodrow Bill, 73
World War II, 8, 99, 147

X̱aniwáshya (maternal great-great-grandfather), 147
X̱ax̱ísh (maternal great-grandmother), 7, 17–18, 23–25, 36–37, 83, 87, 124, 138, 151, 153, 157; dogs, 87; exorcism, 126–28

Yakama, xi, xii, xvi, 4, 6, 10–12, 14, 19, 21–22, 23, 29, 33, 60, 86, 137, 146, 166, 168
Yakama Nation, 164, 167; Yakama Nation Indian Advisory Board, 11; Yakama Indian Reservation, 5, 11–12, 21, 26, 170; Yakama Tribal Culture Committee, 12
Yakama Veterans Association/Organization, xvi
Yakama Warriors, 99
Yakima, x*map*, xii, xiii, 5–6, 8, 11, 13
Yakima Folds, 6
Yakima Language Practical Dictionary, 10, 12
Yakima Meadows, 149
Yakima River, 5–6, 8, 17, 19–20, 88, 121
Yakima Tribal Council, xvi
Yakima Valley, 22, 101, 11
Yallup, Martha, 12
Yallup, Wilfred, xvi
Yallup, William "Bill," 100
Yamada Language Center, 14
Yamomoto, Akira, 11
yarrow, 90
Yuumatálam, 58–59

Zepeda, Ofelia, 13
Zillah, 6, 17–18

VIRGINIA R. BEAVERT is a member of the Yakama Nation and a native speaker of Sahaptin. She is a recipient of the Washington Governor's Heritage Award and the Ken Hale Prize of the Society for the Study of the Indigenous Languages of the Americas. She is the coauthor of *Ichishkíin Sínwit Yakama / Yakima Sahaptin Dictionary*. Photo courtesy of Jeff Magoto, Yamada Language Center.

JANNE L. UNDERRINER is the director of the Northwest Indian Language Institute at the University of Oregon. Virginia and Janne have been working together for the past twenty years. Photo courtesy of Northwest Indian Language Institute.

"I walk hand in hand with knowing the ways of my family and writing them down for those to come."

Virginia Beavert grew up in a traditional Native household with parents and a maternal great-grandmother who were shamans, and her childhood was populated by speakers of tribal dialects and languages: Nez Perce, Umatilla, Klikatat, and Yakima Ichishkíin. At age twelve she met linguist Melville Jacobs while working with his student, Margaret Kendell. Jacobs taught her to read and write the Klikatat orthography he had developed, and she began a lifetime of work on Native languages. After a stint in the US Air Force during World War II, Beavert earned advanced degrees in education and linguistics, and she has spent decades devoted to the preservation of Native language and culture.

In *The Gift of Knowledge / Ttnúwit Átawish Nch'inch'imamí*, Beavert sets down the story of her life and the traditions of her family for the benefit of future generations. It is a treasure trove of memories, teachings, and reflections (many in Yakima Ichishkíin with English translation) about family life, religion, ceremonies, food gathering, and other aspects of traditional Indigenous culture.

VIRGINIA R. BEAVERT (Yakama) is a recipient of the Washington Governor's Heritage Award and the Ken Hale Prize of the Society for the Study of the Indigenous Languages of the Americas. She is coauthor of *Ichishkíin Sinwit Yakama / Yakima Sahaptin Dictionary*. **JANNE L. UNDERRINER** is director of the Northwest Indian Language Institute at the University of Oregon.

"Inspiring and informative.... [Beavert's] passion for and interest in the welfare of her younger readers reverberates throughout every page of *The Gift of Knowledge*, in which her stated purpose is to record the lifeways taught to her by her family."
—*Journal of the West*

"A must-read for those interested in Indigenous Studies, anthropology, history, and the Columbia Plateau.... A shining example of intellectual sovereignty."
—*Oregon Historical Quarterly*

"An accessible and insightful book, animated with tradition and wisdom, a treasure for future Yakama and other Indian peoples."
—*Pacific Northwest Quarterly*

UNIVERSITY OF WASHINGTON PRESS
Seattle | *www.washington.edu/uwpress*

COVER PHOTOGRAPH: *Wáwtuktpa* (At camp), ca. 1922 (the author is the child and her mother is seated). Courtesy of Yakama Nation Museum

ISBN 978-0-295-74612-8

90000

9 780295 746128